A Guide to
Staff & Educational Development

Edited by Peter Kahn & David Baume

SEDA
STAFF AND EDUCATIONAL
DEVELOPMENT ASSOCIATION

Routledge
Taylor & Francis Group

LONDON AND NEW YORK

First published in Great Britain and the United States in 2003 by Routledge

2 Park Square, Milton Park,   270 Madison Ave,
Abingdon, Oxon, OX14 4RN   New York NY 10016

Transferred to Digital Printing 2007

www.routledge.com

© Peter Kahn and David Baume, 2003

ISBN 0 7494 3881 9

British Library Cataloguing-in-Publication Data
A CIP record for this book is available from the British Library.

Library of Congress Cataloging-in-Publication Data

A guide to staff and educational development / edited by Peter Kahn and
David Baume
    p. cm.
Includes bibliographical references and index.
    ISBN 0-7494-3881-9
    1. College teachers--In-service training. 2. Career development. I.
Kahn, Peter (Peter E.) II. Baume, David, 1943-
    LB1778.G78 2003
    378.1'25--dc21
                            2003008165

Typeset by Saxon Graphics Ltd, Derby

Publisher's Note
The publisher has gone to great lengths to ensure the quality of this reprint
but points out that some imperfections in the original may be apparent

Contents

Notes on the editors and contributors

THE EDITORS

Peter Kahn is Teaching Development Officer in the Teaching and Learning Support Unit at the University of Manchester. The role involves having a particular concern for promoting professional development related to teaching and the support of learning. In this capacity he also acts as Project Manager for a regional programme of staff development that aims to build capacity for learning based around processes of inquiry.

This current position follows his earlier experience in mathematics. Following a PhD in the mathematical modelling of brain function at Imperial College London, he was awarded the Society for Research into Higher Education 'Younger Academic Research Award' for 1995–96 while based at the Institute of Education, London. Peter subsequently worked as a Lecturer in Mathematics at Liverpool Hope University College, where he developed wider interests in educational development. He has recently published two books on learning and teaching in mathematics.

He holds a Fellowship from the Staff and Educational Development Association (SEDA) and a Master's degree in Education from the University of Liverpool. He is active within SEDA as the Events Co-ordinator of the committee that oversees the SEDA Fellowship Schemes. In particular, he currently organizes the annual SEDA Summer School for New Educational Developers.

David Baume is a higher education consultant. His current and recent consultancy work includes higher education student progress files; course design; assessment strategies for a nursing programme; project evaluation; university teaching awards; programme evaluation; university leadership development; helping staff to write about their learning and teaching innovations; staff development for part-time teachers; staff development for inquiry-based learning; and supporting tutor development and accreditation. His current research and publications are about the assessment of portfolios produced on a course in teaching in higher education, and about personal development planning and progress files.

Previously he was a Director of the Centre for Higher Education Practice at the Open University, where he led the production of courses on teaching in higher education. He was also a founding member of the National Co-ordination Team for the HEFCE Teaching Quality Enhancement Fund.

David taught in higher education for 20 years before becoming a staff and educational developer. He was founding chair of SEDA from 1990 to 1995 and a founding editor of the *International Journal for Academic Development*. He is a member of the Council and the Accreditation Committee of the Institute for Learning and Teaching in Higher Education (ILTHE). He holds a Master's degree in Higher Education and Fellowship of SEDA. He can be contacted at ADBaume@aol.com.

THE CONTRIBUTORS

Caroline Baillie is a Senior Lecturer in Engineering and the Deputy Director of the UK Centre for Materials Education (UKCME). Her work with UKMCE includes running national workshops and teaching development grant schemes for materials educators as well as personal consultation work with academic staff of over 40 departments. She has over 100 publications in materials science and education to her name and is the author of four books on teaching and learning, with particular interests in the relationship between knowledge development and creativity in research and in student learning.

Rakesh Bhanot describes himself as a 'reformed technophobe' and is an education-focused convert to higher education based on information and communications technology (ICT) rather than a technological pioneer in this area. He is Programme Manager for the Postgraduate Courses in Learning and Teaching in Higher Education at Coventry University.

Christopher Bond is Senior Lecturer in Educational Development at the University of Surrey Roehampton. Chris is experienced in assessing organizational training and development needs, and designing bespoke programmes and marketing training and development initiatives. His publications and conference papers are on the development and delivery of work-based learning and development in organizations and the application of soft systems methodology and reflective practice in creating learning organizations.

John Cowan was Scottish Director and Professor of Learning Development for the Open University when he retired in 1997. Since then he has been active nationally and internationally as an educational consultant, notably in aspects of problem-based learning, self-assessment, and personal and professional development planning.

Diana Eastcott is a Professor and Director of the Staff and Student Development Department at the University of Central England, Birmingham. She is a staff and educational developer with many years' experience as an institutional manager, course leader, facilitator and teacher. Her main focus is on promoting initiatives that have a significant impact on improving the quality of student learning.

Stephen Fallows is Research Co-ordinator for the Centre for Exercise and Nutrition Science at Chester College. In this role, he manages the research phase of a very successful international MSc programme that has 300-plus students from over 20 nationalities and is delivered in the United Kingdom, Singapore and Hong Kong. Prior to returning to his 'home discipline' of nutrition science in 2001, he was Reader in Educational Development at the University of Luton. Dr Fallows utilizes information and communications technology (ICT) methods to support his students world-wide.

Diana K Kelly is Head of Lifelong Learning at the Dublin Institute of Technology, Ireland. Dr Kelly has been facilitating educational development workshops since 1989. At present she is responsible for the Dublin Institute of Technology's Learning and Teaching Centre, which provides workshops, consultations, and conferences for academic staff. Dr Kelly earned her doctorate in Higher Education at the Claremont Graduate University in California.

Helen L King is the currently the manager of the UK-wide Learning and Teaching Support Network (LTSN) Subject Centre for Geography, Earth and Environmental Sciences. Her professional interests are in supporting the continuing professional development of staff and developing student employability skills. After completing her PhD, Helen managed the UK Earth Science Staff Development project, running workshops, disseminating good practice and building up a national network of earth sciences educators.

Val Roche is a Lecturer in Health Services Management at the Edith Cowan University in Western Australia. She has a varied professional background in allied health, higher education, and organizational and professional development in Wales and Australia. Val has led several organizational learning programmes focusing on professional development in transformative change, work-based action learning, health service improvement and innovation as well as co-ordinating research and development projects in rural health and higher education.

Rachel Segal is currently a National Co-ordinator for the Teaching Quality Enhancement Fund National Co-ordination Team, based at the Centre for

Higher Education Practice at the Open University. Originally a Lecturer in Musicology, she was Project Manager for a successful Fund for the Development of Teaching and Learning (FDTL) 1 project and has worked on a series of educational development initiatives. She continues to work with a number of higher education institutions in the UK and Europe, predominantly as an Arts and Humanities Consultant in the fields of performance assessment, study skills, e-learning and disability.

Liz Shrives is Director of Educational Development at the University of Surrey Roehampton. Liz manages the centre at Roehampton that leads academic and educational development, learning support, distributed learning, research into learning and teaching, and quality development. Her work in higher education and senior-level consultancy and training roles enable her to make a significant contribution to educational development at a national and international level. She is an ILTHE Accreditor, a member of the LTSN Generic Centre Advisory Group and the NTFS Advisory Panel, and a consultant for Oxford Centre for Staff and Learning Development.

Lorraine Stefani has recently taken up the post of Professor/Director of Professional Development at the University of Auckland, New Zealand. Formerly she was a Reader at the Centre for Academic Practice at the University of Strathclyde, Glasgow. Her particular interests include promoting the scholarship of teaching and learning and supporting the development of the accessible, inclusive curriculum.

Neill Thew is the Head of Teaching and Learning Development at the University of Sussex, Brighton. He is also a past chair of the SEDA Publications Committee. His main areas of research are into managing effective educational change and improving students' ability to learn.

Bland Tomkinson is currently Director of the Teaching and Learning Support Centre at the University of Manchester Institute of Science and Technology, having previously been Director of its Staff Development Unit. As well as higher education, his career spans central and local government plus a spell in research and consultancy in the public sector.

Gina Wisker is a Professor and Director of Learning and Teaching Development and Women's Studies Co-ordinator at Anglia Polytechnic University, where she also teaches English. Gina is co-editor of the SEDA journal *Innovations in Education and Teaching International*, a member of SEDA's Fellowships Committee and an Oxford Centre for Staff and Learning Development consultant. Her specialist areas are postgraduate student learning and post-colonial women's writing.

Foreword

The Staff and Educational Development Association (SEDA) warmly welcomes the publication of this excellent book, which provides a timely, comprehensive guide to key issues in staff and educational development for higher education. SEDA has travelled a long way over the past decade, initiating, supporting and disseminating practices and policies that enable staff and institutions of higher education to develop and improve institutional and staff capability and, through them, student learning. This book and its companion volume to be published later this year are further parts of this journey.

This book will be of particular value to new entrants to the staff and educational development profession. However, it will also be of considerable interest to more experienced developers. The newly appointed developer will find, for the first time in one volume, specific guidance on how to undertake effectively the challenging and rewarding role of staff and educational development. More experienced colleagues will discover new and inspiring ideas to inform their own professional reflection, practice and development.

Each of the chapters draws on a rich seam of expertise, experience and reflection. The diverse issues they address reflect multifaceted, interlocking and fast-evolving elements of staff and educational development. These range from planning a single staff development event to promoting strategic organizational change. The daunting reality that we face as developers is that our credibility and effectiveness depend on our understanding and our capability in relation to all these elements.

As staff and educational developers, we strive to work creatively, dynamically and credibly within the context of accelerating change in higher education. SEDA is confident that the guidance and support provided by this book will serve as a valuable resource.

Kristine Mason O'Connor and Barry Jackson, co-chairs of SEDA

Acknowledgements

The editors are grateful to James Wisdom, Jonathan Simpson and Stephen Jones for their roles in bringing this guide to publication. We are particularly appreciative of the efforts that the contributors have made in writing their respective chapters. Peter would also like to acknowledge the support of his wife and family, and of his colleagues in the Teaching and Learning Support Unit at the University of Manchester. David thanks Carole for her moral and intellectual support.

Introduction

Peter Kahn and David Baume

A CHANGING FIELD

Staff and educational development, by which we mean the systematic and scholarly support for improving both educational processes and the practices and capabilities of educators, has moved in recent years from complete absence or at best periphery to centre stage in higher education. We have seen the creation of educational development units, whether within institutions or working with subject communities; extensive funding of projects seeking to improve the quality of student learning; new posts for learning development within departments; and substantial resources devoted to learning technology. Large numbers of staff have become involved in staff and educational development, often without receiving any specific professional education for their new role. At the same time, these developers are likely to face a variety of challenges as they seek both to effect educational change and to develop their own careers. More experienced developers also face change in their own work, as they engage in new areas of practice, extend their own professional expertise and assist with the development of newer entrants to the field.

This is a good time for us to capture and share our understanding and practice with each other and with new practitioners. Not to set it in stone, but rather to make it more widely available for use, and test, and further development.

MEETING A NEED

A Guide to Staff and Educational Development aims to facilitate increased professionalism within development work. The book seeks to explore the knowledge, skills and professional attitudes that developers need in order to carry out their work effectively. The main focus is on methods and approaches to and issues in development rather than on specific innovations or practices that you might want to introduce into higher education. The book is thus not directly concerned, for instance, with problem-based learning, peer assessment or good practice in providing for students with disabilities. Instead, it is designed to enable you to understand the processes by which such practices may be introduced.

It is worth emphasizing that the primary focus of this book is on the improvement of education. This focus does, however, also imply a consideration of wider issues. The development of education will also encompass issues that relate to research, staff in support roles within universities, management and in particular to organizational development. Furthermore, the book also aims to provide developers with support for their own development as developers. With the changing nature of this field, it is essential that we developers continually grow in our ability to carry out our work. The book thus concentrates on practical approaches, making appropriate use of literature and research and not avoiding areas of contention or difficulty in development work.

THE INTERNATIONAL DIMENSION

There are, of course, significant variations in the way that staff and educational development is carried out internationally. Indeed, a variety of terms are used to refer to the field of improving educational processes and the practice of educators. While the relevant terms are further explored in Chapter 1, it is worth noting here that the book frequently employs the term 'development' to refer both to staff development and to educational development. Authors do, however, refer separately to staff development or to educational development where they wish to emphasize a particular dimension of development work.

It is also worth noting that although the contributors are drawn from several countries, the book in large part draws on lessons that have been learnt within the context of UK higher education. The issues tackled are, however, not unique to the United Kingdom. Furthermore, each of the chapters remains accessible to an international audience, with any material that is more specific to the UK context clearly identified as such. The number of organizations or initiatives that are involved in development work within the United Kingdom does, though, pose certain challenges. In order to assist the reader, a glossary is therefore provided at the end of the book in order to provide basic descriptions of those that are the most important. As we go to press, the scene within the United Kingdom is changing rapidly, following the proposal for a Teaching Quality Academy to draw together three separate organizations into a single agency (Department for Education and Skills, 2003). These three organizations are the Learning and Teaching Support Network (LTSN), the Institute for Learning and Teaching in Higher Education (ILTHE) and the Higher Education Staff Development Agency (HESDA). The task of advancing learning and teaching within higher education remains the same, however.

OUTLINE OF THE BOOK'S CONTENTS

The various chapters present staff and educational development as an activity that should be both systematic and scholarly. They all recommend a variety of systematic approaches to the particular aspect of the field that they each address, while still encouraging developers to take a principled advantage of opportunities as they arise. Furthermore, these systematic approaches are grounded in a concern for scholarship. Without this, it would be difficult to claim development as a field of professional activity. In broad terms, the book focuses on three specific areas: the process of development, approaches to development and the development of developers themselves.

In Chapter 1, Lorraine Stefani explores the nature of staff and educational development. This chapter sets the scene for the book as a whole by addressing a range of issues that help us to understand the complex and evolving nature of development work. Indeed, it is evident that education cannot be improved without a clear commitment both to engaging with the development of all those involved, whether staff or students, and to considering the strategic goals of the institution.

The development process

The book then goes on to consider a number of features that typically form part of the development process. Chapters 2–6 in turn each consider what might be thought of as key elements of this process. However, the complexity inherent in development work ensures that this process is not simply a linear one. Indeed, much of staff and educational development is managed simultaneously. These elements interact, and are thus not considered in isolation from each other.

An important starting point for development, then, is the identification and analysis of needs. Gina Wisker, in Chapter 2, considers the relevance of addressing the needs of individuals, groups of staff and entire institutions. Wisker in particular contrasts intuitive approaches to needs analysis with more systematic models. She argues that developers need to go beyond informal analysis to more sophisticated techniques if they are successfully to reconcile the needs of the organization as a whole with the development of individuals.

While various development methods could have been considered within this book, we have chosen to focus on two methods in particular. The first of these is addressed in Chapter 3 by Diana Kelly, namely, the use of events. The event forms one of the most visible and powerful methods within the developer's repertoire. Kelly argues that the planning of a successful event must be both comprehensive and careful. Her chapter has a practical focus and draws attention to the many details that go into planning and running effective events.

Development work is complex; so is the work of the clients with whom developers work. It follows that development work needs to be tailored to the individual circumstances of the client. It should therefore not come as a surprise that developers will often need to work as consultants within their own institutions. It is therefore also important to include the use of consultancy as a development method. So, in Chapter 4 Liz Shrives and Chris Bond consider a framework that outlines the key stages of the consultancy cycle. Central to this cycle is the relationship between the client and the consultant.

It is, however, unrealistic to expect that successful development activity can rely wholly on a clear prior identification and analysis of needs and on the appropriate use of development methods. David Baume argues in Chapter 5 that monitoring and evaluation are an integral part of good practice right from the start of any development activity. The chapter begins with a focus on goals and their achievement, while recognizing that the process by which those goals are defined also merits serious consideration. While monitoring and evaluation that addresses only these levels may satisfy the demands of accountability, Baume goes on to consider how evaluation can serve a wider range of purposes and can incorporate an active contribution from the various stakeholders involved in the development activity.

If we are seeking to effect change on more than a very local scale then dissemination of any development is critical. Helen King in Chapter 6 argues that dissemination of an educational development should occur as an integral aspect of the development itself. Furthermore, effective dissemination requires a clear focus on the goals that are sought, and the concerns and context of the end user. Planning is important to ensure that dissemination incorporates these elements.

Approaches to development

The complexity of development work, however, further ensures that the wider context in which the development is carried out is also critical. The book thus goes on to look at four particular aspects of this wider context: the use of information and communications technology (ICT); fixed-term project work; the place of different academic disciplines; and the relevance of national agendas. Indeed, it might be considered that in each of these four cases we go beyond contextual factors to consider distinct approaches to development work. Similarly, it can also be said that the organization itself provides a further dimension to the context in which development occurs.

Technology is indeed increasingly an important aspect of higher education, and this includes its use within staff and educational development. In Chapter 7, Stephen Fallows and Rakesh Bhanot thus focus on ways that developers can use ICT in their work with staff. They emphasize that technology needs to be used appropriately and with professionalism.

A further development approach now increasingly employed, as Rachel Segal notes in Chapter 8, is the fixed-term project. While their short-term nature brings challenges, projects benefit from a clear focus on specific goals. This chapter draws on a wealth of experience that has been acquired within the United Kingdom, not least from the author's own work with the projects supported by the Fund for the Development of Teaching and Learning. The commitment of and the interactions between the various stakeholders in a project emerge as a critical feature of a successful project.

Huge variations in the nature of development work stem from the distinct nature of the various academic disciplines. The manner in which students actually learn is profoundly informed by the discipline concerned. So, a development activity that might work well in one discipline, say physics, may become far less effective or even counter-productive when employed within, for instance, sociology. Caroline Baillie in Chapter 9 addresses these issues, looking at a variety of roles and contexts in which individuals working within discipline-specific educational development are likely to find themselves. Baillie gives valuable accounts of the various groupings of staff that are associated with disciplines, including departments, working groups and national networks or associations.

The final aspect of context we will consider is the plethora of national initiatives and agendas with which development work is often aligned. Diana Eastcott and Neill Thew point out in Chapter 10 that such initiatives and agendas offer great scope for creating positive change within institutions. At the same time, they note that these initiatives should not be pursued in isolation from each other. They further argue that developers should enable their colleagues to take ownership of any local implementation of such national initiatives. This chapter will be relevant to developers in any setting where regional and national development agendas are in play.

Chapter 11 more explicitly considers change at the level of the organization. The complexity of organizational change may well require the developer to use highly sophisticated frameworks or analyses. Val Roche shows how developers can use a variety of such tools to guide change at the level of an entire system. She argues for a more systematic approach to the way in which developers lead and support change.

Developing the developers

In Chapter 12, John Cowan aims both to assist the learning of the developer and to assist the learning of staff and students. In this chapter, we thus begin a transition towards considering the development of the developer him- or herself. The specific approaches to teaching and learning that a member of staff might adopt for his or her students are not a primary focus of this work. As a whole, this book is concerned with how development is carried out rather than the specific approaches to education that one might take. However, this chapter provides a case study that looks at one specific approach to learning, namely learning from experience. Cowan argues eloquently that we need to do more than gain experience: we need to learn from that experience.

Issues of professionalism that are raised in the very first chapter are revisited in Chapter 13 – this time for the individual developer. If staff and educational developers are to help shape and lead the change that is now occurring within higher education then it is essential that they possess the necessary expertise. But what professional expertise do staff and educational developers need? How is the nature of this expertise affected by the context in which they work? How can a developer acquire the requisite expertise? This chapter also looks at the relevance of the experience that new developers bring with them.

Neill Thew in the concluding chapter focuses more widely on the personal and professional development of the developer. Thew is aware of the stresses that are only too common among staff and educational developers. Each chapter in this book requires the engagement of the reader; this chapter very directly encourages the reader to act on its suggestions. Thew offers a variety of ideas and activities to help developers retain control of their professional, and indeed their personal, lives. The aim is to help ensure that we each personally become aligned with our professional role, and that as developers we ourselves develop.

Finally, the Appendix outlines a variety of further sources of information for developers. These sources include books, journals, Web sites and networks. The choice of sources, by Bland Tomkinson, is of course a personal one. It helps to identify relevant resources for newer developers. For more experienced developers it may serve as a helpful reference tool. It is also important that all developers identify a comparable set of resources for themselves on which to help base their practice.

MOVING ON

This brief orientation to the chapters within this book suggests that not only should development work be systematic and scholarly, but it should also be characterized by a number of other factors:

- It is evident first of all that development work is a collaborative activity. The development of educational processes and of the practice of educators is not something that can be carried out in isolation from colleagues, particularly when the development of an entire organization is at stake.

- An appreciation is also required for the context in which the development work occurs. This context may involve specific disciplines, patterns of funding, the experience that developers bring with them to the field, and other factors. Development work must clearly be carefully tailored to the culture of higher education.

- The integrated nature of work in this field also emerges as a critical factor. It is evident that different elements of the development process need to be carried out alongside each other. Dissemination and evaluation, for instance, are elements that are not simply left to the end of the development process.

- Attention needs to be paid to improving one's own practice, including, for instance, learning from one's own experience, as well as to concern for more formal development opportunities.

An additional way to view the field of development is, however, to highlight the way in which professional values should inform the practice of staff and educational development. Such an approach is built into the professional accreditation offered by the Staff and Educational Development Association (SEDA) for both developers and higher education staff more broadly (SEDA, 2000). It is interesting to note that there is significant overlap between some of the factors that have emerged from this overview of the book and the professional values that SEDA promotes. In particular, it is worth highlighting the need for collaboration, reflection on practice and a concern for scholarship.

The extent to which development work has become more of a mainstream function within higher education is also relevant. For one thing, this increases the extent to which the impact of our work is more closely studied, and hence emphasizes the importance of evaluation, dissemination and research within our practice. Alongside this is the enhanced attention paid to the organization as a whole, with greater attention given to strategies, policies and targets. Furthermore, we can regard the growing concern for professionalism within the field of development as a further factor that comes with this position in the mainstream. We may well regard all of these as signs of increasing maturity within a relatively new professional field.

This growing maturity of the field further ensures that a fully comprehensive guide to staff and educational development needs to extend beyond a single text. *A Guide to Staff and Educational Development* is the first of two books that together are designed to provide wide coverage of the practice of staff and educational development. The companion volume, *Enhancing Staff and Educational Development* (Baume and Kahn, forthcoming), will extend some themes and topics from the first book, and introduce further ones. It will be useful to those tackling more advanced academic and strategic development work, including project leaders and unit heads. While again including practical guidance, it will take a more critical approach. Taken together, these two books will provide an indispensable guide for all those engaged in staff and educational development.

So, engage with this first guide to staff and educational development. Implement selected ideas into your own practice and learn from that experience. Draw your colleagues into discussions that follow on from points raised in the chapters. And perhaps above all, ensure that the way in which you use this book is aligned with your professional role; use this book to help you to develop!

REFERENCES

Baume, D and Kahn, P E (eds) (forthcoming) *Enhancing Staff and Educational Development*, Kogan Page, London

Department for Education and Skills (DfES) (2003) *The Future of Higher Education*, HMSO, London

Staff and Educational Development Association (SEDA) (2000) *SEDA Fellowship and Associate Fellowship: Professional Accreditation for Staff and Educational Developers in Higher Education*, SEDA, Birmingham

1

What is staff and educational development?

Lorraine Stefani

INTRODUCTION

The aim of this chapter is to explore the meaning of staff and educational development. In researching this chapter, I came to the conclusion that staff and educational development defies simple definitions owing to its complex and constantly evolving nature. On the one hand, the intention of staff and educational development is to offer the opportunities for all staff and students to develop their full potential. On the other hand, these same opportunities must fit with the strategic goals of the institution in the rapidly changing context of higher education (HE). Managing the complex relationship between an individual's development and institutional strategy and planning presents a major challenge.

This chapter seeks to provide some insight into the nature of staff and educational development as it is generally understood at the beginning of the 21st century. I have attempted to do this by examining the current context in which it occurs, the status given to it within institutions. I offer a broad-brush view of the remits of developers and development units, and consider whether staff and educational development as a field of study deserves now to be recognized and valued as a worthy profession in its own right, crucial to the achievement of goals in HE.

THE HIGHER EDUCATION CONTEXT FOR STAFF AND EDUCATIONAL DEVELOPMENT

As a starting point, the term 'staff and educational development' can be considered to mean the systematic and scholarly support for improving both educational processes and the practice of educators (see, for instance,

Webb, 1996). If used separately within HE, the term 'educational development' would then focus on the improvement of educational processes, while 'staff development' would refer to working to improve the capabilities and practice of educators. These definitions, however, belie the complexity of the role of the staff and educational developer and the multiplicity of activities encompassed within the term 'development' as applied both to staff and to education.

Indeed, this complexity is in part reflected in the range of terms that are used to describe this role. In Australia, for instance, the term 'academic development' is often employed, while in the United States the key term is 'faculty development', alongside 'instructional development'. Both these terms make it clear that we must go beyond a generic consideration of staff development to address concerns that are particularly relevant to the specific context of HE.

In broad terms, it is reasonable to suggest that within a large and complex institution such as a university, the staff and educational development and training needs are vast and multifaceted. Higher education globally is undergoing unprecedented change (Barnett, 1997). Staff are coping with shifts to mass higher education, lifelong learning, diversity of student population, ensuring access to higher education for disadvantaged groups, the information revolution which requires that we equip learners with different skills, and quality assurance and accountability agendas. Global competition for students increases and there are currently drives towards making universities more entrepreneurial. It is no wonder, then, that the staff and educational development agenda has become so complex and wide-ranging, with staff developers having to respond to unexpected demands from a clientele hoping for and expecting answers and solutions to a wide variety of questions and problems.

What, then, within this context is staff and educational development? There is no simple, all-encompassing answer to this question. Potential answers come from a variety of sources. It has often been a cause for concern that there is not a defined educational development discourse (Andresen, 1996), and this may well be for the very simple reason that the agenda has become so vast and unwieldy. In addition, as Webb has articulated, 'development is a site for contestation, it is not a unitary concept which we will one day provide a model for' (Webb, 1996). Perhaps it is this issue more than any other that in fact causes the difficulties of definition. People's understandings of the term 'development' are likely to be very broad, with its having both positive and negative connotations for some staff. Some colleagues outside what might be called the staff and educational development community may have vague notions of what we do. Because development as a concept can be intangible, attention might more fruitfully be paid not so much to what we do as to why and how we do it and what we achieve.

How, then, can we get closer to conceptualizing staff and educational development? In 1995, Elton put forward a vision of the future for staff and educational development in universities. He suggested that:

> staff and educational development will have a primary function as an agent of institutional change. While one of its concerns must always be to meet the legitimate personal needs of staff, its main concern in difficult times will be to meet the needs of students, in their learning experiences, in the services provided for them and in the environment in which they spend three or more important years of their lives. It will be concerned in different ways with changes in knowledge, skills and attitudes of all staff and at every level right up to that of the most senior administrators and the head of each and every university. (Elton, 1995)

Only a few short years have passed since that optimistic statement was published. In those few years we have seen dramatic, continuing and global change in higher education, with far greater emphasis on student learning, as we come to understand more about the impact of teaching on learning and engage with research on student learning strategies (eg Ramsden, 1992; Schon, 1995). But has Elton's vision actually materialized? Is staff and educational development the valued concept that this statement suggests? Does this vision encompass the diversity of approaches, activities and people associated with staff and educational development?

Answers to these questions can be found within institutions themselves, among senior managers who co-ordinate the institutional agenda, among staff or clients who request the 'services' of educational developers and academic practice units, and among the currently practising educational developers. Professional organizations associated with staff and educational development and developers will also have a view as to the definition of our practice. For the purposes of this chapter, it was decided to seek answers to these questions by exploring the literature on staff and educational development, by viewing the Web sites of several HE institutions both nationally and internationally to determine the remits of educational development units and how this remit was presented, and by asking colleagues responsible for managing these units what their definition would be. In carrying out this work, it was highly encouraging to find that a remarkable level of consensus is building up and a growing level of coherence in our understanding of the nature of our field is developing.

THE STATUS OF STAFF AND EDUCATIONAL DEVELOPMENT IN THE INSTITUTION

A contributing factor to the problem of clearly defining staff and educational development may be that among faculty, in this case meaning academic and related staff within HE institutions, there may well be very different understandings of the concept of development. There may well also be different views on the value of development activities to the institution, or to the different constituencies within the institution.

The success and the status of educational development activities depend on the skills of educational developers in initiating effective partnerships and constructive collaborations with their client base in such a way as to fulfil perceived development needs for staff while at the same time working towards the overarching goal of enhancing the student learning experience in HE. Indeed, Hicks (1999) links academic development clearly with student learning. He suggests that 'academic development can be taken to mean: the provision of pedagogically sound and discipline relevant development for academic staff across the broad spectrum of disciplines present within a university so as to impact effectively on student learning'. Hicks elaborates on the three key issues that can be drawn from this definition.

First, he refers to pedagogical soundness, without which there is little point in academic development. To be compatible with the purpose and meaning of HE and the expectations of what one might term those to be developed, academic development must have a theoretical basis.

Second, Hicks suggests, relevance across disciplines is crucial if staff are to value academic development. Indeed, it has been not at all unusual to hear anecdotally of disquiet that the development opportunities for staff are too generic in nature and not necessarily transferable to different disciplines.

The third issue arising from Hicks's definition is the impact on student learning. The current plethora of changes in HE include the shifts towards mass higher education, increasing diversity of the student population, and different routes into higher education through various schemes to widen access to higher education to previously excluded groups of students both in the United Kingdom and further afield (Longworth, 1999; Watson, 2000). This will inevitably mean that staff involved in supporting students through their programmes of study must reassess and reconsider their conceptions of student learning and of facilitating student learning (Gibbs, 2000). To ensure the best possible student learning experience, institutions must ensure that staff and educational development does impact positively on the student experience. This resonates well with the statements of Elton (1995) and Hicks (1999).

Hicks provides an interesting definition of staff and educational development. But does it go far enough? Would all staff involved in staff and educational development be able to identify with this definition, or would they conceivably see it in broader terms?

Professor George Gordon, Director of the Centre for Academic Practice at the University of Strathclyde, provides the following definition:

> I see staff and educational development as providing support to individuals, departments/programmes and institutions in relation to academic practice (teaching, learning and assessment, research and scholarship and academic management and institutional research). Ultimately, all of these endeavours are directed towards enhancing student learning and the student experience and extending understanding and knowledge. Classically, staff and educational development has tended to focus either on individual development or on educational development. External policy drivers have greatly sharpened the institutional focus. That, largely, must be welcomed because it offers important opportunities to connect individual and institutional objectives, departmental and individual etc (personal communication, 2002)

In common with the above-quoted statements of both Elton and Hicks, this definition firmly positions the overarching purpose of staff and educational development as being to enhance student learning, enhance the student experience and to extend pedagogical understanding and knowledge. However, this definition does stretch the remit more widely than Hicks's definition implies, by including the notions of scholarship, academic management and institutional research.

In all the responses received from an e-mail trawl of key international figures in the field of staff and educational development to the question 'What is staff and educational development?', the most common recurring theme related to the intended outcome of staff and educational development is 'to enhance student learning and the overall student experience'. The responses given by a random sample of colleagues across different institutions in the United Kingdom, Canada, Australia and New Zealand, while not as extensive a study as that carried out by Gosling (2001), nevertheless resonate well with the outcomes of his study of the remit of educational development units in the United Kingdom.

Some respondents queried the assumption that staff and educational development ultimately *improves* student learning, and further affirmed the need for research and scholarship and a research culture that underpins the practice(s) of staff and educational development. Other colleagues mentioned a key issue that has the potential to alienate some staff members: that staff and educational development is about facilitating changes in people's practice, changes in ways of thinking and understanding, as regards education and educational processes. It is seen by some that there is an element of counselling or therapy processes associated with our role. This point again emphasizes the notion of development as a site for contestation (Webb, 1996), a recurring theme in much of the research on staff and educational development.

There was remarkable consistency in the definitions of staff and educational development from the e-mail survey mentioned above. However, it could be argued that the terms of reference provided are broad-brush. The primary objective of enhancing the student learning experience is undisputed in the eyes of the developers. However, does the client group with which staff and educational developers seek to work necessarily understand our remit, or indeed recognize staff and educational development as a profession in its own right?

EXPLORING THE REMIT OF STAFF AND EDUCATIONAL DEVELOPMENT

Along with this wider understanding of the nature of staff and educational development, it is also worth looking at how the overall remit of staff and educational development has expanded in keeping with the changing nature of HE, thereby contributing to the elusive, fluid and evolving nature of the field. For example, there is fast-growing interest in and emphasis on the use of information and communications technology (ICT) in teaching and learning. This means that a wider range of different skills is required of people entering the profession than were required in a previous age when ICT developments in teaching and learning were very much left to the technological enthusiasts. Today, there is much focus not only upon raising awareness of the potential educational benefits to be derived from effective use of ICT in the classroom but also on embedding it within mainstream educational development (Fallows and Bhanot, 2002; O'Hagan, 1998).

Another example: the past decade has also seen a gradual shift from generic training events being the norm in terms of delivery of staff and educational development to a demand for more complex educational development projects taking place in the classroom within different disciplinary domains (Katz, 2000). The consequences of this have been a greater emphasis on staff and educational developers working in partnership with staff and students. These partnerships have aimed to develop shared understanding, not just of generic pedagogical frameworks but also of how to turn these pedagogic frameworks into practical classroom actions compatible with the particular academic terrain within which they are operating.

This shift in emphasis has impacted on staff and educational development in very positive ways. First, it has led to a greater degree of professionalization of staff and educational development. Second, it has created more of a culture of scholarship with respect to teaching and learning (Gordon *et al*, 2001).

It has increasingly become the norm in higher education establishments for a central unit to exist for staff and educational development. This appears to be common to HE establishments in Australasia, the United States and Canada, and there has been considerable growth in the number of such units within higher education institutions in the United Kingdom. These units have a plethora of different titles: for example, the Centre for Academic Practice, the Institute for the Advancement of University Learning, the Staff Development Unit, the Centre for Learning and Teaching, the Centre for Staff and Educational Development. However, there is a high level of commonality in terms of their remit. Indeed, that remit can often be seen as an unpacking of the definitions of staff and educational development as highlighted in previous sections. To emphasize this point, I will present examples of the remit of the 'staff and educational development unit' of three very different universities for comparison.

The Centre for Professional Development (CPD) at the University of Auckland, New Zealand (CPD, 2002), puts forward the following points relating to its function:

The Centre for Professional Development:

- promotes and advises on the development of innovative and effective teaching and learning strategies and methodologies and on curriculum design;

- in conjunction with the Centre for Flexible and Distance Learning promotes and advises on flexible teaching, learning and curriculum design;

- advises, trains and supports academic and administrative managers and leaders;

- engages in critical scholarship related to higher education, including conducting and disseminating research;

- provides professional, personal development and computer courses and training for general and academic staff;

- provides teaching evaluation services and follow-up support.

Providing a similar remit in a different format is the educational development unit at Napier University in Edinburgh. From the institutional Web site link to Educational Development, the remit is defined as follows:

Educational Development is responsible for a range of activities which are ultimately concerned with supporting and enhancing the quality of learning and teaching at Napier. This includes supporting the collaborative development of high quality flexible and electronic learning provision to reach its goal in the areas of lifelong learning and growth.

Educational Development has a leading role to play in the authoring and embedding of the Quality Enhancement Strategy and in supporting the implementation of the Learning, Teaching and Enhancement Strategy. This involves encouraging innovation and effective change and offering a range of staff development initiatives designed to embed the culture change that is required to make these strategies happen.

Educational Development delivers services to the University – for example, initial induction courses in teaching and learning, a Postgraduate Certificate in Teaching and Learning in Higher Education, a Postgraduate Certificate in Specific Learning Difficulties (Dyslexia) – and has a development function including: innovation in teaching and learning, staff development for appropriate use of new learning technology, supporting educational research, and providing a staff development programme of activities in areas related to learning teaching and assessment. (Educational Development, 2002).

A further example of the remit of staff and educational development units comes from Coventry University. The information provided on the Web site relating to its educational development unit, the Centre for Higher Education Development (CHED), could almost be written as a case study in itself of what staff and educational development entails and how it is embedded within the culture of the institution.

According to the Web site, CHED is:

a home for Teaching, Learning and Research at Coventry University including on-line learning and support via an electronic learning environment (WebCT). CHED supports staff development in many ways, including courses, workshops, seminars, and individual consultancy in areas impacting on higher education. The Centre offers a full postgraduate programme in learning and teaching in higher education including a postgraduate certificate in learning and teaching for new teachers. (CHED, 2002)

An analysis of these examples brings out a number of points worthy of note. The first point is that in the majority of examples of remits of staff and educational development units examined by means of a trawl of primarily

United Kingdom-based and Australasian universities, there is little mention of working directly with students. This is in stark contrast to the unequivocal agreement found among developers that the outcomes of their endeavours were intended to enhance student learning or impact effectively on student learning. It could be surmised from this that, as Gosling (2001) has suggested, the impact of our endeavours on student learning is 'intended to be indirect, through staff training, projects, policy development etc'. An alternative explanation is that within institutions there has been a reluctance to fully acknowledge teaching and learning as inter-related and complementary activities. This latter point may explain why it is that in many universities, a separate unit/centre has been set up to deal specifically with student learning support. It could be argued that it makes much more sense to set up a unit that has as its remit support and development opportunities for both staff and students such as the Centre for Academic Practice at the University of Strathclyde. Where staff and student development are co-ordinated within a single unit, it is possible to align the development opportunities.

Within the United Kingdom, the remit of most staff and educational development units now includes a postgraduate certificate or diploma-level programme relating to teaching, learning and assessment in HE. It is increasingly common for it to be compulsory for new members of staff to complete such programmes during their probationary period. This requirement for the staff and educational development unit to offer, and for new teaching staff to complete, a qualification means that staff and educational developers are, one hopes, adopting a scholarly rather than a training focus.

Again within the United Kingdom, this development is largely explained by the impetus of the Dearing Report of 1997, the output from the National Committee of Inquiry into Higher Education (NCIHE, 1997). Dearing recommended the professionalization of teaching in HE, and the establishment of an institute to accredit the practice of university teachers. This recommendation resulted in the setting up in 1999 of the Institute for Learning and Teaching in Higher Education (ILTHE). ILTHE was launched with the support of government and all major HE stakeholders. It is a membership organization open to everyone engaged in teaching and learning support in higher education who meets its entry requirements, either by completing an ILTHE-accredited programme or via direct entry route requiring submission of a 3,000-word account of the applicant's approach to and experience of teaching. ILTHE aims to enhance the status of teaching, to improve the experience of learning and to support inno-vation in HE teaching and learning.

In the post-Dearing era in UK higher education there has thus has been a significant focus on the provision of postgraduate-level programmes relating to broad themes of academic practice. These are typically accredited by ILTHE or by the UK Staff and Educational Development Association (SEDA) (see SEDA, 2002). The growth in such accredited programmes is contributing to current promotion of 'the scholarship of teaching and learning' (Gordon *et al*, 2001), encouraging academic staff to put more emphasis on understanding disciplinary-based pedagogy and viewing teaching and learning as legitimate researchable activities. Indeed, the provision of such accredited courses and programmes has now become a major aspect of the work of staff and educational development units. It is not yet the case that all postgraduate programmes on offer place an emphasis on research and scholarship. However, Stefani and Elton (2002) suggest that it must be one of the main features of any really successful programme of continuing professional development (CPD) for academic teachers to convince them that university teaching is a problematic and researchable activity.

Development opportunities with respect to the use of ICT in teaching and learning are often the responsibility of yet another unit. For example, in the case of Auckland University, New Zealand, there is a Centre for Flexible and Distance Learning, while the University of Strathclyde has a unit called Learning Services that encompasses e-learning services and training. In today's climate, this seems something of an anomaly and is perhaps a throwback to the days when use of ICT was confined to a few specialist enthusiasts. The current situation results in the e-learning focus often being primarily targeted towards systems development (ie learning environments such as WebCT and Blackboard) rather than on standard learning development using ICT (Heath and Wiles, 2001).

In a recent article on the role of learning technologists – an umbrella term used to describe all those involved in developing and promoting the use of learning technology – Martin Oliver (2002) describes the emergence of these new professionals in HE, whose practices are sometimes poorly understood. These learning technologists work in partnership with staff from staff and educational development units and in collaboration with academic staff within their disciplines. Many learning technology-oriented staff agree that, first and foremost, their role involves coming to terms with the pedagogy of a discipline, and that the technology is merely a tool. Oliver and others (eg Beetham, 2000; Gornall, 1999) are in the forefront in persuading and encouraging further professionalization of this group of staff. They encourage closer synergy between the remits of educational developers and learning technologists, who in some cases still sit on the margins of academia and yet, with the drive for more integration of ICT into teaching and learning, are crucial to institutions' achieving their strategic priorities (Fallows and Bhanot, 2002).

PEDAGOGY: FROM THE GENERIC TO THE DISCIPLINE SPECIFIC

Regarding the provision of postgraduate-level, accredited professional development programmes, this change in emphasis from provision of generic staff development workshops to accredited programmes marks an interesting shift in the conceptualization of staff and educational development and a historic move forward for institutions. In his definition of staff and educational development, Hicks (1999) mentions the need for relevance to the disciplines. Stefani and Elton (2002) argue that convincing university staff that teaching is a problematic and researchable activity may be best achieved through academic teachers reflecting on problems in their own teaching and then attempting to solve these problems in accordance with the culture of their own disciplinary base. In other words, it is suggested that university staff be encouraged to engage in cycles of experimenting with, and reflection on, their current classroom practice, activities associated with action research (for a discussion on action research, see for instance Zuber-Skerritt, 1992). The importance of development occurring within disciplinary contexts is considered in much more detail in Chapter 9.

Developments of this nature have contributed to the evolution of the profession of staff and educational development. A further indication in the UK of the importance of disciplinary-based development was the setting up of the Learning and Teaching Subject Network (LTSN), funded by the Higher Education Funding Council for England. The LTSN was set up specifically to provide resources tailor-made to the teaching and learning demands of 24 different disciplinary-based subject areas, and for the purposes of disseminating good practice within and across different subject areas (Allan, 2000). This was an explicit signal that educational development could and arguably should occur within the disciplinary base. It was also a response to the difficulties of expecting staff to transfer their learning from generic workshops on issues relating to teaching and learning into their disciplinary base, where they may be trying to effect change as a lone ranger. Within the United Kingdom, the advent of ILTHE, the LTSN and the general marked increase in resources available to disciplinary-based staff are tangible evidence that staff and educational development has made its mark in HE (LTSN, 2002). This invites the question, has staff and educational development, however elusive an agreed definition may be, reached the status of a recognized profession integral to the mission and purpose of HE?

STAFF AND EDUCATIONAL DEVELOPMENT AS A PROFESSION?

Has staff and educational development become a respected and important profession? It may be useful to examine the ways in which people enter this field, what knowledge and skills they contribute, and whether or not the developers and development fit the criteria of a 'profession'.

There is currently much discussion on the training and entry into the profession of the next generation of staff and educational developers. The first generation were the pioneers, the staff who were prepared to go against the grain and set up informal networks to discuss educational development and to encourage other enthusiasts to participate. Staff and educational development was born out of the immense energy and efforts of enthusiasts. Our move towards becoming a profession owes a great debt indeed to these pioneers. The second generation, in many instances, appear to be drawn from academic-related staff who came out of their disciplinary- or academic-related bases, having experienced teaching within their own discipline but perhaps been discouraged from promoting enhancement measures in that setting.

In the current HE climate, we developers are not just working with staff new to the trials and tribulations of teaching large classes. Rather, there is an expectation by senior management that our role will be to shape the future teaching and learning strategy of the institution, and to enable the institution to fulfil the terms of its mission. This then would tend to further affirm the notion that staff and educational development is reaching the status of a 'profession'.

Arguably, the current and potential routes into staff and educational development ensure a more diverse range of people with a wider skills base than other professional territory in academia. It may well be that future educational developers will find it easier to pursue professional development pathways that enable them to make a choice to enter the profession of staff and educational development. Chapter 13 specifically points a way forward for aspiring or newer developers to gain relevant development expertise.

Knapper (1998), in an editorial for the *International Journal for Academic Development* (IJAD), asked, 'Is academic development a profession?' He considers that the hallmarks of a profession might include:

- agreement among practitioners about the definition and scope of the field, including widely accepted standards of practice;

- a formal organization and structure;

- a formal and theoretical base to underpin professional practice;

- perhaps procedures for licensing and accreditation, including a code of ethics and systematic training of practitioners.

It is worth examining how well staff and educational development as a profession lives up to these criteria.

With the development of accredited programmes for academic and related staff, which embody common standards for academic practice, and the bold move by the UK government to establish a professional body for teaching in HE, in the shape of ILTHE, the issue of common standards relating to academic practice and development begins to be addressed on a wider level. Formal organization and structure is becoming more evident, with an increasing range of recognized networks involved in promoting and disseminating current scholarship, and research relating to different aspects of academic practice and development.

There is little question that staff and educational developers require a theoretical underpinning of their practice. In most situations in which educational developers find themselves, if they cannot establish their credentials with their client group, they will not be taken seriously. The growing body of educational development research is enhancing the credibility of the field, particularly as much of this research is becoming more accessible to the wider body of academic and related staff.

There is undoubtedly a need for forms of accreditation for staff and educational developers. Within the United Kingdom, some members of the educational development community have had aspects of their own practice – specifically their teaching work – accredited through ILTHE. Others have submitted a portfolio of evidence of and reflection on good practice that more specifically relates to their work as developers to the SEDA Fellowship Scheme (see Chapter 13 for further details of this scheme). Discussion and dialogue is under way regarding the professionalization of the new professionals in posts specifically relating to the use of ICT (Oliver, 2002). These developments, which appear to be more advanced within UK higher education than elsewhere, in themselves indicate a desire on the part of developers in general to have more clearly defined career pathways and CPD opportunities linked to their own professional development.

With respect to the ethical dimension of a profession, both ILTHE and SEDA request evidence of one's carrying out one's work according to a set of agreed values and attitudes, which is clearly a move towards a future ethical code of practice.

These considerations suggest that staff and educational development increasingly meets the criteria to deserve the status of profession.

IN CONCLUSION

At the beginning of the 21st century, staff and educational development has moved from being seen as a fringe activity pursued by a few teaching enthusiasts to the point of being a respected profession in its own right. It defies simple definition, in part because of the dynamic and fluid nature of the profession. It is by necessity constantly evolving in response to changing imperatives and the expectations of HE stakeholders.

The real challenge for staff and educational developers is to enable all staff to develop to their full potential and to enhance the capabilities of the university. The following chapters expand on the multifaceted and complex aspects and outcomes of staff and educational development strategies and actions.

REFERENCES

Allan, C (2000) The Learning and Teaching Support Network (LTSN): the implications for educational developers, *Educational Developments*, 1 (2), pp 1–3

Andresen, L (1996) The work of academic development: occupational identity, standards of practice and the virtues of association, *International Journal for Academic Development*, 1 (1), pp 38–49

Barnett, R (1997) *Higher Education: A critical business*, Society for Research into Higher Education (SRHE) and Open University Press (OUP), Buckingham

Beetham, H (2000) *Career Development of Learning Technology Staff: Scoping Study Final Report* (accessed December 2002) [Online] http//sh.plym.ac.uk/eds/effects/jcalt-project/

Centre for Higher Education Development (2002) (accessed December 2002) [Online] www.coventry.ac.uk/ched

Centre for Professional Development (2002) (accessed December 2002) [Online] www2.auckland.ac.nz/cpd//aboutcpd.html

Educational Development Unit (2002) (accessed December 2002) [Online] www.ed.napier.ac.uk/about/index.htm

Elton, L (1995) An institutional framework, in *Directions in Staff Development*, ed A Brew, pp 177–88, Society for Research into Higher Education and Open University Press, Buckingham

Fallows, S and Bhanot, R (2002) *Educational Development through Information and Communications Technology*, Kogan Page, London

Gibbs, G (2000) Learning and teaching strategies: the implications for educational development, *Educational Developments*, 1 (1), pp 1–3

Gordon, G, D'Andrea, V, Gosling, D and Stefani, L (2001) *Building Capacity for Change: Research on the scholarship of teaching*, Review Report for the Higher Education Funding Council (HEFCE), HEFCE, London

Gornall, L (1999) New professionals: change and occupational roles in higher education, *Perspectives*, 3 (2), pp 44–49

Gosling, D (2001) Educational development units in the UK: what are they doing five years on? *International Journal of Academic Development*, 6 (1), pp 74–90

Heath, S and Wiles, K (2001) *NetCulture Briefing Paper: Frameworks for staff development in C&IT in learning and teaching* (accessed December 2002) [Online] http://www.netculture.scotcit.ac.uk/

Hicks, O (1999) Integration of central and departmental development: reflections from Australia, *International Journal for Academic Development*, **4** (1), pp 43–51

Katz, T (2000) University education for developing professional practice, in *New Directions in Professional Higher Education*, eds T Bourner, T Katz and D Watson, pp 19–32, Society for Research into Higher Education and Open University Press, Buckingham

Knapper, C (1998) Is academic development a profession? *International Journal of Academic Development*, **3** (2), pp 93–95

Learning and Teaching Support Network (2002) (accessed January 2003) [Online] www.ltsn.ac.uk

Longworth, N (1999) *Making Lifelong Learning Work: Learning cities for a learning century*, Kogan Page, London

National Committee of Inquiry into Higher Education (1997) *Higher Education in the Learning Society: Report of the National Committee of Inquiry into Higher Education* (the Dearing Report), HMSO, London

O'Hagan, C (1998) *Staff Development for Teaching and Learning Technology: Ten keys to success*, Higher Education Staff Development Agency (HESDA) Briefing Paper 53, HESDA, Sheffield

Oliver, M (2002) What do learning technologists do? *Educational Developments*, **3** (2), pp 19–21

Ramsden, P (1992) *Learning to Teach in Higher Education*, Kogan Page, London

Schon, D A (1995) *The Reflective Practitioner: How professionals think in action*, Arena, London

Staff and Educational Development Association (2002) accessed 28 January 2003 [Online] http://www.seda.ac.uk/

Stefani, L A J and Elton, L (2002) Continuing professional development of academic teachers through self initiated learning, *Assessment and Evaluation in Higher Education*, **27** (2), pp 117–30

Watson, D (2000) Lifelong learning and professional higher education, in *New Directions in Professional Higher Education*, ed T Bourner, T Katz and D Watson, pp 3–10, Society for Research into Higher Education and Open University Press, Buckingham

Webb, G (1996) *Understanding Staff Development*, Kogan Page, London

Zuber-Skerritt, O (1992) *Professional Development in Higher Education*, Kogan Page, London

2

Carrying out a needs analysis: from intuition to rigour

Gina Wisker

Development is a crucial link in an institution's enhancement of the quality of student learning. (Barnett, 1992)

INTRODUCTION

Universities today need to be learning organizations in order to rise to the challenges and demands of what Barnett (2002) has called 'an age of super-complexity', involving overload and conflicting ideologies and pressures. Learning organizations encompass shared vision and practice, and also the communication and development strategies that go a long way towards clarifying the attempt to bring this vision into a reality. Staff and educational developers have a crucial role to play here, because we work across all strata of the university to attempt to address changing needs.

At the heart of this essential development role is the needs analysis, which, if it is well managed, can ensure that all involved in the university's activities are fully engaged in the ownership of the vision. This involves institutional development, but development that is also very much produced and owned by individuals. It is individuals who must share the vision and carry out the mission of the university. At the same time, these individuals should be allowed to recognize the need for, and shape the direction and content of, their own lifelong learning.

A changing climate

The current climate of accountability, strategy and rigour in learning and teaching in higher education (HE) calls for a move from the kinds of intuitive, discussion-based need analyses that educational developers conventionally provided. Such a move is certainly required if the tension between the needs of the individual and the needs of the organization are to be reconciled in a way that is both well handled and sensitive. Our roles are very definitely on that changing continuum between national and corporately identified directives, and the rather more instinctive face of everyday interests and needs. Ten years ago, we might have had to be self-starters who decided what to do in a very hands-on fashion, working with the few who turned up to lunchtime workshops and innovations sessions, and then went away and tried out good ideas in the classroom, perhaps never spreading good practice any further. Now we are much more central in our functions, much more likely to ensure that what we organize and deliver is in alignment with strategic priorities. We are also, however, in danger perhaps of addressing the needs of only a few stakeholders, serving the masters with their hunger for paper rather than working with the practitioners.

Our labours are in danger of being a paper construction that lacks action. Of course, it need not be like this, but to ensure that it is not, we must make sure that we do not lose contact with our colleagues who are doing the teaching, who are facilitating the learning, who are setting and marking the assessments, and who would like a say in the kind of educational development activities and provision in which they are increasingly being *told*, and not just invited, to participate.

This new element of compulsion contrasts with the way in which I first began in development work. I was not told to take part and there were no quotas of involvement or performance indicators to check whether I had produced outputs as a result of involvement. It was curiosity, collegiality, community and an interest in developing as a better teacher that invited me and others like me to educational development. But, of course, we also found it difficult to describe how to carry out a needs analysis. It certainly emerged as something that appeared as much more ad hoc and questionable. That is, I just ask people what they want and then try to provide it. If I cannot provide it, then I can call in someone else. This model, the one I favoured, is problematic in many ways. Who am I talking to? How do I know they know how to identify their needs?

Needs versus wants

Needs, of course, should not be confused with wants. This is a fundamental issue in any needs analysis. Wants are likely to be personal and could be out of line with the aims and directions of the university. However, it could be argued that in a learning organization in which members are committed to the vision and the development of the organization, then wants and needs might well coincide. For example, here are some mini-cases of colleagues we might well meet at any university. How might we work with the needs and wants of each of these, in context?

- Bill wants to do a film studies course so that he can actively enjoy films more. He knows he will enjoy this course. But perhaps he also needs to do it in order to stay up to date in the ways in which culture is represented – which is a key outcome in his work as a literature lecturer.

- Andrew is about to retire in a few years' time, and one could argue that there is no need for him to undertake any further development because he won't have to use it.

- Jane can argue that she has 'done that' already. She did a teacher training course (for secondary school teaching) in 1972–73. Why would she need to do anything else now about teaching?

Persuading Andrew and Jane to realize that involvement in updating could make them more effective, engaged and motivated as teachers might be an uphill struggle. Starting with a sharp intake of breath about how long ago they did anything like this would not be the right approach! How is the educational developer to deal with these various colleagues? They variously insist that: I don't need a qualification, I don't want a course, I don't have the time, and I am confident that the study I did do 30 years ago 'will do' for me now. So each could be very offended if you suggest that they need this updating. Others of course are endlessly motivated:

- Bob loves learning! If something new comes along, if there is a workshop or a conference or a course, he will go. He has just been on a course in e-learning and e-moderating in case he starts to work at a distance with students who need some online learning and teaching. He went to a conference on working with students with disabilities in relation to the Disability Act and a day's training on the financial systems package, and he is still struggling with the evening Hebrew classes because of his work with Israeli PhD students.

How do you as an educational developer work with these different people? A more holistic approach involves the individual being able to see him- or herself as part of a large organization. Individuals feel valued as a part of that whole and can accept the need to align themselves with a managed, realistic version of the development needs of the organization. Such an approach should overcome the resistance and confusion of those described above. How then can we carry out needs analyses that avoid resistance and enable co-operation and ownership throughout the organization? And that can then encourage the effective translation of development into action,

inspired by focused vision and identified learning outcomes or needs translated into those achievable outcomes?

The first answer to this question is to look at some more systematic
approaches. In the process, we can begin to appreciate more fully the inad-
equacies of the earlier, informal approaches to needs analysis. The chapter
then looks at a number of substantial case studies of practice in this area.
This provides the second answer to our question. These case studies are all
drawn from work presented as part of the Staff and Educational
Development Association (SEDA) Fellowship Scheme, a scheme that offers
professional accreditation for staff and educational developers. The
practice that is evident within these case studies also provides a further base
for us to move beyond more intuitive approaches, while still retaining
appropriate relationships with all those involved. The aim in these case
studies is to find further ways to overcome both that 'secret sharing' model
and the cat's cradle of paper-based policy.

MODELS OF NEEDS ANALYSIS FOR HIGHER EDUCATION

The first problem we meet is that needs analyses in staff and educational
development are relatively under-theorized. The industry-oriented model
of training needs analysis tends to start with the assumption that there is a
problem in an organization or in the work of one or more people, and that
needs arise from the problem identification (Rae, 1997). This deficit model
is not entirely suited to higher education (HE), although it is certainly
familiar as a response of managers who seek to translate challenge into a
problem to be solved.

A deficit model assumes that someone, usually at the top, identifies a
problem and instructs others to undertake development in order to solve it –
whether it be a problem in the organization, such as lack of trained
managers, courses that don't recruit – or a problem in the individual, eg out-
of-date information and communications technology (ICT) skills, poor
management practice. Of course, some colleagues respond well to being told
they have a problem that training and development will sort out for them.
However, academics in particular are notorious in their distaste for and
rejection of this kind of industrial and commercial problem-oriented model,
and can assiduously refuse it, ignoring the learning process that is supposed
to be part of the development. Relatively autonomous, creative academics
and administrators must be involved in the determination of their needs in
line with the directions in which the university is going in order to ensure that
their learning is active, owned, then put into action in their practice.

The identification of development needs should more properly be seen
as a structured, sensitive, shared activity that involves all those who will be

party to the development – the stakeholders. (It is worth noting that in many contexts the stakeholders will include the students.) If the stakeholders are fully involved in the identification of needs, as well as in the subsequent stages of the development process, then the development that results will be understood, owned and finally translated into action by all involved.

It is also important to address the ways in which information about needs can be gathered. These can include interviewing each individual member working with the whole group in a brainstorming activity; using questionnaires to gather information about needs and preferred ways of addressing them, attitudes, behaviours and so on; and analysing documentary data about achievements, directions and developments. This information, of course, may already have been gathered by others, and it therefore makes sense to develop an appreciation for the specific ways in which this occurs in your own context. Quality assurance processes now mean that degree programmes will be reviewed on a regular process, and the resulting data may well be of use. Information concerning needs will also result from the appraisal process. This is particularly important given the way in which appraisal offers links to institutional targets and goals.

Once the needs are appropriately identified, analysis of the needs arising from this identification is then required. This analysis involves an attempt to translate needs into specific ways of addressing them, as Rae (1997: 5) notes:

> Effective training and development in an organisation depends on the need (i.e. requirement) for the improvement of human performance being identified and satisfied by the provision of appropriate development opportunities. 'Wants' can frequently be 'needs', but the analyst must be certain of the value of any aspect raised and eventually provided.

Development needs analyses can clarify problems that are felt to exist, or help clarify and identify the specific kinds of innovations or moves that are needed. Rae (1997) looks at the blockages that people create to the identification of needs and to attempts to meet these needs. Of course, there is possible blockage from the manager who wants a quick fix and for whom spending time on a needs analysis seems a waste of time when it is already clear (to them) what is wanted. This is akin to the lecturer who knows what he or she wants the student to know and feels that telling them will do the trick – rather than negotiating with them and setting up appropriate learning opportunities. Well-handled needs analyses can help to move from confusion and suspicion to clear identification of what the problem or demand might be. It is possible to suggest specific ways to address the issues concerned. Some training manuals, focusing on problems, see this stage as one that indicates types of solutions. But if the needs analysis is not problem focused as such, it is more likely to prepare the way for negotiation with the staff. It is then possible on a more collaborative basis to identify the kinds of activities and practices that might help address the needs, of which some development activity is a key element.

An effective development needs analysis will become detailed and specific at this point. Rae (1997) identifies several moments, people and tasks for which training needs analyses are needed:

- new workers coming into an existing work situation;

- new workers coming into an existing work situation with some experience that requires updating or change;

- completely new work being introduced;

- remedial action being seen as necessary;

- a need to review new developments and to review existing situations for possible modifications.

In terms of the situation in HE, there are several situations that are worth highlighting. Some work is required at the point of induction for new colleagues or colleagues new to a particular role. This is, of course, particularly evident as staff first take on major responsibility for teaching. Meanwhile, established colleagues will have scope to branch out into new areas of practice or to keep abreast of developments.

Consideration at a detailed level may, however, also be needed for the skills associated with specific jobs or roles. For example, you might encounter an administrator who needs to be able to work with a new finance system, or a head of department who needs to understand new disability legislation and then work with staff to interpret how to make it effective in practice. Within such specific contexts, the role of job development needs can then be identified at a detailed level:

- describing the needs or requirements of the job or role;

- identifying the level of skills that is needed to undertake the job or role;

- identifying the gap between the knowledge and skills, and the specific activities that could help fill this gap.

It is then worth looking at how to move from an analysis of needs to more specific planning of development activities. The UK Industrial Society (1994), for instance, offers an alternative way to move from the analysis of needs to the actual framing of development activities. The initial stages of a broader method are outlined in Table 2.1, with comments added to indicate the HE context. In particular, it is worth emphasizing that it is not sufficient to identify a need. This identification should also be followed by a clear definition of the development objectives. It is this focus on development objectives that helps to pave the way for actual development activities.

However, it is also essential to emphasize within the HE context that this whole process of identifying and meeting needs also incorporates a negotiation with those concerned about how and when to work on this development activity, what achievable outcomes can be identified, what steps of learning, time and place could be put in place, and so on. Tailoring development needs analyses to those involved is essential so that the right kind of development is carried out and impacts on practice. This goes far beyond a view of needs analysis as the identification of a problem that is then left to the developer to meet in an appropriate fashion. The activity that follows is, indeed, closely related to the analysis of the needs themselves.

In terms of the development activities that can result, there are evidently a wide range of activities on which to draw. Events, as considered in the next chapter, are often particularly effective, as is consultancy, which is looked at in Chapter 4. We might also think of mentoring and collaborations with more experienced colleagues. Activities need not always be led by the developers themselves, but simply by those with the relevant experience. Trainers or developers can also be their own worst enemies here. It is only too easy to use only favourite ways of working with people, when something carefully designed would be more appropriate.

Table 2.1 *The endless belt of development*

Stage	Activity	Comments
Stage 1	Recognize a business need	This might be a particular target, such as improving research assessment ratings, or dealing with a problem such as levels of complaints, or launching a new activity or reorganization. A business need does not always generate a training and development action.
Stage 2	Define development objectives	This should be done via appropriate consultation and discussion with stakeholders, the key players being the line manager and the facilitator of the action.
Stage 3	Design learning process	An appropriate route is agreed, wherever possible to ensure that the method is 'bespoke' to the learner.

Source: Industrial Society (1994), developed in Thackwray (1997: 30–31)

It is also worth emphasizing that needs analysis is the first step in an ongoing development that ends with sound evaluation of effectiveness. Bernthal (1995), for instance, views needs analysis in this way. Thackwray also argues that effective evaluation of development must be an integral part of the needs analysis process: 'In essence, higher education must evidently move away from seeing training and development as reactive and separate, and more towards a position where "development" is no longer separate from "management"' (1997: 15–16). Thackwray further comments:

> Many of the difficulties associated with effective evaluation arise because HE institutions are poor at both setting and keeping to objectives. Poorly constructed training and development objectives are usually vague. Vague objectives are not objectives but broad statements of what is required (eg, the objective for the next research assessment is to do better). (1997: 125)

This concern for evaluation follows on from the earlier emphasis on defining development objectives. Far more is required than simply identifying needs and framing activities that are then delivered to staff with inadequate skills or knowledge. Indeed, the process should also include, among other elements, detailed analysis of the relevant needs, stakeholder involvement and clear evaluation. Chapter 5 offers more on this.

CASE STUDIES OF NEEDS ANALYSES

It is, however, important to connect this more systematic approach to the identification and analysis of needs with examples of practice. Since the inception of the SEDA Fellowship Scheme, colleagues have been reflecting on their own practice in this area. In particular, candidates for the scheme are asked to provide evidence to demonstrate that they have 'analysed the development needs of individuals and groups in the organisation and the staff and educational implications of institutional goals and policies'. They are asked to provide three specific examples that they have met this objective, as well as a commentary that both highlights how the evidence presented meets the objective and incorporates reflection upon their own development. In addition, candidates also need to demonstrate that their practice meets a set of professional values, incorporating for instance a commitment to collaborative practice and to equality of opportunity. (See Chapter 13 for a further perspective on the SEDA Fellowship Scheme.)

The cases that follow in this chapter provide only part of the material that the author of the case study concerned presented for his or her SEDA

Fellowship. Taken as a whole, these case studies present selected examples of the full range of practice that candidates for the Fellowship are required to demonstrate. Some readers will, however, find the variety across the case studies as a whole helpful in terms of their own professional development, since changing circumstances and changing demands could easily lead to situations where favoured approaches do not fit and others needs to be developed.

The first of the case studies is provided by Patricia Kelly. She considers the impact that a carefully thought through process of needs identification, analysis and subsequent development activity can have on the practice of an individual lecturer. There is indeed a great deal of pleasure and much professional skill involved in working one to one with the needs of individual colleagues. David Baume then looks at a single workshop that was designed for a specific faculty. In terms of the initial method to collect the information about the needs of the participants, he employed a questionnaire. This provided a basis both for the initial planning and for the subsequent evaluation of the workshop. David also includes a summary of the evidence that he presented alongside the commentary. As well as providing further context, this will also be of use to any reader who is interested in pursuing the Fellowship Scheme, and will help provide the wider context for the needs analysis. I then provide the third case, which considers the development needs of women staff across an entire university. The needs analysis was conducted in relation to the university's mission statement, and in relation to its staff development and equal opportunities policies. The final case is provided by Anne Langley. She looked at the development needs of a small group of residential school counsellors, and in the process advanced her own learning, in part by gaining a renewed understanding of the importance of peer support in development work.

CASE STUDY 1: AN APPROACH FROM AN INDIVIDUAL (BY PATRICIA KELLY)

Given employment uncertainty, funding restrictions and pressure on academic staff to earn revenue, it is easy to look for short-term and instrumental responses to problems. While useful, these responses do not necessarily encourage teachers to question what they are teaching, why they do it in certain ways and whether those ways respond to ongoing changes in the teaching and learning environment. The approach that I took in the extract that follows, from the portfolio that I presented for my SEDA Fellowship, draws instead on a longer-term vision of higher education. What follows is one of the examples that I provided for evidence.

Addressing the core issue

Jim was one of the first staff development challenges I faced. In these days of increasing casualization of academic staff (piece-work of the mind), his situation could happen anywhere. He was a conscientious professional who began teaching after a successful career. He approached our unit to complain angrily about some delayed teaching evaluations. I had to acknowledge and defuse his feelings before I could uncover the real issue. Second, there was an administrative problem that was easily dealt with. Finally, Jim needed professional support to develop a personal and professional programme to improve his situation on a long-term basis. He was a competent, diligent lecturer but because of the situation, he had become rather directive in manner. The following exchange demonstrates his motives at this time.

Jim: 'I was trying to prepare them for the cold, hard world of practice.'
PK: 'It may be tough but it doesn't have to be cold, does it, Jim?'

The core problem was that the students had used him as a focus for their resentment against the administration. They expressed this anonymously through student evaluations and in person through rather adversarial attitudes towards all staff. We designed a programme to 'humanize' the course. I worked with him in the lecture to model the group work and support the changes he wanted to make through:

- an introduction to group work, designed to build team skills and to challenge this elite group of students to communicate more effectively in a diverse cultural and social work environment;

- a negotiated 'agreement' on professional conduct for the (then) year-long course.

As Jim summarized it, 'You've taught me other ways of doing things. I'm explaining rather than telling. It's more open, like a two-way street.' He later completed the Graduate Certificate in Education (Higher Education), his first formal higher education qualification, as well as his SEDA Associate Teacher accreditation, and he was recently awarded a faculty 'excellence in teaching' award. I am proud to feel that I played a role in this.

CASE STUDY 2: NEEDS ANALYSIS FOR A WORKSHOP FOR ART AND DESIGN ON ASSESSMENT (BY DAVID BAUME)

What follows is a lightly adapted version of one of the examples I provided in the portfolio for my SEDA Fellowship in 1995. I have also sketched the supporting evidence that I provided. At the time, I was head of the Educational Development and Support Service (EDSS) at London Guildhall University (LGU).

Invited to run a workshop on Assessment for the Faculty of Art, Design and Manufacture at LGU, I used a planning and evaluation form to collect in advance participants' views on what they wanted from the workshop. I used this form to determine the detailed outcomes for and contents of the workshop, as well as to evaluate the workshop in terms of achievement of participants' own goals.

The commentary for the portfolio further indicated a number of ways in which I met the Fellowship Scheme's values. In seeking to demonstrate the value of 'Understanding how people learn', it is worth noting that the process of involving participants in determining in advance what they want to get from a workshop or course, and then using that information to plan the workshop or course, acknowledges the role of motivation and active involvement in learning. Further values that this example addressed were 'Recognizing individual difference' and 'Focusing on development'. The workshop planning and evaluation forms do these directly and explicitly: they make use of the individuality that each person brings, and they help each individual to clarify his or her goals and hence to develop in directions of immediate concern to that individual.

Evidence presented

The evidence that I presented alongside the commentary comprised a sample completed planning and evaluation form for this workshop, together with the workshop timetable. The planning and evaluation form had five sections. I sent it out to participants some time before the workshop. Part A asked participants, 'What do you want to get out of this workshop?' I used the responses to plan the workshop. Parts B–E were completed at the end of the workshop. Part B asked participants to what extent they had got from the workshop what they intended to get. Part C asked how interesting, relevant, informative and enjoyable they found the workshop. Part D invited further comments. Part E asked what future work would be helpful to them.

Further reflections

How might it be different now? More to do, less time to do it, as everyone would probably say. Beyond that, I find that I still like the reflective approach I tried to take. And I still believe passionately in the importance of needs analysis as a process. It is a thing that can get squeezed when times are tight. But it should not be squeezed. If you miss out the needs analysis and plunge straight into designing the strategy or programme or workshop or Virtual Learning Environment or whatever, you can end up with what I call the Concorde syndrome: an elegant solution to the wrong problem! So, keep analysing needs.

Needs analysis can get very complex. And I'm sure 'need' and 'analysis' are both highly contestable concepts. But asking people what they want or need, and maybe also why, is easy enough, and valuable, and usually well appreciated.

CASE STUDY 3: DEVELOPMENT NEEDS OF A UNIVERSITY'S WOMEN STAFF (BY GINA WISKER)

I analysed the staff and educational development needs of the groups of women staff – both support staff and academic staff – at Anglia Polytechnic University across the multi-site, multi-faculty university in relation to both the university's mission statement and its staff development policy, and its equal opportunities policy. This resulted in the development and ongoing running and monitoring of a programme of staff development workshops aimed entirely at the broad range of women staff across the different sites of the institution, entitled the 'Women as Managers' series.

Women are under-represented in positions of responsibility across the university. I collected this information as part of my work towards a needs analysis of the educational and professional development needs of Anglia's women staff, and part of the groundwork for the senior managers equal opportunities workshops. Spotting this disproportionate representation of women, the newly formed Equal Opportunities Committee and its chair recommended that some training be put on specifically for those women who would benefit from management training. I was asked to develop this training even though at that time I was only very much 'on loan' to the Centre for Educational Development to carry out ad hoc staff development.

To continue my needs analysis, I contacted various women throughout the university to assess the kinds of training activities that they would find useful. I rang the women working in student services and consulted with those managing administrative and support staff, and with fellow academics teaching on the MA in Women's Studies, as well as using informal networks.

What emerged was a series of workshops, initially:

- Women as Managers;
- Women and Time Management;
- Women Managing Stress;
- Women and Assertiveness;
- Women Managing Meetings.

Outside facilitators or speakers were in the first instance called in for three of these events, and I ran the other two. They were felt to be successful, and I then ran each session again on the other campus; that is, if the first session was in Cambridge, I re-ran it in Chelmsford, so as to enable women from all over the university to participate.

Initially all the sessions were to be open to all women, although the first drive was for management training. Nonetheless, it was so unusual to have women-only events to train women in such skills that the sessions were thrown open to all women, and fliers indicated that they were only for women, and for all women. At that point, staff development was curiously paid for by individuals attending, or by agreement by their heads. It was decided by the Equal Opportunities Committee, in consultation with me, that this series would be free, which effectively removed the need for women hoping to attend to have to try to convince all concerned that they deserved and should have the training. Interestingly, and not surprisingly, many women said that this freed them up to come along.

Once the series had been running for a couple of years, with ever new additions called for by individuals and by the committee, it was suggested that in the new series there be some workshops for all women staff, and some especially for smaller groups of those with management roles already, at whatever level. In the light of this declared need, I have developed a programme that reflects the different needs, in particular by focusing on chairing skills.

CASE STUDY 4: THE DEVELOPMENT NEEDS OF RESIDENTIAL SCHOOL COUNSELLORS (BY ANNE LANGLEY)

I found this a difficult objective to demonstrate for the SEDA Fellowship. In theory we all believe that staff development should be based on client needs, but it is all too easy to assume that we know what these are, rather than making the effort to discover what they actually are.

The case study here concerns a small group of residential school counsellors. There had been requests for some years for a resource to support new counsellors at residential school, to parallel the equivalent resource for new tutors. Up till then, a briefing letter had been sent out from the centre about the role, but there was no nationally agreed policy on subsequent briefing and support. In addition, a change in student support throughout the university seemed likely to increase the development needs of new counsellors. This stimulated me to examine their needs and explains the context to this analysis, demonstrating that the project would help to fulfil both group and institutional needs.

I worked on the project with the chair of the relevant committee. We agreed to send out a questionnaire to investigate the needs of counsellors and what briefing and support were currently being provided in order to inform future provision. I devised the questionnaire, analysed the responses, and produced a report for regional colleagues, incorporating suggestions and comments from the chair at each stage. Payment for completed questionnaires ensured an almost 100 per cent response rate! As a result of the analysis, I distilled the good practice revealed: making recommendations on the briefing and support required (including a list of reference material), producing a booklet for new counsellors (a revised version of which is still in use) and initiating a pilot mentor scheme.

Reflecting on the values underpinning this work proved illuminating. The questionnaire was designed to recognize the wealth of experience and skills that individuals brought to their role. It encouraged both new and experienced counsellors to review their role, and the skills and information requirements that underpin it, to reflect and to pass on their experience, all of which enhanced their own personal development. We wanted quotations from experienced staff to enrich the new resource and received some very thoughtful and valuable material. The project was carried out as a team effort with colleagues, especially those who contributed their experience by filling in questionnaires. Residential school raises particular issues around equal opportunities. Harassment (sexual, racial, ageist, etc) can become a problem, and counsellors have a very important role in setting an appropriate tone, defusing situations and if necessary handling formal or informal complaints. I contributed a paragraph on equal opportunity issues to the new resource, following up concerns identified in the analysis, and added material on equal opportunities as part of the core reference material.

I learnt a great deal from this project. I forgot to ask for names on the questionnaire (so contributors could remain anonymous) but needed a name to pay them, so I had to turn detective to discover the names! I was impressed again by the richness of experience and expertise in my colleagues, and the generosity with which they shared this. I drew on my own experience as a residential school counsellor in constructing and analysing the questionnaire. It is a curious role, in which anything can happen (and usually does!), and this brought home to me that no amount of briefing can prepare for all eventualities, thus emphasizing the importance of support for newcomers to the role. I looked again at my own practice (filling in a questionnaire myself), reviewing my own current development needs and those I had when I started. This review revealed the importance of peer support – even for experienced staff – in this very demanding role.

Evidence presented

I included eight pages from the report 'Residential school counsellors: analysis of needs for briefing and support' (Anne Langley and [colleague], 1998, Open University) to show the 'Summary', 'Recommendations', 'Suggested reference materials' and the 'Analysis of residential school counselling support'. The report was based on questionnaires filled in by contributors before, during and after the school. Beforehand, they gave details of their experience with the Open University, their work at residential school, the skills, knowledge and experience they were bringing to the role, the skills they wanted to develop, and any additional briefing and information they thought they needed. During the school, they explained what briefing they had been given, what they had found useful, what they would have liked to be told before they arrived, what support they were being given, their suggestions for improving support and their current reactions to the role. After the school, they described the reference materials, advice and guidance they had found most helpful, and what else they would have liked to be given.

In addition, I presented in my SEDA Fellowship portfolio two e-mails. One was sent from myself to regional colleagues about 'Residential school reference materials and staff development for counsellors'. It represented best practice by listing 'Key reference documents', making suggestions for briefing new counsellors, and recommending the provision of more formal support to both new and experienced counsellors. It ended with three bullet points emphasizing things that had emerged from the analysis. The second e-mail was from the chair of the relevant committee that I had requested in order to confirm my role in the project.

CONCLUSION

The due consideration of needs within the development process requires a thorough approach. While in the past it may have been possible for developers to address needs on a largely informal basis, this is no longer the case. The development of the organization as a whole requires that more systematic approaches be developed. Indeed, the complexity of change within organizations demands that due care be taken. These issues are revisited again in Chapter 11, where a variety of further approaches are considered. It is essential, however, that needs are considered in the context of an ongoing process that incorporates their identification and analysis, and gives due attention to the involvement of the stakeholders. Only then will it be possible to frame development activities that achieve the desired goals and that can be effectively evaluated.

REFERENCES

Barnett, R (1992) *Improving Higher Education*, Society for Research into Higher Education (SRHE) and Open University Press (OUP), Buckingham
Barnett, R (2002) *Beyond All Reason*, SRHE and OUP, Buckingham
Bernthal, P (1995) Evaluation that goes the distance, *American Journal of Training and Development*, **49**, p 41
Industrial Society, The (1994) *The Industrial Society Survey*, The Industrial Society, London

Rae, L (1997) *Planning and Designing Training Programmes*, Gower, Aldershot
Thackwray, B (1997) *Effective Evaluation of Training and Development in Higher Education*, Kogan Page, London

3

Planning and running events

Diana Kelly

INTRODUCTION

After identifying the development needs, it is time to plan the event. Many but by no means all development needs may be met through an event such as a workshop, seminar or conference. Some development needs may be more appropriately addressed through guidebooks, Web-based materials, one-on-one consultations or other methods (see, for instance, the comprehensive guide for planning all aspects of a development programme: Burnstad, Hoss and McHargue, 1997). However, events are often an effective development method because they bring people together who have common interests or needs. More importantly, events provide an opportunity for staff to exchange ideas and learn from each other.

This chapter is designed to take a developer through the entire planning process, from the early organizational stages to steps after the event. It has a practical focus, as an extended checklist to ensure that all relevant aspects of planning and running an event have been considered. The planning process is similar for different types of events, so the term 'event' will be used throughout the chapter as an inclusive term for workshops, seminars, conferences, etc. When specific types of events are intended, those specific terms will be used.

This chapter develops the process of planning and running an event in the following five sections:

1. Before the event: planning the purposes, content and methodology.

2. Before the event: planning the details.

3. On the day of the event: ensuring everything is ready.

4. During the event.

5. After the event.

It is important to consider these five stages in this order because each one builds upon the previous stage. Moreover, this approach will provide developers with a holistic view of the planning, implementation and evaluation of an event (Hilsen and Wadsworth, 1988).

BEFORE THE EVENT: PLANNING THE PURPOSES, CONTENT AND METHODOLOGY

The most important part of the planning process begins after the needs and purposes have been determined and prioritized. It is likely that several important development needs were identified, as described in Chapter 2. Each development need is likely to require a different approach or type of event. To get started with your planning, focus on the need with the highest priority and ask this question: 'To address this development need, is an event necessary, or are other measures more appropriate?' For instance, there may be institutional structural issues that need to be addressed first, as considered in Chapter 11.

Example: 'Student retention' as an identified development need

Many institutions are concerned with the issue of student retention. However, research on this indicates two things. First, focusing on retention alone is unlikely to improve retention. Second, retention is an extremely complex issue, only part of which may be related to learning and teaching, as Tinto emphasizes in an important work on the link between student involvement in learning and student retention (1987).

Should events be held about student retention? Yes – but the purpose of such events would be to raise awareness of the complexity of the issues involved and relevant institutional issues (eg guidance, finance, individualized tutoring provision, flexibility of educational provision, etc).

After it has been determined that the identified need is one that should most appropriately be addressed through an event, the next nine sub-sections may be used for the initial planning process.

1. Determine the purpose and desired outcomes of the event

It is important to consider during the early planning stages the most important knowledge or skills that should be gained from the event. The overall purpose and desired outcomes will determine what type of event you decide to plan. In this chapter, we consider four different levels of outcomes in educational development:

1. stimulating and re-energizing staff;

2. learning new information about teaching and learning;

3. changing behaviours and attitudes – using new teaching methods;

4. making an impact on the organization over time.

It is worth emphasizing here that there are many different types of events that may be designed to meet the desired outcome. Searle (1999), for instance, provides a wide-ranging collection of relevant ideas. Several of the most common types of events are described below.

Table 3.1 then goes on to show how the types of event that are considered below relate to the desired outcomes. One might consider for instance a Level 1 outcome of re-energizing staff, a dynamic demonstration to show staff a new teaching method. In contrast, an interactive workshop in which participants have the opportunity to actually try to use a new teaching method is likely to produce a Level 2 outcome of demonstrating a new teaching skill. Levels 3 and 4 are more long-term outcomes that

Table 3.1 *Types of events matched to an appropriate purpose and outcome*

Level	Typical purpose	Possible desired outcome	Type of event
1	Build awareness about new teaching methods	Hear about new teaching methods	Presentation, demonstration
1	Learn from other staff	Hear about new teaching methods	Conference or series of presentations
2	Learn new teaching skill	Demonstrate new teaching skill	Interactive workshop
2	Understand learning theories	Discuss/solve teaching problems using the learning theories	Interactive workshop
3	Use new teaching methods in classes	Try new teaching method in class, report back to the group	Workshop series, learning & teaching course
3	Gain a deeper understanding of learning and teaching	Self and peer learning about learning & teaching through reflective activities	Week-long intensive learning & teaching seminar/workshop, learning & teaching course
4	Majority of academic staff use learner-centred teaching methods	Institutional culture shift to a 'learning paradigm' model (Barr and Tagg, 1995; Lieberman and Guskin, 2003)	Many different events provided over 10 or more years

normally result from ongoing development programmes such as intensive week-long teaching programmes, postgraduate courses in learning and teaching, and a variety of courses and events provided to staff over many years.

- *Presentation/demonstration*. Usually one hour in length or less, and often given by a keynote speaker. Usually held in a large lecture theatre or a room in which the focus of attention is on the speaker. Interaction is usually limited to question-and-answer sessions at the end of the presentation.

- *Conference*. Some universities, including the Dublin Institute of Technology, hold an annual 'Learning and Teaching Showcase' to provide academic staff with an opportunity to learn from the innovations of their colleagues. This type of event may well involve a series of presentations. Further detail on such events is provided by Lewis, Svinicki and Stice (1989).

- *Short workshop*. Usually two or three hours in length, and usually having some element of work by participants such as small-group activities, problem solving, hands-on activities or other forms of engagement. Workshops are usually limited in number of participants (10–30) and are usually held in a room in which participants may easily form small groups.

- *Full-day workshop*. A workshop lasting six hours or so held over one day allows time for participants to try out new techniques, practise applying what they are learning, and reflect on what they have done and learnt.

- *Workshop series*. A series of workshops may be developed for a special purpose or for a specific group. For instance, Fullerton College developed a series of workshops specifically aimed at part-time academic staff (Kelly, 1990a).

- *Intensive multi-day learning and teaching workshop/seminar*. This type of event is intended to give academic staff an opportunity to focus intensively and reflectively on their learning and teaching, and to learn from colleagues, as evident in the 'Great Teachers Workshop' (Smith, 1995). Similarly, the 'Faculty Learning Academy' run by Pima Community College (Schulz and Gonzales, 1998) is a two-week-long event designed for new academic staff. Usually such events occur in a residential environment and the participants take active roles in facilitating the event.

- *Learning and teaching course or programme*. Some universities offer academic staff an opportunity to participate in a longer-term accredited course or programme on learning and teaching in higher education.

These programmes usually focus on developing knowledge in learning theories and practices, and applying learner-centred teaching methods in their own setting.

2. Determine the topic of the event, including the title and content, using the information gathered through the process of identifying development needs

The purpose, title and content of the event should relate directly to the needs expressed by the staff. University staff are busy people, and unless they see a direct benefit to their daily work and their needs, they are unlikely to consider taking the time to participate in the event. When possible, even use their own words to describe the event. Comments on needs surveys or in focus groups about needs are ideal sources of information.

Example: Teaching adults

Some academic staff who are more accustomed to teaching younger students say in the needs assessment survey that they feel uncomfortable when teaching adults. They explain that working adults in their evening classes have considerable experience; the adults challenge them, and the teaching methods they use with younger students don't seem to work.

'Experiential Learning Methods for Adults' as an event title may sound great to an educational developer, but may not be appealing or clear to academic staff members who have limited background in learning theories.

'Teaching Strategies for Adults in Evening Classes' might be a better title, with a description that includes the concerns expressed, but in a positive way: 'How do adults learn differently from younger students? What teaching methods are the best to use with adults?'

3. Determine the target audience for the event and their level of prior knowledge of the event topic

It is not always necessary to have a specific target group in mind for an event. Many educational development events are open to everyone and are intended for a broad audience. However, events can be targeted to specific groups in order to meet more specific needs.

In some cases, it will be possible to determine in advance the level of prior knowledge of the event topic, particularly when the event is developed in consultation with a target group such as an academic department or a course team. If an event is intended for a particular group, or background knowledge is essential, any publicity should clearly describe the target group: 'those with experience in problem-based learning' or 'those who teach engineering courses'. If this is not specified, participants can become frustrated if one or two do not have the background knowledge or the background for which the event was designed.

If it is essential to the success of the workshop to determine the level of prior knowledge before the event, brief survey forms could be sent to enrolled participants. But often this is not practicable, especially if participants enrol too late to respond. A quick 'Background Knowledge Probe' (see Angelo and Cross, 1993) exercise at the start of the event can help the facilitator or presenter to determine the level of participants' background. (Angelo and Cross (1993) also outline a range of strategies for formative assessment, many of which are useful in workshops.) A responsive facilitator should be able to make minor adjustments in order to recognize the level of prior knowledge so that the event is neither too advanced nor too simplistic for the group.

4. Determine the length of time needed to achieve the desired outcomes

As shown in Table 3.1, the higher the outcome level, usually the longer the event. An event could be a one-hour presentation, or a five-day or more intensive interactive seminar. The event could also be stretched out over time, such as a three-hour workshop once per week for 10 weeks. It is important to think about the desired outcomes and plan the length accordingly. One of the mistakes most often made by new educational developers is to try to do too much in a limited time. Sometimes it is difficult to tell what is 'too much', so it is also important to build in some flexibility to allow for extra discussion time or new issues that may emerge in the course of the event. See the next sub-section for important considerations on learning methods.

5. Decide on the most appropriate learning methods to achieve the desired outcomes, modelling best practice in adult learning

Activities and learning methods in any event need to be carefully planned so that the event models best practice in adult learning. When academic staff experience good learning methods as learners, they will see how to actually put these methods into practice as teachers. Three general principles are important for any event:

- selecting and using the most appropriate learning theory and method;
- promoting active learning;
- using the three Rs of adult learning.

Selecting and using the most appropriate learning theory and method
What is the best way for this particular participant group to learn the specified topic in this particular event? It is important for any learning event to be grounded in good learning theory and corresponding methodology (see Jarvis, Holford and Griffin, 1998, for a helpful review of a wide range of learning theories and practices).

Example: Workshop on Experiential Learning

In designing a workshop on experiential learning, it is very useful to consider using the Kolb Experiential Learning model (see Jones, 1988; Kolb, 1984; and also Chapter 12 for a description of this model) as the curriculum design model for the workshop. Not only will participants gain an understanding of the methods of experiential learning, but they will also go through the full cycle during the workshop as learners.

Promoting active learning

Most participants in educational development events say that the part of the event they enjoyed the most was the opportunity to interact with colleagues about learning and teaching. When planning the learning methods for the event, build in the opportunity to interact. So, during the workshop planning stage, decide when and how active learning methods will be incorporated.

Active learning also includes reflection, so it is important to plan for some reflective activities during the workshop. These give participants an opportunity to think and write before taking part in discussions in pairs or small groups. Again, plan the reflective activity carefully: Why will it be done? At what point in the event will it be done? What will it accomplish? What reflective questions will be asked of participants? (For examples of reflective activities see Angelo and Cross, 1993.)

Example: Workshop on Learning Styles

In a workshop on learning styles, best practice would say that it's a good idea to know something about the learning styles represented in the group. So, the workshop might start by having participants use a brief learning style instrument (if it is not feasible for them to do it prior to the workshop). During the course of the workshop, participants should experience a wide variety of learning and teaching styles, and have a chance to reflect on and discuss their reactions to the various styles. Finally, participants should have a chance to think about how they might incorporate a wider range of teaching methods to address the variety of learning styles in their own classes.

Use the three Rs of adult learning

These 'three Rs' are Respect, Relevance and Responsibility (Kelly, 1990b), and are general good practice with adult learners. Principles of good practice in adult learning are outlined in detail in several classic books (Brookfield, 1986; Cross, 1981; Knowles, 1984; Wlodkowski, 1988) and are very appropriate to apply to academic staff who participate in educational development as adult learners.

- Show *respect* for the teaching experiences of the participants by inviting them to share experiences relevant to the topic being discussed. Build in activities to draw out their experiences.

- Help participants to see the *relevance* of the various topics of the event, either by providing specific examples of classroom situations in which they may be used or by asking participants to discuss their own ideas on how they might apply what they are learning.

- Give participants the *responsibility* for doing some thinking and problem solving during the event rather than simply listening to a presentation.

6. Decide on key players to be involved in presenting or facilitating the event

Is the event on a topic with which you, as the educational developer, are very familiar? If not, it would be best to find others within the institution (or outside, if funding permits) to work with you in designing and delivering the event. Most workshops can be facilitated by one person, unless the group is very large. However, more complex events, such as a conference or a seminar series, will involve a number of different academics who have expertise in various aspects of learning and teaching. For this reason, it is important to get to know the teaching and learning interests and expertise of academic staff to determine who might be able to work with you in facilitating different events.

Indeed, it is often a good idea to have a member of the 'target group' assist with both planning and running an event and provide examples. For instance, if the event is intended for those who teach in engineering, it would be a good idea for someone with an engineering background to provide case studies or examples that demonstrate how these teaching methods are being used successfully in engineering.

7. Decide on materials to be included in the event packet

Participants in any event appreciate having a well-organized packet of materials relevant to the event, even if it's only a short two-hour workshop.

It is much easier to provide a packet at the beginning of the event than to take time to hand out materials as needed throughout the event. Some presenters have reservations about handing out everything in advance because they feel that people might look ahead. However, if the event is involving and interactive, this should not be an issue. Also, participants are much more relaxed if they have all their materials at the beginning and they know that they will not need to write furiously to get all the words from a PowerPoint presentation. Copies should always be clean, crisp, and in a font size and style that are easy to read. Ideally, handouts should be arranged in the packet in the order they will be used during the workshop.

8. Determine the media to be used

Many studies have shown that people learn best when they have several stimuli (National Training Laboratories, 1998; Staley, 1998). In particular, it is important to incorporate audio-visual media, which help to focus the attention of the participants and to show visual images that may be memorable after the event. If possible, it is a good idea to use several different types of audio-visual media. However, let the learning goals drive the use of media, and don't use technology simply to be flashy. The use of media should enhance learning, not distract from it. The following examples may help.

- *Flipcharts, whiteboards, overhead transparencies*. All of these can be used for taking notes during discussions to make notes of the major points made by the participants. The simple act of writing down points raised by participants (so that everyone can see them) makes participants feel that they have made a valuable contribution to the discussion.

- *PowerPoint slides or overhead transparency slides*. Although PowerPoint is becoming over-used, it is a very useful tool to focus the attention of the participants on the major points being made during a presentation portion of an event. PowerPoint should not be used for showing every word of a presentation, but rather to highlight major points and raise questions for discussion. Font size and type are crucial when showing any type of slides. *Do not* show a typed overhead transparency with tiny type and detailed graphs – these are much better as handouts. *Do not* use all the 'bells and whistles' of PowerPoint in a presentation, because they can distract rather than enhance learning.

- *Video/DVD*. Video is a very effective way to demonstrate major ideas in a very short time. By showing some concrete examples on video, the participants may be able to grasp a complex idea much more easily than through a lengthy presentation. However, it is important to use very short videotapes, no longer than 15 minutes and preferably very much less. If the video is longer, stop the tape at selected points for a discussion to help the participants refocus. Before playing any video, it is important to let participants know why it is being shown and what they should look for during the video, and that the video will be the focus of a discussion afterwards. At the conclusion of the video, it is a good idea to immediately give participants a few minutes to reflect on what they have seen, write it down or talk with a partner, before debriefing the video in the larger group.

● *Video cameras and audio tape recorders.* In some cases it is a good idea to use a video camera or audio tape recorder during an event to record the proceedings (with the prior permission of any presenters and/or participants if they will appear on the tape). These tapes may allow other staff members to see the event even if they were not available to participate in the event. Videotaping may also be used for short teaching demonstrations done by participants and discussed within the workshop group.

9. Plan an evaluation strategy for the event, including feedback methods

As mentioned in the first section, we can consider four levels of outcomes for educational development events: 1. Stimulating and re-energizing staff; 2. Learning new information about teaching and learning; 3. Changing behaviours and attitudes – using new teaching methods; 4. Making an impact on the organization over time. It is important to evaluate events in order to determine their effectiveness in reaching the intended outcomes, as described on page 57 in the section 'After the event' and as emphasized in Chapter 5. Whether or not the intended outcomes were achieved, the evaluation process will inform the planning of future events. Way, Carlson and Piliero (2002) argue that such continuity is needed in order to achieve long-term impact on an organization.

Level 1 evaluation: participant reaction
Participant reaction is normally obtained through brief evaluation forms at the close of an event. Participants have the opportunity to rate various aspects of the event and comment on the event. At this level, the desirable reaction is one that is positive and indicates that the participants were stimulated and re-energized by the event. It is important to allow sufficient time (a minimum of five minutes) for participants to complete this brief evaluation. If they do not complete it while in the room, it is unlikely they will ever return it.

Level 2 evaluation: learning

How much did participants actually learn from the event? Their reaction may have shown that they enjoyed the event, but did they actually learn anything new? Questions on a brief survey or an anonymous reflective exercise (Angelo and Cross, 1993) at the end of an event may be designed to ask participants to think about what they learnt about the topic and how they might think about applying what they learnt. If the event lasts a full day or longer, it is a good idea to check in with the participants by providing several opportunities for them to provide feedback on what they have learnt so far, and what more they are still hoping to learn, as well as any topics that have been covered that are confusing to them. This gives the facilitator an opportunity to make adjustments to the event while it is in progress.

Level 3 evaluation: behaviours and attitudes

Participants may have enjoyed the event, and they may have also learnt something new, but do they actually use what they have learnt? A follow-up survey may be used to ask participants whether their behaviours or attitudes have changed since the event. Have they followed up on their good intentions to apply what they had learnt? Other ways to measure this level of change would include a pre- and post-event analysis of teaching behaviours by peer observers, or curriculum content changes made as a result of what was learnt in the event, or changes in attitude towards the topic of the event measured through pre- and post-event assessments.

Level 4 evaluation: impact on the organization and students

Impact on the organization and students is the most difficult to measure, because it usually takes quite a few years to influence institutional change, as Smith and Beno (1993) emphasize. However, longitudinal research can be done if there is an institutional research office in place at the time when educational development events start.

Most programmes of educational development tend to focus on Level 1 evaluations, but it is important to consider and plan for the other levels in order to strategically evaluate the long-term benefits of educational development for individual staff members, students and the institution. In planning events, it is important to determine which level of evaluation will be most appropriate for the event so that the event may be evaluated in a way that will inform the future planning of educational development.

BEFORE THE EVENT: PLANNING THE DETAILS

Select the day and time for the event

In scheduling the event, it is important to consider how it fits into the academic timetable and the availability of the target group. Is one day of the week or one time of day better than another? Does the event need to be held in the evening or on a Saturday to accommodate the needs of part-time staff? To ensure good participation in the event, it is important to find a day and time that suit the most people and do not conflict with other pressing deadlines or events.

Select the location to ensure a positive learning environment

It is important to select a location that best suits the type of event being planned. There are several questions that need to be answered regarding location. First, should the event be held on-campus or off-campus? Second, what is the most appropriate seating arrangement for the event? Third, what are the structural considerations of the facilities to be used?

On-campus or off-campus
For shorter events, such as a half-day workshop or a two-hour seminar, it is generally most convenient to hold the event on-campus. For longer events, such as conferences or full-day workshops, if funding is available it is better to hold the event off-campus. This change in environment helps the participants to focus on the event and reduces distractions. Also, getting away from the campus usually helps participants to relax and be more open to new ideas without the constraints of the familiar campus.

Seating arrangements
An interactive workshop is best held in a flexible room with a flat floor and small tables for group work. A large lecture theatre is more appropriate for a presentation than for interaction. A seminar room with a conference table works well for a small group of 8–10 participants who will be using highly interactive methods, including brainstorming, discussions and problem-solving activities.

Structural considerations
In evaluating any room for suitability, it is important to consider the following attributes of the room to be used for the event.

● *Obstructions in the room*. It is best if there are no posts or other structures that would obscure the view of some participants to others in the room or to visuals on a screen.

- *Lighting*. Ideally, the room should be well lit so that it is easy to see others and to read printed materials. However, the lighting should be adjustable so that lights do not shine on screens being used for overheads or PowerPoint.

- *Acoustics*. The room should have good acoustics so that it is easy to hold a large-group discussion without outside distracting noises from the street or from the next room.

- *Temperature*. Care needs to be taken with the room temperature as participants lose concentration if the room temperature is too high or too low.

- *Audio-visual facilities*. Does the room have the necessary outlets so that the planned audio-visual equipment may be used? If Internet accessibility is important for the event, does the room have reliable access to the Internet?

- *Refreshment facilities*. Ideally, the room where the event is taking place should be large enough to allow space for refreshments. If this is not possible, it is important to locate a space immediately adjacent to the room of the event that may be used for refreshment breaks. Otherwise, valuable time may be lost in getting to the place where the refreshments are located and participants may drift away in many directions during the break. Don't provide alcohol with lunch – it will damage the afternoon!

- *Toilets*. Ideally, toilets should be sufficiently near to the meeting room that it is possible for workshop participants to leave for a moment if needed.

Plan for catering

Refreshments are an important part of the breaks in any event, no matter how long or how short the event. Generally it is best to take a refreshment break about every 90 minutes. This break time provides participants with the opportunity for informal networking and discussion with others. Very often these informal exchanges during the breaks provide participants with some good ideas and useful contact that often continue after the workshop.

Plan event publicity

After the initial planning has been completed, it is important to provide good publicity for the workshop to attract the interest of the target audience.

Create a workshop flier

Ideally, create a one-page flier that will attract the interest of the target group for whom the event is intended. This should be clearly stated near the top of the flier (eg 'Workshop on Using Problem-Based Learning in Teaching Physics'). Graphically, the flier should be easy to read, with large, bold letters and simple and strong graphics. It should *not* be overly wordy with long explanations. It should clearly indicate date, time and place, and include information on how to register and full contact details. If the target group uses e-mail for announcements of this nature, publicity should be sent by e-mail. If e-mails tend to be ignored, then a hard copy of the flier should be sent to campus mailboxes of the target group.

Provide incentives to come to the event

The flier should incorporate several of the following incentives to attract the attention of the target audience:

- A brief statement of the teaching and learning challenge to be addressed.

- Examples of the teaching methods or tools that will be included.

- If a well-respected speaker is featured, this should be highlighted.

- The fact that space is limited or that it is a limited opportunity (if it is a one-time or annual event).

- Refreshments provided.

If many events are being planned for the academic year, it is best to develop a full listing of all events to distribute to staff at the beginning of the academic year so that they may plan well in advance to attend the events of their choice.

Determine convenient and efficient methods for event registration

Generally it is good to provide multiple methods of registration for events, including online, phone, fax, e-mail, and a tear-off registration form that may be mailed in. If possible, it is a good idea to install software that may be used to keep a running database of registrants for various events.

Print name badges and/or folding name cards, for a professional welcome

Printed name badges or folding name cards let the participants know that they were expected and are welcome to the event. Name badges are important for events in which staff from many areas are participating.

ON THE DAY OF THE EVENT: ENSURING THAT EVERYTHING IS READY

Post directional signs

It is best not to assume that participants are familiar with the location of the event unless all events are always held in the same location. For this reason, it is important to post directional signs leading to the room from several different directions, and post a sign on the door of the room to let participants know that this is the right place.

Arrive early to check on room arrangements

It is *essential* to arrive in the room at least half an hour before the event is due to begin, perhaps even an hour. This is the best way to avoid any unanticipated problems with room layout and equipment. However, if there is a dedicated room that is always used for educational development and is always set up in a particular way, a quick check 20 or 30 minutes prior to the starting time is probably sufficient. For conferences and larger events, usually it is best to do the set-up the evening before the event.

Upon arrival in the room, the room arrangements should be carefully checked:

- Are the seating arrangements correct, as specified?

- Is the audio-visual equipment in the room where it should be? Does it work?

- Are the refreshments in place or will they be arriving on schedule as ordered?

Greet participants as they arrive and register

Ensure that someone is ready at least 15 minutes in advance at the registration table to greet participants as they arrive. This greeting is essential in making participants feel welcome and relaxed.

DURING THE EVENT

Provide a brief introduction to the structure and methods of the event

Participants want to know what to expect during the event. What types of activities will be used? At what time will the event finish? Any ground rules should also be covered here, including the role of the facilitator in keeping the workshop moving, encouraging participation, and discouraging any one person from dominating the event. Spending a few minutes at the beginning to review the agenda for the event will alleviate concerns and help participants to focus on the topic. Participants appreciate a well-organized event in which their time is used productively and effectively.

Provide a brief introduction of event participants

In very large events such as conferences or large presentations, introductions of participants are usually not done. Unless this is to be an ongoing group, introductions of participants in workshops should be very brief. Many participants consider that lengthy introductions take away valuable time from the workshop. For this reason, it is important for the facilitator to first explain the rationale behind doing introductions (eg for networking with colleagues, etc). Then, encourage participants to keep the introductions brief. Usually name and department are sufficient, perhaps with a sentence on their interest in the topic of the event. Make sure the first person you ask gives a good short answer, or maybe demonstrate this with your introduction of yourself!

Provide a non-threatening opening activity in which participants demonstrate their prior knowledge of the topic

A focused listing activity or a background knowledge probe (Angelo and Cross, 1993) can give participants an opportunity to reflect on a carefully constructed question that is posed after the introductions but before the presentation begins. This serves three important purposes. First, it helps participants to focus on the topic of the event rather than thinking about the work they need to do or the traffic they just came through. Second, it helps participants to realize that they do know something about the topic and that their prior experience will be valued. And third, it lets the facilitator know the level of background of the participants so that certain areas of the workshop content may be emphasized more than others, if necessary.

Usually a 'think–pair–share' method works most effectively for this activity because it results in a richer, more thoughtful discussion with greater participation. Participants first think and write down their response to the question posed. This thinking process, even though it may occupy only a few minutes, gives participants an opportunity to gather their thoughts and ideas before starting a discussion. Second, participants pair up and compare their responses. By having the opportunity to share their ideas with only one other person, they often receive positive feedback about their ideas, which makes them more confident about sharing in a larger discussion. And then they share these ideas with the larger group voluntarily, as the facilitator writes them down on an overhead transparency, whiteboard or flipchart. Writing the ideas down indicates to the participant that his or her idea was important and contributed to the discussion and group knowledge.

If appropriate, provide an opportunity for participants to state their learning goals

This activity may take the place of the previous activity as a way of helping participants to focus on the topic. If participants are asked for their learning goals, this should be done before the facilitator describes the learning goals for the event. Whether or not this is an appropriate activity depends on the topic and the background of the participants. In some cases, participants may feel that they do not know enough about the topic to state clear and specific learning goals – they have a general interest in the topic. However, some participants may have very specific problems or challenges they want to resolve and they are hoping that this event will provide the answers. This activity can be useful in letting the facilitator know whether the group of participants has any issues that they feel are particularly important. Then the facilitator can make decisions about how the issues might be addressed during or after the event. But be careful that in asking participants for their learning goals for the event, you do not set up unrealistic expectations, such as that the event will guarantee to meet all their learning goals! Encourage them to take responsibility for using the event to achieve the goals they have each identified for themselves.

Provide rationale for each activity or presentation prior as a transition

When introducing a new activity during the event, it is important first to explain why the activity is being done. Sometimes academic staff feel that group work is a 'waste of time' because they were expecting a presentation format. These frustrations can easily be alleviated by a quick explanation about the learning benefits that come from problem-solving in small groups so that participants can apply what they have just heard about.

Use proven adult learning methods throughout the event

Adult learning methods draw upon and value the prior experiences and observations of the participants. Participants, as adult learners, appreciate practical information with concrete examples that illustrate any theoretical information. But it is also important to include opportunities for participants to begin to think about how they might apply what they are learning.

Finally, it is important to encourage self-directed learning after the event by providing readings or references that may be pursued individually.

Ask participants for feedback at points throughout the event, and at the end

In an event of any length, there are three major points at which it is a good idea to ask for feedback: beginning, middle and end. In a multi-day event, this process may be used each day. The feedback is focused on the needs, questions and learning issues of the participants, rather than on the overall evaluation of the event. This is much better than learning at the end of the event that participants were confused or not learning what they had hoped to learn.

Here is a brief description of this three-step process. First, as noted in the section about learning goals (page 56), it is a good idea to ask participants at the beginning if they have any 'burning issues' that they feel are critical – issues that they must have resolved before leaving the event. Second, just before the mid-point in the event, ask participants to write down any questions or concerns about the topic that have not yet been addressed. These anonymous responses can be reviewed quickly during the break by the facilitator and responded to after the break. Finally, at the end it is important to allow sufficient time for participants to complete a brief evaluation of the event.

AFTER THE EVENT

Analyse the feedback and evaluations of the event participants

Tally the results of the workshop evaluations to determine what participants felt was most useful, what they learnt, and what they felt should have been included in the workshop. These results will also provide input on the most appropriate length for the workshop because participants will mention if they felt it was too rushed or if they did not have sufficient opportunity to interact or discuss. This feedback will provide good information for planning future events on this topic.

Conduct additional medium- and long-term evaluations of the event

If appropriate, follow up the initial evaluation with more evaluations of Level 2 or Level 3 outcomes (as described in the first section). This will be particularly important for long-term and ongoing events, such as workshop series or courses.

Plan for follow-up events and activities

Research has shown that one-off workshops or events are not always effective for long-term change in teaching, although Rust (1998) shows that such long-term change may be achieved. For this reason, it is important to provide additional opportunities for participants to get together to continue to learn and to reinforce what was learnt at the initial event. This follow-up can take several forms:

- additional events on this topic, held in specific departments or for specific groups of staff;
- additional workshops at a more advanced level;
- development of special interest groups that meet regularly to discuss this topic – either in person, or online via online learning discussion groups or e-mail listservs.

CONCLUSION

In planning and running events, it is essential to take the time and effort to systematically plan all the details well in advance. This process becomes more routine over time, and may be applied to running many different types of events. It is important to consider that events are probably the most visible elements of the role of the developer. University staff are busy people, and do not want their time to be wasted through a poorly organized event that does not meet their needs. Equally, through a well-planned event, staff will be enthusiastic about what they have learnt, and will be more likely to participate in future events. Finally, events should be treated as an opportunity to model best practice in learning and teaching, and only a careful and detailed planning process will allow this to happen.

The most important part of the planning process is to consider the intended outcomes for the event, and how they fit into an overall strategy for educational development. How is this event contributing to the educational development goals of the institution? Through a comprehensive planning and evaluation process, it will be possible to see the results, over time, of the educational development events.

REFERENCES

Angelo, T A and Cross, K P (1993) *Classroom Assessment Techniques: A handbook for college teachers*, Jossey-Bass, San Francisco

Barr, R and Tagg, J (1995) From teaching to learning: a new paradigm for under-graduate education, *Change*, November/December, pp 13–25, American Association of Higher Education, Washington, DC

Brookfield, S (1986) *Understanding and Facilitating Adult Learning*, Jossey-Bass, San Francisco

Burnstad, H, Hoss, C and McHargue, M (1997) *Growing Your Own Staff Development Program*, National Council for Staff, Program, and Organizational Development, San Bernadino, CA

Cross, K P (1981) *Adults as Learners*, Jossey-Bass, San Francisco

Hilsen, L and Wadsworth, E (1988) Staging successful workshops, in *Professional and Organizational Development in Higher Education: A handbook for new practitioners*, ed E Wadsworth, ch 8, New Forum Press, Stillwater, OK

Jarvis, P, Holford, J and Griffin, C (1998) *The Theory and Practice of Learning*, Kogan Page, London

Jones, W (1988) Leading experiential workshops, in *Professional and Organizational Development in Higher Education: A handbook for new practitioners*, ed E. Wadsworth, ch 11, New Forum Press, Stillwater, OK

Kelly, D K (1990a) *A Human Resources Development Approach to Part-time Faculty in the Community College*, US Department of Education, Washington, DC, ERIC #ED 316 279

Kelly, D K (1990b) Three R's of adult learning: respect, relevance, and responsibility, unpublished paper, Claremont Graduate University, Claremont, CA

Knowles, M (1984). *The Adult Learner: A neglected species*, 3rd edn, Gulf Publishing Company, London

Kolb, D A (1984). *Experiential Learning: Experience as the source of learning and development*, Prentice-Hall, Englewood Cliffs, NJ

Lewis, K, Svinicki, M and Stice, J (1989) A conference on teaching for experienced faculty, *Journal of Staff, Program and Organizational Development*, **7** (3), pp 137–42

Lieberman, D and Guskin, A (2003) The essential role of faculty development in new higher education models, *To Improve the Academy*, **21**, pp 257–71 (journal of the Professional and Organizational Development Network in Higher Education, Anker Publishing Company, Bolton, MA)

National Training Laboratories (1998) *Average Retention for Learning Activities*, National Training Laboratories, Bethel, ME

Rust, C (1998) The impact of educational development workshops on teachers' practice, *International Journal for Academic Development*, **3** (1), pp 72–80

Schulz, R and Gonzales, G (1998) The faculty learning academy, *Innovation Abstracts*, **20** (25), pp 1–2

Searle, B (ed) (1999) *Tools and Tips: A collection of practical staff development opportunities and ideas*, National Council for Staff, Program, and Organizational Development, San Bernadino, CA

Smith, C (1995) *The Great Teachers Format: Why does it work?* Community College League of California, Sacramento, CA

Smith, C and Beno, B (1993) *A Guide to Staff Development Evaluation*, Community College League of California, Sacramento, CA

Staley, C (1998) *Teaching College Success: The complete resource guide*, Wadsworth, New York

Tinto, V (1987) *Leaving College: Rethinking the causes and cures of student attrition*, University of Chicago Press, Chicago

Way, D, Carlson, V and Piliero, S (2002) Evaluating teaching workshops: beyond the satisfaction survey, *To Improve the Academy*, **20**, pp 94–106

Wlodkowski, R (1988) *Enhancing Adult Motivation to Learn*, Jossey-Bass, San Francisco

4

Consultancy in educational development

Liz Shrives and Chris Bond

INTRODUCTION

This chapter aims to unravel the ways in which different approaches to consultancy can be used, and to suggest how careful and informed use of consultancy can achieve a range of goals and benefits. Consultancy generally involves a sustained relationship between client and consultant. The quick-fix solutions that many sought in the 1980s often failed. For a time, some higher education consultants colluded with the more general idea that a short intervention by a consultant – often resulting in the production of a glossy report – could address and resolve key client issues. It is arguable whether such short and often surface-level interventions are true consultancy or whether they are simply the contracting out of short pieces of work to an external or internal agency. In any event, they are often ineffective.

Throughout this chapter, we use the term 'educational developer', or simply 'developer', in its broadest sense. The developer may be a member of staff who works full time in a dedicated educational development unit. He or she may be a member of a school, department or faculty who has been seconded for a period of time to work with academic colleagues on educational development issues. He or she may be an independent developer. These are the people who undertake consultancy. Their clients may be individual staff or the department, school or institution.

Within this chapter, we also explore educational development in its broadest context. We hope that the discussion of educational development consultancy will be useful to discipline-based academics as well as to members of educational development units. The initial part of the chapter summarizes some issues in educational development consultancy, complementing the more detailed account of educational development in

Chapter 1. The main body of the chapter reviews the consultancy cycle and how this applies to educational development. A short illustrative case study is provided for each stage of the consultancy cycle. Finally, we consider some of the advantages and disadvantages of the developer as internal consultant.

SOME ISSUES IN EDUCATIONAL DEVELOPMENT CONSULTANCY

In a view perhaps derived from (bad) practice in management consultancy, educational development consultancy is sometimes seen as an expert telling others what to do, and may thus be regarded as a directive and intrusive process. This view arises from misconceptions of what good consultancy actually is or means, and is associated with questions about the validity of the process, about the perceived high costs, and about the effectiveness of consultancy in creating and effecting desired change.

Of course consultants are hired for their expertise. But this expertise may be in the content of the consultancy, or in the consultancy process, or, it is to be hoped, in both. We consider this further in our account on page 64 of the consultancy cycle, especially under step 2, contracting (pages 66–67). Using consultants well is as much, and perhaps sometimes also as difficult, a skill as acting as a consultant.

A large part of the day-to-day work of an educational development unit takes the form of consultancy. Many educational development groups or units also use the more formal models of consultancy, contracting consultants from well-established organizations or contracting the services of well-respected individuals within the sector. For instance, within the United Kingdom, such organizations would include the Oxford Centre for Staff and Learning Development (OCSLD), the Staff and Educational Development Association (SEDA) and the Higher Education Staff Development Agency (HESDA). There may be several reasons to use an external consultant. Such external consultants may bring particular knowledge not available within the educational development unit; they may bring particular skills; they may well bring a good reputation. Additionally, consultants may be used by the educational development unit to confront issues that the educational development unit, which needs to maintain its good relationship with the rest of the institution over the long term, prefers to avoid confronting, so as to prevent damage to that relationship.

More and more discipline-based academic staff are becoming involved in the development of learning and teaching, as reflected in Chapter 9, which considers development in the disciplines. These are often people who are not, and do not wish to be recognized as, educational developers.

The growth of short-term secondments of discipline-based staff to educational development units, teaching prizes, fellowships and awards results in a more diverse range of staff being involved in educational development activity. Within this diverse context, consultancy should be used as a versatile and effective approach for supporting and enabling change and the development of staff.

The models and strategies of educational development consultancy need to address how people learn. Conceptions of learning should inform the strategies and approaches to be used, as they should any planned learning activity. (There may sometimes be merit in making these models, strategies and approaches explicit in the work; the very idea that there are fruitful models of the process of learning is still not universally accepted by academics of disciplines other than education!) Professional development is an aspect of learning and a way of enabling practitioners to understand the process of learning that change requires (Nicholls, 2001).

The emergence of project-based work within learning and teaching development has become widespread and was initially viewed as being effective in achieving and embedding change. Project-based work in educational development within the United Kingdom has been supported by the funding councils through initiatives such as the Fund for the Development of Teaching and Learning (FDTL) and the Teaching and Learning Technology Programme (TLTP). It is also recognized as a mechanism for enabling change by the National Teaching Fellowship Scheme (NTFS), and indeed many institutions have adopted similar approaches in their own learning and teaching grants, bids and awards schemes. This approach supports academics within their discipline to develop a specific area of practice. However, innovation alone is not enough to make a major impact across an institution and within the sector. Dissemination through conferences and reports alone is not sufficient to ensure that the new practices transfer to other institutions. Models of educational development that use process consultancy (Schein, 1987) can address some of the difficulties associated with transferability and educational change. Chapter 11 on change also considers the challenges of effecting change, as does Chapter 6 on dissemination.

Before we consider in more detail how a model of educational development based on consultancy might operate, it will be useful to develop an understanding of what consultancy is. Cookman, Evans and Reynolds (1992) suggest that consulting is what happens 'when someone with a problem or difficulty seeks help to solve that problem or resolve that difficulty from someone who has special skill'. They further propose that consultants are 'people who find themselves having to influence other people, or advise them about possible courses of action to improve the effectiveness of any aspect of their operations, without any formal authority over them or choosing not to use what authority they have'. The educational developer may well have to work with influence and collaborative inquiry (Reason, 1994; Weil, 1998) rather than with formal authority.

Cookman, Evans and Reynolds (1992) claim that within an organizational development context consultants can help their clients to:

- perceive the situation more clearly;
- devise alternative strategies for solving the problem;
- evaluate the alternatives;
- decide on a course of action (from a list, including doing nothing);
- plan the implementation and take action.

THE CONSULTANCY CYCLE

How can educational development consultancy operate in practice? We have chosen to consider the consultancy cycle to explore this. In its simplest form, the consultancy cycle can be viewed as being about three discrete phases of activity. These are:

1. getting in (establishing a relationship with a potential client and securing agreement to undertake work);
2. getting on (gathering necessary data and information, working with the clients on evaluation and implementation);
3. getting out (concluding the consultancy assignment and withdrawing from the situation).

In a more detailed form, the phases that make up the consulting cycle can be defined as:

1. *gaining entry*: making initial contact and establishing a working relationship;
2. *contracting*: finding out what the client wants;
3. *collecting data*: finding out what happens now;
4. *making sense of the data* and diagnosing the problem;
5. *generating options*, making decisions and planning;
6. *implementing* the plans and taking action;
7. *disengaging*: arranging any necessary follow-up action.

An account of each stage of the cycle is followed by a short case study. We conclude our review of the stages of the consultancy cycle with a set of statements and a skills set that we believe underpin effective practice as an educational development consultant.

GAINING ENTRY

Gaining entry is about making initial contact with academic staff and gaining the required access to the school, department, unit or group. It is of course easier to gain entry when invited. However, as we consider on page 66 under 'Contracting', an invitation does not solve all problems; for example, an invitation from a head of department does not guarantee an enthusiastic reception from every member of the department. But, unlike vampires, educational developers may sometimes have to enter uninvited, for example to promulgate some university policy. Gaining entry involves building up a relationship based on mutual trust and respect. It is about forming and sustaining relationships or trust with academic colleagues, with the eventual aim that academic colleagues will view the educational developer and the educational development unit as the first port of call when they have a problem or issue related to learning, teaching or assessment. As an educational developer operating as a consultant, you may have to gain entry at several levels within the organization. For example, although you may have good relationships at a strategic level with a head of school or subject leader, much of your project or consultancy work is likely to take place at the course team or module group level. Unless you can also gain entry with this group of staff, it is unlikely that you will be able to effect much change or value added through your interventions.

The following case study demonstrates some of the complexities associated with gaining entry in a complex organizational system. This case study on plagiarism amplifies how it may be necessary to work on gaining entry at several levels and with a diverse range of stakeholders simultaneously.

CASE STUDY 1: PLAGIARISM

The Academic Standards Committee is concerned at the number of cases of plagiarism that have arisen during the last examination period, and has requested that this be addressed. This is a university-wide issue, but there is a challenge in identifying the most appropriate place to 'gain entry'. Working directly through the committee will not involve the key groups of staff who can effect change, but the development of an institutional policy would go a long way to raise awareness and get staff to think about the issue. If programme leaders are to be the initial contacts, how do you ensure that you access them all and ensure fair representation of views about current practices? Working with staff will go some way in addressing the larger issue by enabling them to identify plagiarism during the process of assessing work and informing them of how to deal with it. However, such work alone will not solve the problem; that will require intervention with students. Clearly, the presenting problems are multifaceted and decisions need to be made carefully about who is to be involved if effective change is to be achieved.

This problem was addressed through a multidirectional approach that required gaining entry with a number of groups in a planned and systematic approach. Programme leaders across the university were encouraged to attend a workshop. The take-up was patchy, but because the same workshop was offered a number of times and marketed widely, word spread and take-up gradually increased to the point where staff in each school were concerned enough about the issue to request further guidance and support. We were then able to involve heads of schools, working with them in a cross-university group to identify good practice and develop guidelines. The initiative to work with students followed as a natural development, and groups of staff worked with the educational developers to create materials and session outlines for them to use with students.

By careful management of the initial entry, the entry to other groups of staff followed as a logical progression, ie heads of schools and students.

CONTRACTING

Once entry has been gained, the next phase in the consultancy cycle is contracting. This phase is of critical importance, but is often overlooked or rushed. Contracting is concerned with making as explicit as possible as many of the staff's needs as is possible, but also with letting them know your needs as well. Block (1983) talks about 'client needs and consultant wants', and stresses the importance of securing an adequate balance of these in any contract. It is common for educational developers to concentrate exclusively on finding out what the staff they are working with want from them and fail to declare their own needs. Cookman, Evans and Reynolds (1992) suggest that balance can be achieved through the consultant's being willing to explore such areas as:

- what I can and cannot do;
- what my own values are in relation to the proposed project or activity;
- what I need from the client and the client system.

Higher education (HE) institutions are highly politicized environments with many different priorities, explicit and tacit, in play. We may have reached an agreement with a head of school or unit on a particular piece of work to be carried out, but we will still have to contract with the staff involved. To do so involves high levels of integrity as well as skill from the educational developer.

We may, for example, have been asked by a head of school to introduce a system of peer appraisal of teaching to help the school meet a quality assurance requirement. While we can agree and contract on the broad outcomes of such a project with the head of school, we may have our work cut out to promote the concept to academic staff, who may view it as an intrusion on their professionalism and yet another management tool for getting more for less. We may need to contract for additional outcomes with the staff. Possible examples are reviewing the time involved in peer observation and reporting on this to management, or agreeing a system that is developmental and not linked to other formal appraisal mechanisms. The following case study on peer review of teaching demonstrates how we may need to contract with several groups of staff in the context of a single project or consultancy intervention. It reinforces the notion that contracting must be an inclusive process that involves all key stakeholders, not just senior managers, if change and development are to be effected.

CASE STUDY 2: PEER REVIEW OF TEACHING

A university agreed a directive that all schools should develop and implement a scheme for the peer review of teaching. Schools approached the educational developer for help in moving this forward. Contracting required the educational developer to clarify the agenda of the school as well as the developer's own agenda.

At the stage of contracting, one clear need is to establish the purpose or aim of a peer review scheme within any particular school. The educational developer could provide advice and examples of practice elsewhere in the university and sector, but would also need to establish the principles and values that the particular group of staff wish to underpin the development. If it were to be a scheme to weed out poor staff then it would need to be approached differently from a scheme that was designed for the purpose of identifying and sharing good practice.

Contracting here would also need to make explicit what scale of involvement the educational developer was prepared to make in the development process, and what time and resources the school is expected to invest in the activity. Is it expected that the educational developer actually devises the scheme, or will the developer facilitate a group of staff to do that? How will the implementation actually happen? Will all staff try a first cycle of the scheme and then commit to evaluating the scheme, or will a pilot operate in which the educational developer may be an additional observer?

This would also be the point at which local practices, customs and cultural nuances would need to be identified. Is there a culture of anonymity, or are staff happy to share and be open about the feedback they receive? Is the structure of the school such that reporting of such activity is expected to be formal, perhaps through the committee structure? Are staff used to seeing colleagues teach, or do staff tend to work behind closed doors? To what degree do the staff reflect and evaluate practice as part of the discipline or their everyday practices?

Answers to these questions will enable the developer to identify the commitment to change and the scope of the activity required in order to develop and implement a scheme effectively

DATA GATHERING

The third phase of the consultancy cycle is concerned with data gathering. Again this stage is often passed over too quickly by pressed educational developers who may be tempted to rush in with their prescription to cure all teaching ills. The data-gathering phase is about collecting as much relevant information as possible about the issue or problem that you have been called in to address. Although formally phase 3 of the cycle, data gathering will of course begin from the initial point of contact. How the staff or group frame the issue or problem they want you to look at, who the approach comes from and the type of advice they ask for – all these are valuable data. Data will be collected through both formal and informal channels and quantitative and qualitative instruments: observation, perception, surveys, focus groups, reports, etc. It is important not to evaluate the data before a full picture emerges. Once again, many consultants and some educational developers fall into the trap of making a diagnosis based on woefully inadequate data. For our academic colleagues who are grounded in a tradition of scholarly activity and research, this will seem shallow and unprofessional.

Block (1983) suggests that data gathering is about collecting information to develop a better understanding of what is happening to create problems for the client. Block also notes that the very act of gathering data is a significant intervention into the organization. In this respect, we have to recognize that our conversations with colleagues can have an impact on the work we are undertaking. This accords with notions of process consultancy that are advocated by Schein (1987).

The case study below is concerned with data gathering about students' numeracy skills. It reminds us that we need to ensure that we use a diverse and appropriate range of devices and instruments to gather data. Too narrow an approach may mean that we have insufficient data to inform choices about the problem or issue that we are involved in trying to explore. Inappropriate use of data-gathering techniques, or failure to explore the problem in its broadest context, may lead to inappropriate choices being made when we move to the next phase of the cycle, which is making sense of the data and generating options.

CASE STUDY 3: EMBEDDING SKILLS IN THE CURRICULUM

A school of life and sport science became alarmed about the increasing difficulties students were experiencing in dealing with numerical elements of first-year courses. They approached the educational developers to see if they could provide any help or guidance in how they should deal with the issue. It is easy to make a diagnosis that the students are coming to the university with lower standards of numeracy skills, but this may not be the case, and it is important that the real nature of the problem be identified. Is it that students do not have the skills required or that they do not understand the problem as presented? It is also important to establish the extent of the problem. Is it all students, or only some? Is it all students on all courses, or do particular courses pose a higher degree of difficulty?

In this case, the data can be solely quantitative, but value might be gained from actually talking to staff who teach the students and to the students themselves in order to identify the difficulties being experienced.

These data are crucial to establishing where the problem actually lies, and without the data it is impossible to work towards an effective solution.

MAKING SENSE OF THE DATA AND GENERATING OPTIONS

The next stage in the cycle is concerned with making sense of the data. This is about assisting the staff you have been working with to reflect upon, question, challenge, problematize and discuss the data gathered in order to make sense of them in relation to the issue or problem that is being worked upon. A real challenge here is to assist staff to interpret the data in the context of the real issues and not just against the symptoms that may present.

Cookman, Evans and Reynolds (1992) remind us that 'often the client will remain firmly focused on the content of the problem' and that 'your challenge is to get them to consider the process aspects of solving the problem'. For the developer, this raises a crucial issue of ensuring that staff with whom we are working still retain ownership of the problem or issue that they are seeking to resolve. Too often developers may enter with their magic wand, introduce changes to curriculum or assessment practice and then disappear in a puff of smoke. If we have not helped develop sustainable skills and change in our colleagues then it should be of little surprise if staff revert to their former practice.

As part of this phase, or independently, we may generate a number of options for action. Once again, here the educational developer needs to work closely with the staff to generate actions and options that are appropriate to the organizational context and the project being undertaken. It is also important that the educational developer assist colleagues to find ways of working that will challenge but not overwhelm hard-pressed academic staff.

The following case illustrates how a collaborative approach to interpretation of data and the generating of options for action can ensure that the staff we work with retain ownership of the area under consideration. We review briefly a case around student perceptions and expectations of study. This was conducted collaboratively between a programme team and members of a central educational development unit.

CASE STUDY 4: EXPLORING STUDENTS' PERCEPTIONS AND MOTIVATION

Failure rates on a first-year course in business and computing were high. The perception of the academic staff was that the students were lazy and had poor commitment to the course. The educational development unit arranged focus groups, where the issues of lack of commitment and apparent lack of preparation for lectures and sessions were raised with the students. The input at the focus groups concentrated on the students' expectations of the university, themselves and the staff.

Analysis of the data was difficult owing to the diverse nature of the outcomes from the focus groups. The educational developers were careful not to prejudice the findings by the perceptions of the staff. However, analysis of the qualitative data from the focus groups and additional quantitative data revealed that:

- Students had a high regard for staff.

- Students struggled with the lack of individual attention they received through lectures and workshops. The transition from school to university was difficult in this respect.

- Staff provided extensive bibliographies and the students were overwhelmed with these. They were unable to identify which texts they should read.

- Students found the learning outcomes really useful in outlining what they should be learning but staff had not been using them in the sessions.

- Students found some technical elements of the course very difficult, while others repeated what they had done in the final year at school.

From these outcomes, staff were then able develop strategies to further support the students.

It is evident here that the outcome was heavily dependent on an objective analysis that considered a wide range of data and not just those presenting as the initial problem. The success was due to the fact that the educational developer was able to take the staff's thinking beyond the content of the problem.

IMPLEMENTING

The implementation phase of the cycle requires data gathering and reflection both in and on action (Schon, 1987). The best-laid plans are those that are changed in response to changed circumstance and perception. The educational developer needs to support the staff he or she is working with in engaging with both the intended and the non-intended outcomes of any particular interventions that are agreed.

CASE STUDY 5: KEY SKILLS IN THE CURRICULUM

A consultancy project to embed key skills into the curriculum through working with groups of staff in schools developed a series of workshops to use in schools. These workshops would support staff in redesigning elements of curricula. Academic staff attending the workshops were particularly resistant. They would not buy into the concept of key skills, at the same time claiming that they were already implementing key skills. But the data gathered, from course documentation and student feedback earlier in the process, indicated that they were not already implementing key skills. The implementation strategy was therefore changed in order that the outcomes agreed could still be achieved. This involved the production of guidance documentation that tackled the issues and provided examples of good practice.

DISENGAGING

The final phase of the cycle is disengaging. Lippitt and Lippitt (1978) argue that 'a professional responsibility and goal of most consultants is to become progressively unnecessary'. Such an approach accords with the notion of process consultancy that Edgar Schein advocates (1987). Ideally, disengagement should be a gradual process of withdrawal over time rather than an acute or abrupt ending. Many writers on consulting suggest that the best time to talk about ending is at the beginning; that is, during the contracting phase. Gilmore (1997) notes that although much research has been conducted about the other phases of consulting activity, little has been undertaken or written about ending consultations.

In the context of educational development, there will be many beginnings and endings. The nature of the role means that relationships are ongoing, but these should be focused around different needs and issues at different times. It is inevitable, and indeed sometimes productive, that some of these boundaries will become blurred. Nevertheless, it is important that the consultant identify when closure of a particular consultancy intervention is appropriate.

The following case study is based on the development of a Research Supervisors Development Programme in collaboration with the research office at a university. The case illustrates how it is essential that educational developers plan, with staff they are working with, strategies for building capacity and for disengaging from projects with which they are involved.

CASE STUDY 6: RESEARCH SUPERVISORS DEVELOPMENT PROGRAMME

An educational development unit was approached by the university's research office and asked to design and deliver a programme of professional development and skills training for research supervisors across the university. The university had ambitious aims to expand both its portfolio and its numbers of research students, but realized that such aspirations would need to be coupled with a programme of staff development. The developer agreed to work collaboratively with the research office and to project-manage and pilot the development of such a programme. It was agreed that the project would involve the developer for two years, and that after that time a product and process would have been developed such that responsibility for the co-ordination, delivery and management of such a programme would be handed over to the research office. Throughout the project, it had been essential to build capacity among the research office team and to start the process of disengagement as various phases of the project were completed.

SKILLS SETS FOR DEVELOPERS WORKING FROM A CONSULTANCY PERSPECTIVE

The cycle is intended to be holistic in nature. However, we recognize that each of the stages that we have explored places particular demands on developers. Table 4.1 highlights key aspects of the process at each stage of the cycle, and proposes an associated skills set to accompany these. For developers and/or staff who are new to this model of working, these could form a framework for skills development through self-audit and continuing professional development (CPD).

Table 4.1 *Key stages and skills required for effective consultancy in higher education*

Action	Skills
Gaining entry Establish who is involved Decide who you need to talk to first Identify the key stakeholders	Networking at operational and strategic levels, listening, empathy, communication
Contracting Who gives the agreement? Who provides the resources to support the consultancy? Agree the outcomes and deliverables Establish and agree the project plan Agree roles and responsibilities Agree a strategy for disengaging	Negotiating, setting key targets and outcomes, defining roles and responsibilities
Data gathering Background information on the group, issue and context Decide and agree which instruments and process to be used to gather data Check against outcomes and deliverables	Research skills
Making sense of the data and generating options Analyse, interpret, evaluate and reflect on the data Apply appropriate theoretical and conceptual frameworks Frame the data in the context of the original problem Frame the data in the context of the agreed outcomes Present possible scenarios Evaluate options against cost/benefit Secure agreement of all key stakeholders to proposed actions	Reflection and analysis, presentation skills, evaluation skills, thinking strategically. Facilitation skills
Implementing Involve all appropriate staff Establish that any additional resources are secured Ensure that evaluation and monitoring are continuous Agree roles and responsibilities for implementation Do it!	Facilitation, leadership, project management
Disengaging Assist all stakeholders to review and reflect on all processes and outcomes Conduct final evaluation Ensure that follow-up action is arranged Let go!	Negotiation, assertiveness

FINAL THOUGHTS

As we have shown, much of the educational development work that occurs within an institution can use a consultancy approach. Through institutional learning and teaching strategies, centrally organized programmes, institutionally based projects and guides for good practice, we try to shift or reframe pedagogic and andragogic practice within the institution. This is achieved mainly through influence and persuasion, as we actually have little control over what goes on in the classroom or the lecture hall.

Working in a development role requires constant consideration of the most effective approaches. Gone are the days when the universal solution was to 'run a workshop'. The demands in the system for quantifiable, effective change that supports the strategic intentions of institutions have resulted in a more considered and sophisticated approach to educational development across the sector. As with all approaches to educational development, there are advantages and disadvantages to the use of consultancy. Table 4.2 suggests the specific advantages and disadvantages of using the consultancy approach in your own higher education institution.

As with any approach, the benefits and disadvantages need to be considered, particularly against the desired outcomes of change and the pros and cons of using any other approach. We hope that we have managed to show in this chapter the appropriateness of the consultancy model for use in educational development. We believe that the true advantages of this

Table 4.2 *Advantages and disadvantages of working as a consultant in your own higher education institution*

Advantages	Disadvantages
You can take longer gaining entry	You are part of the culture you are trying to
You will probably know the client(s)	change
You may know something about the	Your department may have a poor image
staff's problems	You may have a poor image
You know the history of the institution	You may be imposed rather than chosen
You may share the same values	You may know things about the client(s)
You may spot non-genuine reasons for	you can't disclose
calling you in	You may have problems over confidentiality
You know where to get information	You may be part of the problem
You can find the real client more easily	You may have to confront friends
You may have an established good	You may be discounted as a prophet in
reputation	your own land
You may be able to ask for help from	You may fear the effects on your career
other internal consultants	prospects
Implementation and follow-up are easier	

Source: Adapted from Cookman, Evans and Reynolds (1992)

model lie within the process of working with staff in identifying real (as opposed to initially perceived) problems and in steering these staff to implement substantial, grounded and sustained (as opposed to superficial) change. We have seen that employing this approach in our own work at the University of Surrey Roehampton has resulted in a dramatic increase in the sense of understanding of the issues and ownership of the process of solving educational problems. This has been the case when using the consultancy approach to work with staff on a one-to-one basis, with a small group or in taking a whole school, department or unit through a period of change. We have found as practitioners that the framework of the stages of the consultancy cycle stages provides a coherent structure and a principled, productive set of key activities for approaching situations and problems where effective change is required.

REFERENCES

Block, P (1983) *Flawless Consulting: Guide for getting your expertise used*, Learning Concepts, Austin, TX

Cookman, P, Evans, B and Reynolds, P (1992) *Client Centred Consulting: A practical guide for internal advisers and trainers*, McGraw-Hill, London

Gilmore, T (1997) The social architecture of group interventions, in *Developing Organisational Consultancy*, ed J E Neumann, K Kellner and A Dawson-Shepherd, pp 32–48, Routledge, London

Lippitt, G and Lippitt, R (1978) *The Consulting Process in Action*, University Associates, La Jolla, CA

Nicholls, G (2001) *Professional Development in Higher Education*, Kogan Page, London

Reason, P (ed) (1994) *Participation in Human Inquiry*, Sage, London

Schein, E (1987) *Process Consultation*, vol 2, *Lessons for Managers and Consultants*, Addison-Wesley, Boston

Schon, D A (1987) *Educating the Reflective Practitioner*, Jossey-Bass, San Francisco

Weil, S (1998) Postgraduate education and lifelong learning as collaborative inquiry in action: an emergent model, in *Beyond the First Degree*, ed R Burgess, pp 119–39, Society for Research into Higher Education and Open University Press, Buckingham

5

Monitoring and evaluating staff and educational development

David Baume

INTRODUCTION

Terminology

This chapter is intended to support the monitoring and evaluation of any activity involving staff or educational development. 'Activity' is intended to serve as a wholly inclusive term, covering a workshop, a programme, a single intervention, a small, medium or large project, or the whole of the work of a staff or educational development unit.

Focus

I devote most of the chapter to evaluation. However, much of what I say about evaluation can also be applied to the monitoring.

Methodology and utility

This chapter begins with a broadly positivist approach, a concern with goals met and deliverables delivered as well as with processes satisfactory. I offer other approaches later in the chapter. The chapter progresses from basic through more sophisticated and varied accounts of the monitoring and evaluation of staff and educational development. It addresses how monitoring and evaluation can lead to increased understanding and to changed (it is to be hoped improved) practice. The later methods described are not necessarily better; fitness for purposes is all. Some ideas from the early methods underpin later methods. However, I believe that the urge for accountability will outlive at least some fashions in monitoring and evaluation. I further believe that, whatever more sophisticated answers and understandings monitoring and evaluation will provide, we developers will still be asked to show how we have achieved goals, delivered deliverables, and done so through good processes; hence my advocacy of a positivist approach as at least a part of any evaluation.

Purpose

My main aims with this chapter are to demystify monitoring and evaluation; to suggest that monitoring and evaluation are an integral part of good practice right from the start of any development activity, rather than optional add-ons; and to offer some particular approaches, with the hope that you will variously review, adopt and adapt these approaches to your own setting.

Perspective

I adopt two points of view in this chapter; mainly that of the evaluator, but also sometimes that of the staff or educational development unit or project to be evaluated, which I often call the evaluand.

Progression

The early parts of this chapter describe and review a selection of methods in the literature and in current practice. Later in the chapter I propose an alternative account of the purposes of evaluation and offer a new under-pinning approach to evaluation.

SOME BASIC IDEAS IN MONITORING AND EVALUATION

At its heart, *monitoring* is a very simple and common process. It runs alongside, or indeed is integral to or frequently interspersed with, most conscious human activities. Monitoring involves first asking a question such as 'How is it going?'

Given some answers to this question, monitoring further involves asking and answering a further question along the lines of: 'So (how) should we change what we are doing?'

Evaluation is at its heart a similarly simple process, undertaken at the end of or at waypoints during an extended staff or educational activity. Evaluation first involves asking a question such as 'How did that go?'

If the evaluation is being carried out at some intermediate point in the life of an activity, then the answers to this question should inform the answering of further questions along the lines of 'So what should we do next?'

If the evaluation is being undertaken at the end, a different further question will be more appropriate; perhaps 'So what do we learn from this that may be of use or interest to others?'

Thus far, then, I have suggested that both monitoring and evaluation are concerned with goals achieved or not, and with processes satisfactory or not. In all that follows, I encourage you to test the ideas against your own thinking and experience, and also to apply the ideas to a project or unit that you are interested in monitoring or evaluating or having monitored or evaluated.

WHAT WOULD IT MEAN FOR AN ACTIVITY TO BE GOING OR HAVE GONE SUCCESSFULLY OR WELL?

I shall first sharpen the distinction implied in the question above between succeeding and going well. In what follows I shall take *succeeding* to mean achieving *goals*, and *going well* to mean adopting satisfactory or excellent *processes*. Why is this distinction significant? Consider: An educational development project may have achieved all its goals, but have operated in such a clumsy way as to damage relationships and render further successful collaboration most unlikely. By contrast, a staff development unit may run in a wholly harmonious way, with procedures, budgets and codes of practice properly followed, but with few or none of its goals achieved. Good process, we should hope, is more likely to be accompanied by attainment of goals, and vice versa. But the correlation is well short of 100 per cent.

Having established this distinction, I shall now consider goals and processes, and the rather distinct approaches required to evaluate each, separately.

Goals and their achievement

Goals of three kinds can usefully be distinguished. A staff and educational development activity may specify its goals in terms of what it intends to do; in terms of its *activities* – for example, 'We shall run twenty workshops.' It may specify what it intends to produce; its *outputs* – for example, 'We shall produce six booklets and a Web site.' (Clearly, as in the case of workshops, some activities may also be considered as outputs. Sometimes outputs and output-type activities are lumped together as 'deliverables'.) A staff and educational development activity may – one hopes it does – also specify what effects it intends its activities and its outputs to achieve; these effects we may call its *outcomes* – for example, 'The department will describe the learning outcomes of all its units and will achieve and assure the constructive alignment of learning outcomes, teaching and learning methods, and assessment methods and criteria.'

There is a rather inconvenient relationship among these three kinds of goals. Activities and outputs are easy to describe and quantify, and thus to establish as goals, as suggested in the short examples above. I suggest below further ways to do this. Establishing goals and targets for activities and for outputs makes for easy monitoring and evaluation, and little more than competent management and administration are required to achieve them. But, as developers, we know that we undertake activities and deliver products in order to have effects, on the practices and perhaps also on the knowledge and understanding and world-view of colleagues or whole departments, subjects, institutions. And such outcomes are harder to define and to measure – though never impossible, as I hope the example above suggests and arguments below will confirm.

How might we measure the outcomes of staff and educational development? To the extent that staff development is a form of teaching – and I know that this is a sensitive issue, our clients also being our professional colleagues and deserving of appropriate respect – still, to the extent that staff development is a form of teaching, we can establish intended learning outcomes for our staff development processes, and find out how well participants have attained these intended learning outcomes. This is unexceptionable for programmes for new staff, for example the by now almost ubiquitous Postgraduate Certificate in Learning and Teaching in Higher Education, on which the work of participants is assessed. By contrast, the idea of assessing colleagues at the end of a staff development workshop may produce a sharp intake of breath, from us as we contemplate it and from participants if we try it. My own view is that we all, developers and our clients, need to become a little more robust about this. But what follows does not require this!

So, let us find another approach to assessing the achievement of outcomes. I shall concentrate here on assessing the outcomes of staff development events, not forgetting that the purpose of this exploration is to find ways to evaluate the workshops and, more generally, to evaluate any staff and educational development activities, here to evaluate in terms of extent of goals achieved. This requires a brief excursion into workshop design.

The classic approach to designing a teaching or training event is a linear one. It starts with context, then considers content, participants and aims, then moves through intended learning outcomes to learning and teaching methods and then to learning resources and materials and finally to assessment and evaluation. This classic approach can cause a problem. It can lead to intended outcomes that are, for any number of reasons, unassessable, which also renders the workshop in this important respect unevaluable. The solution to this problem is to iterate in the design, to go back at each stage of design to the previous stage to ensure consistency or, in John Biggs's helpful and mellifluous phrase, constructive alignment.

(Constructive alignment means more than consistency. It also acknowledges learning as a process of constructing rather than absorbing knowledge. I am happy to use Biggs's phrase in its full intended meaning. See Biggs (1999).)

What does consistency mean here? It means that we need to ensure that the workshop outcomes are of a form that can be assessed. This may mean that instead of setting a final test, we can provide a task towards the end of the workshop and invite some or all participants to share their achievements on the task. This is not very difficult, but it does require both sensitivity to the needs and status of our clients and clarity and consistency of thinking on our part. Again; to the extent that staff development is a form of teaching, and further to the extent that we, as developers, will inevitably be judged for what we do as developers and how we do our development as well as for what we say during it; then sensitivity to clients and clarity and consistency of thought are virtues worth practising.

But we may well have outcomes that cannot be assessed in a workshop. For example, we may intend that participants should be able to adopt a new approach to the design of their course, or to create and implement a new assessment strategy or student support system. Such outcomes cannot be achieved in a single workshop. What to do?

We could run a series of workshops, consultations or other processes over time, and at or after the end assess how far our intended outcome for the whole staff development has been achieved, thus informing our evaluation. This long-term approach has much to commend it.

Proxies

There is another approach. We can search for a proxy, an intermediary, some activity on the part of our clients which, while not exactly the intended outcome of our development work, can give us fair confidence that our intended outcome has been achieved.

Chris Rust (1998) has shown how this can be done for staff development workshops. In a careful study, he followed up the effectiveness of 33 workshops delivered by 14 consultants of the Oxford Centre for Staff and Learning Development to over 500 participants. Completing end-of-workshop evaluations, 69 per cent of participants felt that they were very likely to change some aspect of their practice as a result of this workshop and a further 21 per cent considered it possible that they would make such a change. But this was only a statement of intent. What did they actually do?

Four months after the workshop, Rust sent a further questionnaire to those workshop participants who had said that they would be willing to respond to such a questionnaire. Twenty-five per cent of respondents claimed to have changed their practice to a great or a fair extent, and

89 per cent to have made at least some change. A further telephone survey asked a sample of questionnaire respondents about the kinds of changes they had made. Each interviewee provided one or more specific examples of changes they had made as a result of the workshop they had attended. All believed that their changes had been successful. Rust's conclusions merit reporting in full:

1. Workshops can promote at least some changes in the practice of most participants, and extensive changes in some participants, and these changes [in their practice] can be judged to have been successful.

2. Workshops can successfully reassure the participants and provide them with extra confidence in what they are already doing and confidence to innovate.

3. Workshop ratings are reasonable predictions of likely impact, and indications by participants of how they are likely to change [their practice] are good predictors of likely impact. (Rust, 1998: 72–80)

Rust offers cautions against deducing too much from his findings. The workshops also scored very highly on participants' satisfaction. The workshops were concerned with practical topics, and changes to practice were intended outcomes. However, even accepting these cautions, these results are surely encouraging for those who plan to facilitate change through workshops. The findings also offer some support to the evaluator who uses participants' plans to make particular changes as indicators that they will in fact make these changes.

We can draw a broader implication from this result. Where a large project with many similar processes or events is to be evaluated, or an educational development unit is running a number of similar events, Rust's paper suggests a defensible approach to evaluation. Briefly, this approach is first to identify participants' stated intentions, and then to follow up a sample to see if their intentions are carried through into practice. This approach could be applied to any monitoring process and to evaluating any development process designed to stimulate changes in behaviour, not just to workshops.

Planning evaluation

I have focused here on staff development activities. Similar principles apply for planning and then evaluating educational development projects, where the demand for evaluation may be even stronger than for staff development. I suggest:

- Plan the evaluation as you plan the activity.

- Ensure that your evaluation methods will be able to evaluate how far the goals of the project have been achieved.

- If you realize that your evaluation methods will not sufficiently evaluate how far the goals of the project have been achieved, consider modifying the goals of the project to make them more readily evaluable.

Is this not suggesting letting the tail of evaluation wag the dog that is the project? Perhaps, but only a little. And I feel that there is something incomplete – perhaps even, though not everyone will agree with me, a little dishonest – about a declared goal, the achievement of which you know in advance that you cannot properly evaluate.

An implication may be drawn from what I have just said that attention to how far the attainment of a goal can be measured invariably leads to a softening of the goal. This is not the case. I have seen an early draft project goal that spoke of 'having a positive impact on the teaching of...'. This could scarcely have been made softer. What it needed was clarifying, sharpening, strengthening. The revised project outcomes spoke of two goals (among others). The first goal was to be the (high) proportion of the teachers in the discipline who would have at least heard about the project, through the proxies of using a number of different and realistic specified methods of reaching them all. These outreach methods were activities or out*put* measures, admittedly, but they provided plausible proxies for modest out*comes*. The second goal was to be the (rather smaller) proportion of lecturers in the discipline who would have begun to explore how they might apply some of the project outcomes to their practice, this time through attendance at workshops (activities, yes, but activities that require, or at least very strongly encourage, particular out*comes*).

Evaluating processes

I have looked at some length at goals and the evaluation of their achievement. What are possible indicators of a satisfactory or unsatisfactory process? At its most basic, a staff and educational development activity and those who provide it need to comply with legislation and with institutional guidelines, for example on employment and equality of opportunity. Beyond that, it is difficult to provide generally applicable indicators of a satisfactory or unsatisfactory process. Fortunately, it is also unnecessary. We all have instincts for what comprise satisfactory dealings and relationships with others. These instincts get us part of the way there; but probably not the whole way. We also have the ability to talk and listen to colleagues about what they require, expect and aspire to in our dealings with each other. We may need to apply our considerable expertise in facilitation and negotiation to extract these accounts of requirements, needs and aspirations. We should then probably record them, perhaps in the form of local guidelines and ground rules. (I know that ground rules are a staff development cliché, but they have become so only because they are widely used and often found valuable.) We also need to monitor adherence to them and deal with excursions from them.

Process goals might include the following:

- Everyone is clear about goals and methods.

- Everyone (or a specified subset) has had the opportunity to contribute to project plans.

- Everyone feels that his or her contributions are taken suitably seriously.

- Meeting notes are circulated within 48 hours of the end of the meeting.

- Goals and methods are subject to regular review.

TWO OUTER LOOPS

The evaluability of goals

The discussions above of the need to iterate between various elements of a staff development programme, and about the possible need to modify project goals to make them more evaluable, both embody a broader principle. They both suggest an outer loop of reflection and action, of monitoring and evaluation, as also addressed in Chapter 12. In the case of the workshop, the outer loop checked that the various elements of the workshop were aligned, consistent with each other; that they pulled in the same direction. In the case of the educational development project, the outer loop involved letting the planning of the evaluation inform the setting of the goals of the staff or educational development activity – if you can't evaluate its attainment, it may not be the most useful goal.

The continued appropriateness of goals

There is a further outer loop; a further-out loop if you will. This further outer loop additionally asks what may sound a heretical question: even if they are evaluable, are the stated goals, the planned processes, still appropriate?

Why do we need to ask such a question? Surely goals and at least some procedures and processes are fixed? Surely the funders will object if we go around changing goals?

The environment in which the activity is being undertaken will surely change, gradually or abruptly or both. Other initiatives will come along that may render the current activity obsolete, or that may duplicate some of the planned goals, or with which some form of co-operation is clearly the only sensible course. For such reasons, we need to check the continued appropriateness of goals. Changes of goal may of course require high-level exploration and approval. But such changes are very likely to become appropriate in the life of a two- or three-year development project, and certainly in the life of an established unit. Better to seek them out than be buffeted by them; better to monitor and evaluate the project or unit in its wider environment than to try to hide from the world.

AN INTERIM CONCLUSION

The suggestions so far would provide a secure basis on which to plan the evaluation of most staff and educational development activities, most projects or development units. The resultant evaluations would be likely to meet most of the needs of those funding the activity or the evaluation.

The second part of this chapter goes beyond, offering some further and richer approaches to evaluation. But if your current needs have been met, this is a good place to stop, for now at least.

A 10-STEP WAY

Staying with the evaluation of goals and processes, but acknowledging more of the complexities that can arise around staff and educational development, a 9-step approach for evaluating staff development was proposed by Baume and Baume (1995), based closely on work by Nevo (1986), here expanded to 10. To the account already given in this chapter, this account particularly adds the identification of stakeholders, their interests and questions, and also the identification of the criteria for the judgement of answers to stakeholders' questions. It is suggested that substantial additional effort be applied to the planning of evaluation – the first 5 of the 10 steps are about planning. This extended framework also contains a useful wider list of possible types of object to be evaluated.

In brief, the proposed steps are:

1. Identify the *object(s) to be evaluated*. What you wish to evaluate may be a policy; a development unit or service; a programme; an event or activity; or a project. (It may sound, or even be, glaringly obvious that you should start by deciding what you want to evaluate. It is still worth

taking the few seconds necessary to be sure, as huge amounts of time can be wasted evaluating the wrong thing. And if the few seconds reveal some confusion about what exactly is/are to be evaluated, then the consequent few minutes or hours of further analysis will for the same reason be very useful.)

2. Identify the main *stakeholders* in the objects(s) to be evaluated. In Weiss's helpful account, stakeholders are 'members of groups that are palpably affected by the [object to be evaluated], and who will therefore conceivably be affected by evaluative conclusions about the [object to be evaluated], or the members of the groups that make decisions about the future of the [object to be evaluated], such as decisions to continue or discontinue funding or to alter modes of operation of the [object to be evaluated]' (1986). If we adapt Weiss's list, the main stakeholder groups are likely to be intended clients and users of the development activity, and their managers; policy makers; staff development unit managers; individual developers; and project staff.

3. Identify the *questions or concerns* of each major stakeholder or group. These may be about goals, strategies and plans, the approach and activities taken, and the outcomes achieved. A good way to identify their questions or concerns is to ask them what their questions or concerns are.

4. A particularly valuable step is to go beyond stakeholder questions to stakeholder *criteria for a satisfactory answer to the questions*. These criteria may address four classes of issues:
   - How far are the expressed stakeholders' needs met? (Broadly, these needs should form the goals of the things to be evaluated.)
   - How far are broader institutional or national policy goals achieved or supported?
   - How far are agreed standards, norms and processes met and followed?
   - How effective are the methods compared to other methods that could have been followed?

5. Plan and pilot the *methods and instruments* to be used.

6. *Carry out* the evaluation.

7. This is the new step: as well as answering stakeholder questions, also seek to *understand* the object(s) being evaluated, to make sense of why what was done had the effect that it had. I explore this in more detail below.

8. *Report to stakeholders* on answers to their questions and concerns.

9. *Change staff and educational development practice* as appropriate

10. Periodically *review* evaluation methods and processes.

Baume and Baume (1995) contains a worked example of this method in action.

DEEPER PERSPECTIVES ON EVALUATION

The message 'you are about to be evaluated' rarely lifts the spirits of the impending evaluand. However hard we work to make evaluation an objective, neutral, non-threatening process, being evaluated may well feel like being interrogated, judged and, quite possibly in at least some respects, found wanting. The following approaches will not entirely overcome this evalu-phobia; nothing can. But they variously seek to make evaluation more illuminating, more complete, more appreciative and readier to give due weight to process.

Seeking to illuminate

'It is little exaggeration to assert that educational research has had negligible impact on the workings of educational institutions and on the ways in which academic men and women reflect upon their professional activities' (Miller and Parlett, 1974, preface: 3). Almost 30 years later this is still mostly true, and probably as true for educational evaluation as for educational research. Parlett and Hamilton (1972) propose, and Miller and Parlett (1974) illustrate, a new approach to evaluation. It still feels fresh and highly attractive. The chief aim of the illuminative approach 'is to explore, describe, analyse, elucidate and portray – in other words to illuminate – the practices and processes of teaching and learning, broadly defined, as they occur in their national settings' (Miller and Parlett, 1974: 2). 'The illuminative approach... [is]

- ... *problem centred* – beginning (as all applied research does) with issues and concerns as defined in real life settings;

- ... *practitioner-oriented* – designating its chief function to provide information and insight from professional educators;

- ... *cross-disciplinary* – drawing especially on psychology, sociology, psychiatry and social anthropology for concepts and ways of thinking;

- ... *methodologically eclectic* – interviews, questionnaires, observation and analysis of documents are used in various combinations, according to the circumstances, defined problems and stages of investigation;

- ... *heuristically organised* – the research progressively focusing and refining the areas of inquiry as the study unfolds, in the light of accumulating experiences and as the crucial issues-to-be-studied become uncovered' (Miller and Parlett, 1974: 2).

Seeking the whole picture

'Above all, evaluation is the discernment of the good.' Robert Stake (2002), author of this statement, speaks and writes about and practises what he calls responsive evaluation. Stake calls for evaluation to be more holistic, more thoughtful, more experiential. Evaluation, he feels, should find and tell the evaluand's story, should ask 'What's happening here?' He contrasts what he calls responsive evaluation with criterion-based, analytic, information-based evaluation – in fact, with the kind I have advocated in the first part of this chapter.

Stake's evaluations have some of the qualities of a story, giving a rich picture of the setting, the people, the atmosphere, the environment as well as what is happening and why. He advocates a criterion-free response. We cannot, Stake acknowledges, fail to be analytic or use criteria – but we should let analysis emerge, let criteria float to the surface. At the same time, he is happy to approach an evaluation with a question in mind – such as 'Were the goals of the activity achieved?' Stake can be seen as taking forward the illuminative approach described immediately above while maintaining focus on goals achieved if not on criterion met.

Seeking to appreciate

Imagine asking, as a lead evaluation question, 'Think of a time in your entire experience of this [staff or educational development project or unit] when you have felt most excited, most engaged and most alive. What were the forces and factors that made it a great experience? What was it about you, others and your organisation that made it a peak experience for you?' James Ludema and his colleagues (2000), who suggest this evaluation question, call it an unconditional positive question, reflecting the unconditional positive regard that is one of the cornerstones of humanistic psychology. They offer strong rationales for this question as part of an approach that they call appreciative inquiry. I should stress here that Ludema *et al* are describing a method for inquiry, typically into the functioning of organizations, rather than evaluation. I take responsibility for adapting what they say towards evaluation, although in truth very little adaptation is needed.

First, they suggest, surely one of the goals of an evaluation is to understand and thereby to extend the best, as well as to understand and thereby remediate the worst.

Their second rationale needs a little more space. It hinges on what they see as the quite inappropriate and destructive power of the dominant paradigm, critical inquiry. They quote in Ludema *et al* (2000), with approval the deliberately militaristic comments of Gergen (1994), who speaks of 'the mammoth arsenal of critic weaponry at our disposal... There is virtually no hypothesis, body of evidence, ideological stance, literary canon, value commitment or logical edifice [or, we might add, staff and educational development activity] that cannot be dismantled, derided or demolished with the implements at hand.' Staff and educational developers are for the most part nice and constructive people, and I am sure that such behaviour is not common – although not all evaluations of staff and educational development are undertaken by developers! Gergen lists some damaging consequences of this relentlessly critical approach, but for our purposes as staff and educational development evaluators or evaluands we should concentrate on the claimed benefits of an appreciative approach, which Ludema and colleagues offer as 'continuously to craft the unconditional positive question that allows the [staff development activity] to discover, amplify and multiply the alignments of strengths in such a way that weaknesses and deficiencies become increasingly irrelevant' (Ludema *et al*, 2000).

Seeking good outcomes in good process

'There is a lot to be said for commenting on the quality of the thinking and processes that [educational development units, organizations and] project teams develop and trusting that good processes tend to evoke good outcomes.' This proposition from Peter Knight (2003) challenged me. I talk above about the importance of monitoring process as well as outcome. But at first it seemed to me to be hopelessly optimistic to trust that good outcomes will follow from good processes.

On the other hand, I note that whether in evaluation or development or many other forms of professional activity, we devote much more attention to making, finding and using good processes, good practices, than to evaluation. This observation in turn suggests that where ultimate goals are impossible to identify, for example within the timescale of the project, and proxy goals cannot be found, then attention to good process may be a plausible proxy for the achievement of good outcomes.

THREE PURPOSES FOR EVALUATION

I have selected above ideas and practices from a large literature about evaluation, and from a much smaller literature about the evaluation of staff and educational development, a range of approaches that I hope will be useful. However, I am conscious that on first (and quite possibly also second) reading they may seem to point in very different directions. Let me offer a synthesis and resolution, in the forms of (in this section) an account of three primary purposes of evaluation and (in the next section) a unifying approach to the evaluation of a staff or educational development activity.

The literature on monitoring and evaluation suggests two kinds of and purposes for evaluation: 'formative evaluation' to improve an activity or project as it progresses, and 'summative evaluation' to judge its effectiveness. The distinction has become, I feel, rather dysfunctional. For example, it ignores the often substantial and fruitful overlap in method and data collection of the two forms of evaluation, and thus discourages a more coherent approach to evaluation. It also discourages more fundamental forms of learning from evaluation. I propose instead three possible purposes for the monitoring and evaluation of staff and educational development activities. Like formative and summative evaluation, these three purposes overlap. But their use clarifies, for evaluator and evaluand alike, what a particular evaluation is intended to achieve. These three purposes are to account, to improve and to understand.

To account
To *account* (another term would be audit) means to assure those who funded the project that the project has done and achieved what was said would be done and achieved, and done these things to an appropriate standard and in an appropriate way. The standards and the methods of accounting or auditing must be negotiated and agreed. For example, will 'deliverables delivered' do, or is it necessary to go into the more elaborate processes of operationalizing goals described earlier in the chapter? And what do the two appropriates mean in this particular context? But evaluation as accounting or auditing is a definable and useful function, primarily concerned with satisfying (or of course not) the client, the funder, other stakeholders. Accounting is a part, and may be the whole, of summative evaluation.

To improve
'Evaluation can be a form of consultancy and, as such, do a lot for enhancing the thinking and work of those being evaluated' (Knight, 2003). This is a usefully extreme account of what is sometimes called formative evaluation. It suggests the evaluator as critical friend, as someone who is at

once a part of and apart from the project team, supportive of the broad purposes of the project but all the time looking out for possible inconsistencies in thinking and practice, for mis-steps about to be made or opportunities about to be missed, for productive questions to ask and productive suggestions to make – and often for productive, appreciative silences where no intervention is needed! Evaluating to improve can mean using most of the methods described throughout this chapter, and others as newly discovered or invented as appropriate. Evaluating to improve is not limited to the description that opened this paragraph. But the particular role or roles of evaluator as improver need initial negotiation and periodic renegotiation.

To understand

It is not necessary to understand a staff or educational development activity, in any beyond a superficial way, to account for it or to audit it. By contrast, it is essential to understand what is working and what isn't, and how, and above all why, in order to make confident proposals to improve the activity being evaluated. But, beyond supporting improvement, understanding is surely a valid aim for the evaluation of any staff or educational development activity? Seeking to understand can mean the construction and testing of models and theories and explanations. It can mean employing any of a vast range of disciplinary paradigms, methods, ways of thinking and arguing.

Seeking to understand, almost whatever 'understand' means to the evaluator, evaluand and their clients, is a properly scholarly and academic aim. The negotiation around evaluation to understand will need to address, among other issues, what the parties would find useful forms of understanding and explanation. Claims of increased understanding can be tested in public, like any other academic idea or proposal. If well received, the new understandings can be applied to future projects.

Evaluation as seeking to understand provides a way for academics to be properly academic, to research their practice. I have discussed the crossing from evaluation to research in more detail elsewhere (Baume, 2002). The concept of evaluation as seeking to understand also necessarily puts research back into development projects, from which it is sometimes excluded by funding bodies presumably anxious that funds for development are not side-tracked into research. This phenomenon is described by Wisdom (2002: 128) in the context of a project, History 2000, undertaken under the Higher Education Funding Council's (HEFCE) Fund for the Development of Teaching and Learning (FDTL): 'It is important to remember that the HEFCE had not established a research fund. FDTL was about the implementing of educational change. There would have been little point in finishing History 2000 with the words "Well, that didn't work, but at least we know why.'" Indeed. The HEFCE would not have been pleased. But how valuable to be able to say, for example, 'The project worked in these respects, and here are our explanations for why...'?

NEGOTIATING AND NEGOTIATED EVALUATION

The more usual account of an evaluation boils down to someone (the evaluator) doing something (monitoring and evaluation) to someone or something (the evaluand). Instead, I here characterize the planning of an evaluation, and also much of its undertaking, as a negotiation.

The first outcome of a negotiation about evaluation would be an evaluation plan or contract. This would identify the purpose or purposes of the evaluation, perhaps using the three-part typology of purposes – to account, to improve and to understand – offered in the previous section. It would also describe evaluation methods, reporting, and also the resources to be applied to the evaluation. And it would include the inevitable outer loop, this time a process for reviewing and renegotiating the evaluation process and contract. I concentrate below on some less obvious features of an evaluation agreement:

- An agreement about who will provide and verify which data, and when. For example, the evaluator does not need to attend a workshop to know that it ran, or count heads to know how many attended. More generally, the activities involved in, and the outputs of, staff and educational development are relatively uncontentious. They happened or they didn't; they were produced or they weren't. But the evaluator needs to agree how such data about deliverables delivered will be collected and audited, and to what standard of proof. This would support the *accounting* function.

- Agreement on quality measures or descriptions for the activities and outputs referred to above, or an agreed process for defining these quality measures or descriptions – again supporting *accounting*.

- An agreed process for sharpening at least some of the project goals to the point where it could be determined to what extent they had, by the end of the project, been achieved. (Another term for this process is SMARTening, which refers to the suggestions that goals should as far as possible be Specific, Measurable, Attractive, Realistic and Timebound.) For example, a project might aim to 'develop a reflective approach by students to showing how they had attained programme outcomes'. This will need sharpening, or smartening, if its attainment is to be evaluated. This process is concerned with *improving*, and also with making proper *accounting* possible.

● Agreement on the likely headings for a very short evaluation report very early in the life of a project. This report should focus on the *a priori* appropriateness of the project goals, and also on the appropriateness of project methods and plans in terms of their likelihood of achieving the goals, together with any recommendations for change. This supports *improving* but also gives a stronger base for *accounting*.

So, the evaluation plan can be negotiated and agreed. There are subtleties to this. For example, who is the client for the evaluation? Is it the funder of the activity to be evaluated; the activity itself (the staff or educational development project or unit); or some independent agency? The answer to this question affects the power relationship that underpins and informs both the negotiation and the evaluation. When the client for the evaluation is the project itself, and the evaluator's duties include 'accounting' in the sense described above, the evaluator must be willing if necessary to bite the feeding hand.

But what about the evaluation itself as a negotiation? Negotiation implies conversation, exchanges of information and of interpretations, the collaborative development and testing of evolving models and conceptions.

Conversation and negotiation may not seem essential for evaluation for accounting, once the evaluation plan and standards and criteria are agreed. And indeed they are not essential. The evaluator reports, accounts and is finished. But the evaluation is much more likely to be accepted and embraced by the evaluand when the evaluation has been discussed, negotiated and, as far as possible, agreed. And the negotiated evaluation is much less likely to contain errors of fact or interpretation, errors ripe to be pounced on by the evaluand and used to assault the credibility of the evaluation and the evaluator, should the evaluand so wish, for example because the evaluation elsewhere contains well-founded criticisms.

Conversation and negotiation are fundamental to evaluation for improvement. The staff or educational development activity being evaluated for improvement is unlikely to respond warmly to ideas for improvement that fall new-minted from the evaluator's brain. There are two reasons why: the ideas themselves are likely to be much less good, less grounded, less tested, than if they had evolved in conversation with those involved in the project or unit; and staff and educational developers are not wholly immune to that syndrome that makes academics at once so effective at testing and advancing knowledge and so infuriating to work with – the Not Invented Here syndrome.

And as for negotiation in evaluation to understand – negotiation and debate are simply fundamental to the whole academic enterprise and process, of which evaluating to understand is a part.

Should everything in the evaluation be negotiated? I suggest that it should, for the reasons of quality assurance and acceptability and effectiveness suggested above. Should everything in the evaluation be agreed between evaluator and evaluand? As far as possible – but, ultimately, no, not everything. The evaluator's terms of reference should be included in the evaluation agreement. These terms of reference should include the forming and expressing of reasoned and evidence-supported independent judgements. Some of these judgements may differ from those of the evaluand. A good evaluation process provides opportunities for the evaluand to comment on the evaluation process and on the reports and judgement the evaluator makes. But the evaluator must evaluate and report.

CONCLUSION

What do I hope you will take from this chapter? Answers to all your questions and solutions to all your problems about evaluation, of course. But, specifically:

- A determination to negotiate and agree the purposes for and the processes of the evaluation.

- A concern to identify stakeholders and the nature of their stakes in the project.

- A concern that evaluation be systematic, which can include being systematically eclectic in methods.

- A concern that evaluation be as far as possible collaborative.

- A concern for the clearest possible project goals as a basis for evaluation; a realization of the limits of the process of clarifying project goals; and some approaches to take when these limits are reached, such as the use of proxy goals or proxy processes.

- Enthusiasm to try a wide range of approaches to monitoring and evaluation.

- A view of evaluation as a scholarly function and a resolution to make it so.

- A determination to build in evaluation, not to bolt it on. Indeed, a determination to make monitoring and evaluation as natural as breathing.

ACKNOWLEDGEMENTS

My thanks for conversations, for sources and indeed sometimes for negotiations about the evaluation of staff and educational development to Jo Tait, Peter Knight, Mantz Yorke, Carole Baume, James Wisdom and members of the various projects to which I have been and am an evaluator.

REFERENCES

Baume, D (2002) Dialogues: research and teaching, *Educational Developments*, **3,** pp 26–27

Baume, D and Baume, C (1995) A strategy for evaluation, in *Directions in Staff Development*, ed A Brew, pp 189–202, Society for Research into Higher Education (SRHE) and Open University Press (OUP), Buckingham

Biggs, J (1999) *Teaching for Quality Learning at University*, SRHE and OUP, Buckingham

Gergen, K J (1994) The limits of pure critique, in *After Postmodernism: Reconstructing ideology critique*, ed H W Simons and M Billig, pp 58–78, Sage, London

Knight, P (2003) Evaluation of the Learning and Teaching Support Network (LTSN) Generic Centre, unpublished report to the LTSN Generic Centre, COBE, The Open University, Milton Keynes

Ludema, J D, Cooperrider, D L *et al* (2000) Appreciative enquiry: the power of the unconditional positive question, in *Handbook of Action Research: Participative inquiry and practice*, eds P Reason and H Bradbury, pp 189–99, Sage, London

Miller, C M L and Parlett, M (1974) *Up to the Mark*, Society for Research into Higher Education, London

Nevo, D (1986) The conceptualisation of educational evaluation: an analytic review of the literature, in *New Directions in Educational Evaluation*, ed E R House, pp 15–29, Falmer Press, Lewes

Parlett, M and Hamilton, D (1972) *Evaluation as Illumination*, Centre for Research in the Educational Sciences, University of Edinburgh, Edinburgh

Rust, C (1998) The impact of educational development workshops on teachers' practice, *International Journal for Academic Development*, **3** (1), pp 72–80

Stake, R (2002) Evaluating education, handout from author at workshop at Coventry University, 9 April

Weiss, C H (1986) Toward the future of stakeholder approaches in evaluation, in *New Directions in Educational Evaluation*, ed E R House, pp 186–98, Falmer Press, Lewes

Wisdom, J (2002) Making an impact: the evaluation of History 2000, in *Managing Educational Development Projects*, ed C Baume, P Martin and M Yorke, pp 125–39, Kogan Page, London

FURTHER READING

George, J and Cowan, J (1999) *A Handbook of Techniques for Formative Evaluation*, Kogan Page, London. Quite simply: this book lives up to its title, and will be very useful indeed to anyone contemplating, planning, undertaking and using formative evaluation. A wide and well-chosen range of approaches and instruments are described, and richly illustrated in case studies.

Hamilton, D, Jenkins, D *et al* (eds) (1977) *Beyond the Numbers Game*, Macmillan Education, London. This is a rich and exciting collection of descriptions of, methods for, debates about and reports of educational evaluation. It centres on illuminative approaches.

Wisdom, J (2002) Making an impact: the evaluation of History 2000, in *Managing Educational Development Projects*, ed C Baume, P Martin and M Yorke, pp 125–39, Kogan Page, London. This is a valuable, well-written and thoughtful account of the evaluation of a large educational development project. It pays particular attention to the changing context in which the project takes place.

6

Disseminating educational developments

Helen King

INTRODUCTION: WHAT IS DISSEMINATION?

The word 'dissemination' first appeared in 1603. The *Shorter Oxford English Dictionary* (published in 1959) defines the word thus:

> Lit. 1) To scatter abroad, as in sowing seed; to spread here and there; to disperse, so as to deposit in all parts, to distribute.
>   Fig. 2) To spread abroad, diffuse, promulgate.
> *From the Latin 'disseminare'*
> *(dis: in different directions, apart, asunder & semen: seed)*

In order to disseminate something effectively in any context, and to evaluate the success of that dissemination, we must first be clear what we intend to achieve. Do we want simply to 'scatter abroad' the information or resources, to 'sow' (specifically directing the scattering), and/or to 'propagate' (reproduce, breed or grow)? The first of these options may simply involve publishing papers, sending out advertisements, contributing to newsletters, sending e-mails, etc. This requires the disseminator to be relatively passive and the end user to be relatively active if they are to take up the information. The third option – propagation – suggests a much more active role for the disseminator in order to nurture the growth of the 'seed' in designated areas and to support it over time.

If the definition of scattering abroad is taken, then dissemination is relatively easy to achieve and to evaluate. However, if we take the propagation approach then *implementation* is necessarily implied. In this latter case, dissemination requires considerable pro-activity, support and follow-up to the end user, and is consequently more difficult to evaluate. This broader definition of dissemination is often used by learning and teaching projects. For example, the Teaching Quality Enhancement Fund National Co-ordination Team (TQEF NCT) (1997) states with regard to the Higher Education Funding Council for England (HEFCE)'s Fund for the Development of Teaching and Learning (FDTL) that 'Dissemination is a primary purpose of FDTL, but it means much more than simply telling academic colleagues about excellent practice. Dissemination has been successful when educational practice has changed in response to the disseminated excellent practice.' Similarly, in the literature, terminology such as 'knowledge utilization', 'tracking', 'awareness' and 'change' suggests something much broader, more active and focused than simply random scattering abroad.

Dissemination is an integral part of what we do as educational developers. 'Educational development is... about "improving", "promoting", "supporting", [and] "developing" learning and teaching, assessment and the curriculum' (Gosling, 2001). Whether we are working within an educational development unit within an institution or working on a multi-institutional or nation-wide project, we need to have some strategy in place to enable us to share our information, resources and ideas with those who are at the chalkface of learning, teaching and assessment. Dissemination is therefore about communication; and effective dissemination can be achieved only through effective communication.

In many cases, we are involved in disseminating information or resources that we have not produced. For example, we may be sharing examples of good practice between departments or from other institutions, supporting the implementation of a new learning technology, or providing guidance on government policy. In such cases, dissemination is effectively the end process for that resource or information, with the users being involved only at this end point.

Sometimes, particularly if we are involved with specific learning and teaching development projects, we may be sharing information or resources that we have developed ourselves. In this case, dissemination can be an integral process in the project from the beginning, and the users may be involved from the outset.

Of course, in both of these cases, dissemination is rarely a one-off action, hence the use of the word 'process' in the two descriptions. It is often continuous and evolving, requiring ongoing reflection, evaluation and redevelopment of strategies and tactics. To help consider how this process can be put into operation, it is useful to break it down into separate elements.

Elements of dissemination

The greater part of the literature on dissemination is related to medical and social science research, where academic and industrial researchers need to pass on their findings to practitioners such as doctors, nurses and other health care workers (eg Barnes *et al*, 2000; Hutchinson and Huberman, 1993; National Center for the Dissemination of Disability Research (NCDDR), 1996a). However, the processes and considerations are very similar to those required by educational developers when disseminating information and resources to teaching practitioners (eg Fincher, 2000; Gravestock, 2002). For simplicity, the word 'resource' is used to describe collectively the types of information, materials, methodologies, etc that might be disseminated. On review of this literature, three common elements of dissemination feature very strongly:

- dissemination objective;

- practitioner focus;

- context explication (after Fincher, 2000).

Simply understanding the dissemination objective will help to you to plan the methodologies you will use. *Why* you want to disseminate something will be reflected in *how* you do it. But this is not the whole story: 'effective dissemination is, however, not an easy goal to achieve. Simply making material available is not dissemination, and telling someone how you think they should change their teaching is not transfer of practice' (Fincher, 2000). In order to develop your plan into an effective dissemination *strategy* you need to consider the other two elements: the practitioner focus and context explication. That is, what are the practical needs of the end user, and what context is the end user working in? These are crucial considerations that will help to shape and enhance your plans, developing them into a strategic approach to dissemination.

The remainder of this chapter will further discuss these three main elements of dissemination, provide some guidance to support you in developing your strategy, and offer two examples of dissemination strategies from UK higher education (HE).

ELEMENTS OF DISSEMINATION 1: DISSEMINATION OBJECTIVE

For many project-type activities, dissemination is often seen as an end process – we have developed these resources or put together this information and now we're going to send it out to our users: 'From the point of view of disseminators – notably development projects and their managers – dissemination is often considered to be a single thing, with a simple, single aim. "We'll publish it on the web site" "We'll have a series of workshops" are lines often heard, and read' (Fincher, 2000).

But projects and, in particular, educational development units can be much more strategic and we can think about dissemination as a continuing process with various iterations and adaptations along the way. Being clear about the purpose of your dissemination will help you to consider the various methodologies available and to adopt a strategic approach to using them. The potential purposes of dissemination can be categorized into three dissemination objectives. These objectives, rather than being distinct, or even sequential, are more descriptions of the spectrum of dissemination purposes and activities:

- dissemination for awareness;
- dissemination for understanding;
- dissemination for action (Fincher, 2000; TQEF NCT, 1997).

Dissemination for awareness

Dissemination for awareness is the simplest dissemination objective and is closely associated with advertising and marketing. It may require little more than identifying who you want to tell about your activities, services or products, and then telling them. Ideally, your target for awareness should be the whole of the intended audience of your project or initiative. Clarity is crucial here. You must be clear what you want to say and to whom. How you say it must also be clear. Is the language articulate and to the point? Have you used too much jargon? Is the message clearly relevant to your audience? Don't forget, this is about marketing – be bold, be inspirational, even be controversial, but most importantly be memorable! For example, the Learning Development Unit at Liverpool John Moores University used this approach when developing its learning and teaching magazine:

Illustration: dissemination for awareness

'We chose the magazine route because of its reach (every member of staff, whether they are interested in it or not) sees the magazine, so it at least raises awareness of the importance we were placing on [learning and teaching]. We tried to make the design punchy to encourage readers to open past the first page and adopted techniques such as including "At a glance" boxes to each article in acknowledgement that staff were busy, and to encourage them to "dip into" each article. A golden rule was NO JARGON. Article titles were aimed at being meaningful to the person at the chalkface' (Learning Development, Liverpool John Moores University). For examples see http://cwis.livjm.ac.uk/lig/ltweb/vol_2.htm (accessed November 2002).

For educational development units, other methods might include personalized mailshots, e-mails and hard-copy flyers sent to departments, presentations at departmental away-days, membership of learning and teaching committees, etc. For wider-reaching projects, methodologies might include conference presentations or posters, messages to electronic listservs, flyers and press releases. In order to help you think about which methodologies would be appropriate for you to use, consider the following questions:

Exercise: dissemination for awareness

Think about how you receive information (e-mails, mailshots, etc).

- How much of this do you dismiss as 'junk'?
- What is it that makes certain items stand out?
- What ideas can you apply from these notable items to your own awareness-raising strategy?

Dissemination for understanding

'Once people are aware of your "product" they may or may not wish to "buy" it. They cannot make a decision on awareness alone – they must have a greater knowledge of your activity before they can make an informed decision' (Fincher, 2000). There are two types of activity you can adopt to help your audience to better understand what you are disseminating:

- active dissemination: going out and actively providing information, eg events, workshops, newsletters, etc;
- passive dissemination: providing information where it is accessible to your audience when they need it, eg Web sites, library and Web-based archives and catalogues, guides, etc.

Not everyone will be able to attend your events or read your publications at the time they are produced. Similarly, your end users might not need the resource at the time that you publicize it. The passive dissemination methodologies ensure that the information is available whenever it is needed. For example, the Learning Development Unit at Liverpool John Moores University used its Web site to support its learning and teaching magazine:

Illustration: dissemination for understanding – passive dissemination

'Whereas the magazine had a wide reach (all staff), inevitably it cannot house much information so we produced a sister Web site to act as a depository for articles, guidelines, Web links, case studies, strategy news, etc. It is a huge resource (over 2,000 pages and links). We followed the same design philosophy for continuity, and again tried to be as practically focused as possible' (Learning Development, Liverpool John Moores University [online, accessed November 2002], http://cwis.livjm.ac.uk/lig/ltweb/).

Dissemination for action

'The ultimate aim of dissemination is to have your ideas/methods/techniques/activities adopted' (Fincher, 2000). There is no point telling people about something if nobody ever uses it. If somebody does use your resource then this must involve their changing their practice in some way.

Change is, therefore, central to dissemination. However, not only must the end users change their practice in the light of the new information or resource, but the disseminator must also accept that the resource itself will be changed during the process. It is highly unlikely that an idea for getting students to interact in a large lecture, for example, will be transferred and used in exactly its original form. Changes will be made depending on the topic being learnt, the numbers of students, the teaching resources available and so on. So, if you wish to transfer your idea or resource to another practitioner then you must also be prepared for it to be transformed.

Dissemination for action, therefore, will involve methodologies that enable end users to adapt and use the information, idea or resource in their own context. However, 'most academic staff will not make radical changes to their understanding or practice of learning and teaching without some face to face encounter' (Beetham, 2001). Such encounters might include institutional conferences, faculty or departmental workshops, or one-to-one consultations. A variety of change strategies are further considered in Chapter 11.

Illustration: dissemination for action

'[Our internal learning and teaching conference aims] to bring together as many people as possible for an enjoyable event, to reinforce a sense of community, and to stimulate interest in learning and teaching through the exchange of good practice. Anecdotally, we are aware that staff do take away issues that they have picked up at a [conference] seminar. Sometimes just providing staff with the opportunity to talk to colleagues informally has facilitated exchange of practice' (Barlow, France and Hayes-Farmer, 2000).

However, it is rarely possible to arrange such events for all your potential end users. It is then necessary to design some other means for representing the resource that supports the end user in adaptation and adoption. Case studies and guides are often the preferred mechanisms: 'when pressed about the kinds of representation that had actually had an impact on their own practice, academics were much more likely to cite narratives from colleagues about *"what they did, what went wrong, and how they survived"*' (Beetham, 2001).

This section has briefly considered dissemination objectives and their associated methodologies. However, dissemination strategies involve more than simply preparing leaflets, running events and developing guides. In order to be really effective, the activities must be relevant and appropriate to their audience. The next two sections explore this further by discussing the remaining two elements of dissemination: practitioner focus and the context explication

ELEMENTS OF DISSEMINATION 2: PRACTITIONER FOCUS

When disseminating new ideas or resources, it is crucial to consider the practical needs of the end user. An old marketing analogy can be applied to illustrate this: just because you have designed a better mousetrap, this does not guarantee that consumers will rush out to buy it. In order to become interested in your mousetrap, potential users must:

- have mice;

- be concerned enough about the presence of mice to take action;

- feel comfortable enough with the effects of your mousetrap on the user, the user's household, the mice and perhaps the broader environment;

- have confidence that they will be able to operate your mousetrap properly;

- be able to afford your mousetrap; and

- be confident that your mousetrap is enough of an improvement on the mousetraps they have already bought, or could buy, to warrant the investment.

Additionally, and perhaps most crucially, they must trust the information they have obtained about the safety, reliability, effectiveness and ease of use of your mousetrap.

If the phrase 'learning and teaching problem/issue' is substituted for the word 'mice' and 'learning and teaching resource' is substituted for the word 'mousetrap', the above observations ring true within any educational sector, particularly when costs and investments are considered in terms of time and effort on the part of the teaching practitioners. So, the process of dissemination should take place *after* some market research in order to ascertain areas of need and to ensure the resource is worthwhile and effective. It is not desirable, nor does it make good business sense, to produce and attempt to disseminate materials without thought of the consumers' needs. It is further worth pointing out that in the context of HE the issues of reliability and so on are most often related to research evidence. Is there reliable evidence from research that the resource is effective? A willingness to evaluate, as considered at greater length in Chapter 5, and indeed to carry out research is thus often an important counterpart to any dissemination exercise.

The following exercise provides a rough framework for considering your end users' needs, although further advice on the analysis of needs is available in Chapter 2. Ideally, if possible it would also be useful to consult directly with them through, for example, questionnaires, focus groups or one-to-one interviews.

Exercise: needs analysis, or marketing your own mousetrap

Consider a resource that you might have to disseminate (eg some learning software, a technique for making lectures more interactive, or a new policy issue). Translate the above analogy about mousetraps so that it fits your resource and end users. What issues do you think the end users might have in connection with your resource (eg time, financial or other contextual constraints)?

What can you do to prepare to support staff in addressing these issues?

You may find that different end users have very different needs. For example,

users who were already knowledgeable about the area of practice involved, and who had the time and intellectual resources available for reflection, preferred texts about practice such as articles and case studies over the more prescriptive guidelines and toolkits. These people were also resistant to the use of [software] tools that they felt constrained their own learning and teaching practice. Users with less expertise or less time, however, wanted faster solutions. Their preferred representations were short guidelines, tips and tricks, snippets of advice and rubrics for 'making things work'. (Beetham, 2001)

If you are about to begin the development of a new resource (eg a book, workshop or Web site), or have access to a variety of means of disseminating existing information, then you have the potential to match the methodologies to the different users. To do this you have two options:

1. Flood the market: develop the resource in as many different media as possible (guides, workshops, case studies, hints and tips, Web site, etc). But you can't always satisfy all the people all the time. So, you could instead

2. Build canals: decide on a focus, specify your target audience, identify their needs and provide specifically for them.

Note that either or both of these approaches may be necessary, depending on your dissemination objective.

Of course, you may not always be disseminating a resource that staff have a choice about using. Information conveyed on institutional or government policy, for example, may not be very welcome but must be taken on board. As well as understanding the practitioners' practical needs, you must also take into account the context within which they are working so that you can provide them information with optimum relevance, clarity and empathy. The next section discusses this third element of dissemination: context explication.

ELEMENTS OF DISSEMINATION 3: CONTEXT EXPLICATION

Information and resources are not produced by robots in a vacuum. Nor, to use another metaphor, are they disseminated automatically by pouring information from one source into the receptacle of the end user. In the same way that teaching activities are moving away from this knowledge-transfer notion towards a more student-centred approach (see, for instance, Biggs, 1999), so dissemination must also take account of the end users' context and consider that this context may be different from that of the originator.

Findings by the NCDDR (1996a, b, 2001) further emphasize the importance of understanding the context from and to which the resource is being disseminated. For example, the credibility of information sources was found to be more important to end users than the actual quality of the information. Credibility related to perceived *expertise* and perceived *trustworthiness*. 'The more intensely people are involved with an issue, the more likely they are to question both the expertise and the trustworthiness of those whose information contradicts their own understandings' (NCDDR, 1996b).

The context of both the resource creators and the potential end users must, therefore, be considered. Where these contexts are different, effective communication and understanding are vital to ensure that the information is accepted, let alone used. In the majority of educational development situations, contexts will be different: the initiators and users will often belong to different discourse communities (eg learning technologists and discipline-based academics; this latter group is considered at greater length in Chapter 9) with different values and ideologies (Hutchinson and Huberman, 1993). In order to disseminate effectively, there must be a working relationship built on trust between the potential end user(s) and the source of information about the resource, whether that source is the creators themselves or a mediator such as an educational developer.

In building these relationships, it is important to appreciate how people learn about new ideas. Ackerman (1995, quoted in NCDDR, 1996b) explains that 'from a learner's point of view, there are no such things as misconceptions. There are only discrepancies, either between points of view or between a person's activity and some unexpected effects of this activity.' To put it more simply, the extent to which an individual's existing knowledge or understanding may be 'right' or 'wrong' is irrelevant; what is important is how well those understandings are used to help the person make sense of their environment. Hence, simply telling someone that their practices are wrong, ineffective or out of date, or that a better mousetrap is available, is usually an inadequate and often counter-productive approach to encouraging change.

Illustration: developing relationships with end users

'[When we were organizing department-based workshops] it was important to know the internal influences that were facing a department, as these often offer a greater lever for change than external influences. A telephone interview was conducted between the workshop facilitator and the departmental contact prior to the workshop to ensure that the material presented would be tailored to their needs.'

Additionally, 'Change can only take place by the actions of the end-users and it is essential that they have an ownership of a project. In [our] case the ownership was not only through the fact that the project was discipline-based, but also because the end-users were also contributors, supplying the core material – the case study abstracts – for the resource database and the guides' (Gravestock, 2002).

In the earlier stages of dissemination in particular, educational development that supports change in practice does not necessarily always mean getting people to change their teaching *activities*. Sometimes you may need to change their *ideas* about teaching first, owing to the fact that 'a lecturer's conception of teaching plays an important role in his/her decisions about teaching'. For example, 'a teacher who holds transmission conceptions [of teaching] would see the problem-based strategies advocated in a workshop as not useful for his/her purposes or even a waste of time. Therefore, the focus of staff development should be more on changing lecturers' conceptions of teaching and less on teaching strategies' (Ho, 1998).

In order to be able to communicate (and, hence, disseminate) information effectively, you need to have a clear understanding of your own context and that of your end users. The following exercise provides a few questions that may help you to consider this further:

Exercise: understanding contexts

Your context:

- What is your background (discipline based, learning and teaching specialism, numbers of years' experience in the job and other relevant experience, etc)?

- How do you like to receive information (eg e-mails, paper-based documents, Web sites, software, workshops, one-to-one consultation) and which form most enables you to transfer the knowledge to your own situation?

- What is (are) your preferred medium (media) for working with teaching staff (eg do you prefer running workshops and/or writing guides, etc)?

- What is (are) your preferred approach(es) to educational development; for example:
  - romantic (focused on individual personal development);
  - vigilant opportunist (appropriate timing; topical developments);
  - researcher (interested in the interface between theory and practice);
  - professional competence (building teachers' confidence; classroom expertise);
  - reflective practitioner (iterative learning process)? (after Land, 2000).

Your end users:

- Who, specifically, are they, eg new lecturers, programme directors, field course leaders, or mixture; what discipline(s)?
- What are the key issues in learning and teaching for them (eg falling student recruitment, lack of funding for practical work, mainly working with postgraduate students, etc)?

- What support is available to you to help understand them better (eg personal contacts, 'champions' in departments, discipline-based professional bodies and other organizations)?

This section has emphasized the need to understand the context of both the disseminator and the end user in order to ensure effective and efficient communication of information about the resource being disseminated. It has also illustrated the need to appreciate how people learn and to understand their initial conceptions before attempting to change their practice.

DEVELOPING STRATEGIES FOR DISSEMINATION

The above three sections have provided some in-depth discussion on the three main elements of dissemination:

- dissemination objective:
  - dissemination for awareness;
  - dissemination for understanding;
  - dissemination for action;
- practitioner focus;
- context explication.

Experience of dissemination in HE in the United Kingdom and review of the (albeit limited) literature have together indicated that consideration of the end user is critical at all stages of the dissemination process. The disseminator must develop an understanding of the practical needs and context of the various types of end user including the broader environment of their discipline/profession, department and institution. A working relationship needs to be built up such that the users feel the product/initiative to be from a reliable and/or trustworthy source. Perhaps one of the best ways to achieve such a relationship and to really tune in to the users is to involve them in the research and development activities prior to dissemination. Such personal interaction is the most effective channel for assuring take-up and implementation of resources.

These ideas can now be turned into actions by developing a dissemination strategy and an associated dissemination plan. The development of a strategy will help you to work through the above issues in your own context. The development of an associated plan will help you to identify what actually needs to be done and by whom, working within time and financial constraints. This final section provides a couple of exercises to help you develop your strategy and plan; illustrative examples are given to provide ideas and advice.

Developing a dissemination strategy

Ideally, developing a dissemination strategy should be done through discussion with your colleagues, if you are working with others to disseminate materials. You might find the following questions helpful in working through the process:

- *What* do you want to disseminate (information, resource, example of practice)?
- *Who* is your target audience?
- *Why* do you want to disseminate it (awareness, understanding, action)?
- *How* are you going to do it (methodologies and context)?
- How might you *involve* your target audience throughout the process?
- Have you allowed time for *evaluation, reflection* and replanning?
- How will you know that your dissemination has been *successful*?

Note that in terms of building relationships, the size of the audience is crucial. For example, national projects will find it much easier to fully support the take-up and implementation of a product within a target group of five institutions than across the entire HE sector. When designing a dissemination strategy it is vital to be clear on the scope of the targeted market; the benefits of ensuring implementation within a small group must be weighed against the need to make the audience as broad as possible. One solution is to develop a strategy that delineates several levels of target audience: a small group for in-depth, interpersonal support and larger groups for broader, information-sharing purposes (NCDDR, 1996b).

The following illustrations describe two different dissemination scenarios mapped against the questions listed above. The first scenario describes a national project looking to disseminate good learning and teaching practice, and the second discusses an educational development unit's approach to raising awareness of its institution's learning and teaching strategy.

ILLUSTRATION 1: A NATIONAL (ENGLISH) PROJECT LOOKING TO WIDELY DISSEMINATE EXAMPLES OF GOOD PRACTICE

Project: Dissemination of Good Teaching, Learning and Assessment Practices in Geography

Contact: Phil Gravestock, Project Manager

Background: This project was run by the Geography Discipline Network (GDN – http://www.glos.ac.uk/gdn/) and funded by the UK Fund for the Development of Teaching and Learning (FDTL – http://www.ncteam.ac.uk). The project team consisted of a consortium of nine HE institutions with a geographer and an educational developer representing each.

What, why and who? In 1995, the Higher Education Funding Council for England (HEFCE) published the Subject Overview report of the Quality Assessment of Geography provision. There were many positive points but also some areas where there could be improvement including under-graduate dissertation supervision, assessment, over-dependence on lectures, the need to strengthen links with employers, and opportunities for sharing good practice (Healey and Gravestock, 1997).

The aim of the project, therefore, was to identify and disseminate good teaching, learning and assessment practices in geography to staff in English HE. This was achieved, in the main, through the production of 10 guides focused around a selection of case studies. These guides were developed for geography HE staff both nationally and internationally.

How? Dissemination for awareness: active dissemination was initiated from the beginning of the project through mailings via departmental contacts. Once examples of practice starting coming in, a Web site was set up to act as an ongoing repository and to provide an immediate 'product' to advertise through promotional handouts, conference displays and e-mail listservs.

Dissemination for understanding/action was achieved through face-to-face interactions with the end users at a national residential conference and many department-based workshops.

Involving: One of the intentions of the project was to involve the end users in as many stages of the project as possible. This was achieved by:

- producing a resource for which there was demand by the end user;
- involving end users in the project team;
- obtaining the examples of practice from the disciplines.

Evaluation and knowledge of success: Evaluating the extent of change brought about as a direct consequence of any project is extremely difficult, partly because of the many other variables affecting departments and their curriculum design strategies. Responses obtained from conducting telephone interviews with departmental contacts three to six months after the workshops indicated that many departments had noticed a change in their teaching, learning and assessment practices.

ILLUSTRATION 2: A UK EDUCATIONAL DEVELOPMENT UNIT LOOKING TO RAISE AWARENESS OF AN INITIATIVE WITHIN ITS INSTITUTION

Department: Learning Development, Liverpool John Moores University (LJMU)

Contact: Martyn Stewart

Background: The Learning Department is an educational development unit with the primary function of implementing the university's learning, teaching and assessment (LTA) strategy. It has a mixture of core full-time staff with remits for various generic fields (eg assessment, work-based learning/ employability) and part-time staff seconded from various academic schools or service teams.

What, why and who? Dissemination was identified early on as a major part of the implementation of the LTA strategy, and one of the full-time posts was responsible in part for overseeing dissemination. The primary goal was to raise awareness of the strategy and other developments in teaching and learning among as many staff as possible. It was recognized that staff work in different ways and had very busy schedules, so those concerned set out to create a number of dissemination vehicles.

How? A glossy booklet served as an introduction and overview of the LTA strategy. The full document was sent out in paper and electronic format. The aim with this was to raise awareness of the strategy in as many staff as possible, so the booklet was sent out to all staff involved in teaching and supporting learning. For the online version see http://cwis.livjm.ac.uk/lig/ ltweb/lta/lta_abridged/intro.htm (accessed November 2002).

A biannual magazine was also established. Rather than produce a simple newsletter, we set out to create a more user-friendly magazine, which we called the *Learning and Teaching Press*. After a fair bit of investigation (see below), it became clear that what was needed by staff was not a centrally produced publication ('this is what we think you need to be doing') but something that teaching staff could relate to, that they had a sense of ownership of. So, it was decided to focus the attention on disseminating case studies of interesting and innovative practices that might inspire the readership (the magazine was sent out to all teaching/learner support staff). Humour, a few tips, guidelines and news of resources were added but the prime aim was to focus on articles either written by teaching staff, or via interviews with staff (given their limited time). As the magazine evolved, more emphasis was placed on realism – there is a tendency for case studies to sound overly fantastic and wonderful, so the magazine dealt with issues such as what didn't work, how it was received by colleagues, etc. It also dealt with the challenge of implementing change. For examples see http:// cwis.livjm.ac.uk/lig/ltweb/vol_2.htm (accessed November 2002).

The magazine had a wide reach, but inevitably it cannot house much information, so it was decided to produce a sister Web site to act as a depository for articles, guidelines, Web links, case studies, strategy news, etc. The same design philosophy as in the magazine was adopted, for continuity, and again the Web site tried to be as practically focused as possible. See http://cwis.livjm.ac.uk/ltweb/ (accessed November 2002).

A number of one-day dissemination events were held, including a student support 'Sharing Practice' Day and an 'Assessment Matters' conference. There was also a large, two-day general Teaching and Learning conference.

Involving the end user: Martyn Stewart spent a few weeks travelling around the university simply to talk openly to individuals from as many disciplines as possible – mainly the departmental learning and teaching co-ordinators – about what types of things would work and what wouldn't, showing mock-ups of different styles of magazine, etc. Understandably, the key needs were for no jargon, useful and practical information, and something for teaching staff *by* teaching staff. These same principles were borne in mind for the other initiatives.

It was difficult getting staff to contribute articles at first and many were obtained via interview. There is something to be said for this, though, as it provided an excellent opportunity to discuss practical aspects of teaching, of which very few opportunities exist, and was mutually beneficial.

Evaluation: The magazine was well received, particularly by the second and especially third issues, by which time it had settled down and found a format that worked. Feedback questionnaires liked the practitioner focus, bits of humour, etc. The dissemination events/conference were also very well received as they represented the first substantial opportunities for staff to meet new colleagues in different disciplines.

The LTA strategy's Evaluation Scheme Final Report stated that the strategy as a whole had played a major role in creating a culture change around teaching and learning in the university, with bottom-up/top-down methods being successful. To quote a comment from the external evaluators specifically about dissemination, 'The Press has been an important mechanism in disseminating and embedding good practice across the University. It remains one of the major success stories of the Learning, Teaching and Assessment Strategy. Its impact is self-evident and deserves continuing support' (LJMU Learning, Teaching and Assessment Strategy: Evaluation Scheme Final Report, by Professor Vaneeta-marie D'Andrea, Critical Change Consultants for Higher Education, April 2002).

Lessons learnt: Martyn Stewart comments: 'I always apply the same investigative approach that I learnt as a researcher to similar professional problems. Understand the issues – observe, listen, analyse and interpret! Cut out potential mistakes by trying to identify them first.

'Talking mainly with reference to the magazine, but true also generically, treat it the same as any other form of dissemination (including teaching, TV documentaries, etc); try to generate interest first – grab people's attention, try to inspire (case studies can be very inspiring if presented well). It needs someone who can empathize with *all* of the audience. It is possible to be all things to all people if you think carefully about content (ie something for junior lecturers and for senior lecturers). There is also no point trying to spend great efforts to reach those who will never be interested.'

Developing a dissemination plan

The notes you have made to the previous questions should have got you well on the way to developing your strategy. Once you have a general strategy in place, you then need to consider how to operationalize this; that is, to plan your specific goals, when you want to achieve them and what resources you might need to support them (eg time, money, personnel). You may find it useful to tabulate your plans under the following headings:

- purpose;
- target groups;
- method (eg questionnaire);
- vehicle (eg e-mail, focus groups);
- timing;
- person(s) responsible;
- cost.

For simplicity of planning, and clarity, you will need to separate out your dissemination activities. In reality, these will often overlap or coincide – it is rarely a linear process.

Table 6.1 provides some examples to illustrate the type of detail that might be included under each heading. The illustration is part of an exemplar framework provided by the TQEF NCT. The full table is available from http://www.ncteam.ac.uk/documents/dissemination.html (accessed November 2002).

CONCLUSION

This chapter has brought together some of the current literature on dissemination, illustrated with ideas and advice from current practice in UK higher education. Experiences from national projects, institution-based educational

Table 6.1 Framework for dissemination planning

Purpose	Target groups	Method	Vehicle	Timing	Person(s) responsible
• Raise awareness of the work of the project	• Institutional senior management	• Institutional committees • Informal meetings	• Steering Group members	• Ongoing – reaching 50% of departments by the end of year 1, and 75% by the end of year 2	• Steering Group members
• Share experiences	• Peers in own institution • HE community • Subject discipline groups	• Presentations • Written project case studies • Workshops • Reports • WWW pages	• Internal workshops/ departmental away-days • Publish case studies in paper form and on Web site • ISL 1999 • Regional workshops	• Presentations are ongoing • Case studies produced every 6 months beginning year 2 • National conferences are ongoing • Web pages developed and regularly updated	• Esmerelda Dickinson will write the case studies and Joe Smith will be responsible for mounting them on the WWW • Project team will make presentations and attend national conferences
• Promote findings of the project	• HE/FE communities • Professional networks • Software publishers	• Papers • Publications • Press • WWW	• End-of-project conference	• May 2001	• Project team

Source: Reproduced, with permission, from the Teaching Quality Enhancement Fund National Co-ordination Team (2001)

Note: Although the above framework is focused on national projects, the basic structure (and many of the included ideas) is also relevant to institution-based activities. You may also find it useful to add a 'cost' element to the framework if you are working with a limited budget.

114   *A guide to staff and educational development*

development units, and individuals have shown that dissemination is no longer considered as an add-on at the end of a resource development process. Rather, dissemination is an active and important component of the everyday work of staff and educational developers that provides opportunities for liaison, collaboration, brainstorming and practice sharing with colleagues across institutions, nationally, and even internationally. Many of the ideas here are closely related to those expanded on in other chapters in this book. You are encouraged to view this chapter as part of a holistic overview of your role within staff and educational development, rather than a stand-alone activity unrelated to other aspects of your work.

REFERENCES

Barlow, J, France, L and Hayes-Farmer, N (2000) Disseminating good practice: the role of the internal learning and teaching conference, *Innovations in Education and Training International*, **37** (4), pp 356–60

Barnes, V L, Clouder, C, Hughes, J, Purkis, J and Pritchard, J (2000) Dissemination as evidence? Deconstructing the processes of disseminating qualitative research, *Qualitative Evidence-based Practice Conference*, Coventry University, 15–17 May 2000 (accessed December 2002) [Online] http://www.leeds.ac.uk/educol/documents/00001375.htm

Beetham, H (2001) How do representations of our practice enable change to happen? *Educational Developments*, **2** (4), pp 19–22

Biggs, J (1999) *Teaching for Quality Learning at University*, Society for Research into Higher Education and Open University Press, Buckingham

Fincher, S (2000) From transfer to transformation: towards a framework for successful dissemination of engineering education, *30th American Society for Engineering Education/Institute of Electrical and Electronics Engineers Frontiers in Education Conference* (accessed December 2002) [Online] http://fie.engrng.pitt.edu/fie2000/papers/1269.pdf

Gosling, D (2001) Educational development units in the UK: what are they doing five years on? *International Journal for Academic Development*, **6** (1), pp 74–90

Gravestock, P (2002) Making an impact through dissemination, in *Managing Educational Development Projects: Maximising the impact*, ed C Baume, P Martin and M Yorke, pp 109–23, Kogan Page, London

Healey, M and Gravestock, P (1997) Identifying and disseminating good practice in the teaching and learning of geography in higher education (accessed December 2002) [Online] http://www.glos.ac.uk/gdn/confpubl/iagaag.htm

Ho, A S P (1998) A conceptual change staff development programme: effects as perceived by the participants, *International Journal of Academic Development*, **3** (1), pp 24–38

Hutchinson, J and Huberman, M (1993) *Knowledge Dissemination and Use in Science and Mathematics Education: A literature review*, National Science Foundation, Washington, DC (accessed December 2002) [Online] http://www.nsf.gov/pubs/stis1993 /nsf9375/nsf9375.txt

Land, R (2000) Orientations to educational development, *Educational Developments*, 1 (2), pp 19–23

National Center for the Dissemination of Disability Research (NCDDR) (1996a) *Improving Links between Research and Practice: Approaches to the effective dissemination of disability research*, Guides to Improving Practice 1 (accessed December 2002) [Online] http:// www.ncddr.org/du/products/guide1.html

NCDDR (1996b) *Improving the Usefulness of Disability Research: A toolbox of dissemination strategies*, Guides to Improving Practice 2 (accessed December 2002) [Online] http://www.ncddr.org/ du/products/guide2.html

NCDDR (2001) *Developing an Effective Dissemination Plan* (accessed December 2002) [Online] http:// www.ncddr.org/du/products/dissplan.html

Teaching Quality Enhancement Fund National Co-ordination Team (TQEF NCT) (1997) *Dissemination*, Projects Briefing Paper 2, TQEF NCT, Milton Keynes (accessed December 2002) [Online] http://www.ncteam.ac.uk/resources/project_briefings/briefings/ brief02.pdf

7

Educational development through information and communications technology

Stephen Fallows and Rakesh Bhanot

INTRODUCTION

Within higher education (HE), as elsewhere, information and communications technology (ICT) has become ubiquitous. For many of us (and perhaps most of the readers of this chapter), it has become the automatic first action on arriving at our desks to turn on the PC to check for e-mail messages and to ready ourselves for the tasks of the day. For academics at the start of the 21st century, PC-based ICT provides the platform through which we undertake many of our basic work tasks. This circumstance is quite different from that applying even just a decade ago, and completely different from that of a generation ago. The educational environment in which we operate (in our several roles as developers, researchers, teachers and academic administrators) and in which students study has never evolved with greater speed than it is doing at present. And change continues to accelerate.

Rapid and accelerating change presents tremendous challenges for those with an educational development role. Educational developers are often given responsibilities as agents (or even champions) of change, and this can present conflicts between personal, professional and institutional interests. This chapter considers a number of the key issues that apply when ICT impacts upon developmental activities, and focuses on solutions and approaches that may be found realistic and appropriate.

DEFINITIONS AND CONTEXT

The following definitions provide the authors' thinking for this chapter. They may be marginally different from those given by the editors of the book, but the principles are fundamentally the same.

Information and communications technology (ICT)

Information technology (IT) is taken to refer to computers and the software used with them. The addition of the word 'communications' to the term recognizes the current phenomenon through which the overwhelming majority of computers are today linked though the Internet.

ICT represents the latest manifestation of the use of technology in learning and teaching, one that is having profound effects across all phases of education and is changing the nature of HE in a wider range of ways than the educational technologies – 'teaching machines' and the like – that preceded it. We should remember that amazing and largely unfulfilled claims have been made for the likely impact of other developments. What future technological changes will emerge to eclipse the current technology? Whatever emerges, we suspect that the educational impact of these achievements will follow the current and past pattern: impact will be more dependent on the skills of creative educators than on those of the technological innovators, and on the ability of the new technologies to meet the needs of the educational community.

Educational development

There are many definitions of an educational development. In this chapter (and previously, Fallows and Bhanot, 2002), we suggest that educational development comprises *any novel action taken with the intention of either enhancing the teaching of a particular subject or enhancing the students' learning of the subject.*

Thus, as professional HE practitioners, we choose to locate our discussion of educational development soundly within a teaching and learning context. Others may consider this definition to be quite narrow, but in practice it can be interpreted to include a wide range of circumstances.

The reference to particular subjects is deliberate; that which is novel in one area of study may be long-established practice elsewhere. Some subject areas have been homes for early innovative practice while others have tended to continue with their more traditional approaches for much longer. However, as indicated previously, the ICT-based changes are affecting all disciplines, albeit to differing degrees.

The enhancement of teaching and learning is important since standards should at least be maintained, and preferably raised, when any new development is introduced. Enhancement itself can take many forms. It can involve raising the quality of educational output. It can also mean the continued achievement of standards under conditions of restricted resources; that is, it can mean raising the efficiency of the educational process.

Use of the word 'efficiency' within the context of the educational process may be anathema to many of us within higher education. It may particularly offend those in the most privileged quarters of the academic world, where the increased costs of the status quo may simply be passed down the line. But all but a minute minority of today's institutions of higher education need to do more with less (or at best the same) resources. This consideration has been the norm in the United Kingdom for the past several years and has been one major driver for national ICT initiatives. The key premise has been that ICT-based approaches will be able to deliver the curriculum to a greater number of students for little additional cost. The evidence for this premise is rather thin, and the payback on many ICT initiatives over the years has been minimal. In some instances, the concepts ran ahead of the generally available technological capability; this mismatch is less of an issue today as substantially powerful PCs have become the norm for home and institutional use. Sometimes the ICT concepts also ran ahead of what was organizationally possible or educationally reasonable.

Educational developers and ICT

It is useful here to consider the people working in the educational development, the units in which they work and the functions that they perform. Gosling (2001) has provided the necessary information in a recent review of the work of educational development units; this followed an earlier study (Gosling, 1996). The key point to emerge from these studies is that there is no single model of educational development in UK higher education; the situation world-wide is even more diverse.

The diversity of educational developers and their roles carries forward into their approaches to and uses of ICT. The ICT skill requirements of the educational developer whose primary emphasis is pedagogy and curriculum development are clearly very different from those of the person (perhaps not even located within an educational development unit) whose educational development responsibilities are focused principally on ICT-based programme delivery. However, while it is (just about) possible to envisage an educational developer without any ICT skills, such a person would, and indeed probably should, be a very rare individual. ICT has reached such a central position in the operation of higher education that everyone surely needs at least a basic portfolio of ICT skills. While it is not essential that every educational developer is an ICT specialist, it is increasingly important that those whose educational role is concentrated on innovation and improvement should be (at least) aware of the capabilities associated with ICT and education. Such awareness need not necessarily be combined with in-depth personal technical ability – provided that the links are in place to specialists who can provide support with this technical dimension.

ICT curriculum for educational development?

It is increasingly apparent that ICT is an integral element in the toolkit of the educational developer. Present-day educational developers cannot ignore ICT, either with respect to their own professional personal practice or, more broadly, as a fundamental mechanism for delivery of and support for the curriculum.

So, what is the curriculum content of 'educational development'? If anyone can give a universal answer to this question, the authors of this chapter would be pleased to hear from that person! Similarly, we remain uncertain about whether ICT is a direct part of the educational development curriculum or a means of delivering this curriculum. We shall work on the basis that it is both. Both elements are clearly of importance across higher education.

One question that remains to be answered is 'Can a student or a tutor operate within higher education in the 21st century without a competence in ICT?' Although a student or tutor who is 100 per cent ICT-illiterate might just about survive in today's higher education, they would do so only on the verge of extinction. That is, individual survival would depend on a high level of competence in other areas. For the overwhelming majority of the population, and for the longer term, we see ICT proficiency as an essential life-skill alongside the ability to read and write. Clearly, we expect this need to apply to the university student ahead of the general public, and we feel that universal ICT competence should be a target and indeed become the norm within the next few years. For students with disabilities, for whom ICT raises particular issues, it is worth noting here that ICT has the potential for bringing both serious problems and great benefits.

Although we make all these comments as a universal expectation for developed countries, we recognize that internationally for many years there will be students who make the transition from technology-deprived school education to an increasingly technology-enhanced higher education. Evidence suggests that students placed in this position cope very well.

BRIEF OVERVIEW OF USES OF ICT IN HIGHER EDUCATION

It is useful to review just a few of the various modes through which ICT is contributing to learning and teaching within higher education:

- For some time, it has been the norm for library catalogues to be held in searchable electronic format. Nowadays, more and more of the library's academic content is also likely to be held electronically. Online versions of academic journals are purchased in preference to their traditional paper-based equivalents. This has a fundamental impact on the nature and the use of the resource. Every registered student, regardless of physical location, can access a single issue of a journal at the same time. No more 'When I got to the library, the journal was being used by someone else.'

- The students' educational world is no longer confined to the institution at which they are studying and its local resources. The introduction of the World Wide Web makes available an immense range of sources of information. Not all these resources are those that we, as tutors, would recommend. This opens a major debate on a shift of emphasis within education towards evaluation of the plethora of materials. Students now need much greater ability to select and judge the worth of materials than was the case when they were limited to the local paper-based resources.

- Individual and group tutorials can be conducted using a range of ICT methods. At the simplest level, a one-to-one (tutor to student) dialogue can be conducted using electronic mail. Conference options extend this to function to the group. The ICT approach redefines the concept of 'group'; no longer do group members need to be based in a single location. International group tutorials, with students studying the same curriculum but located in different countries, can be used to enhance learning very significantly.

- ICT-based presentations using software such as Microsoft PowerPoint have become routine in many lecture halls – with varying degrees of effectiveness, it should be acknowledged! Such tutor presentations can also be made available online for use by (for example) any students unable to attend the particular lecture session or by those at remote locations. Furthermore, it is not simply the tutor who will use such packages; students' presentation skills are often similarly boosted through their use of presentation software, not just the skills of using the software but the skills of condensing and sequencing material to make presentations that work as well as dazzle.

- Almost all academic administrative tasks are today conducted using some form of ICT. Computer databases and spreadsheets are the standard modes for collation of information in areas such as student registrations and assessment results. We doubt that any of us would want a return to the old-style methods. But we need to remember the personal privacy issues that can be compromised through inappropriate use of ICT-held information. In the United Kingdom, computer-held data that can be linked to a named individual are subject to the conditions of the Data Protection Act.

- Electronic mail is the preferred mode of communication between members of the HE community (student to student, tutor to student, tutor to tutor, administrator to student or tutor, etc). This communication is within institution, within country and international. This opens options that did not exist previously. Tutor–student dialogue on the development of a dissertation by a student on the opposite side of the globe is no longer a fantasy or requires an extremely expensive phone call; it simply needs the synchronizing of e-mail access. Late-morning inputs from a tutor in the United Kingdom can catch a student at home in the evening after work in Hong Kong with a reply to the tutor within the UK working day.

- The days of the hand-written student assignment are dead; we nowadays expect all students to have sufficient ICT skills to be able to offer documents presented to a standard that only a professional and, in some aspects, very competent secretary could manage not so long ago in the days of the manual typewriter. However, since an ICT-based offer is now the norm, we must all be very careful of focusing our attention on the slick presentation of the mediocre over the visually poor exposition of genius.

The above list is obviously not intended to be definitive. Rather, it indicates many of the ways in which learners and their teachers in HE have available a range of ICT-based opportunities that were not readily available only a few years ago. Further, it has to be noted that although each of the above elements can be utilized individually, the introduction of virtual or managed learning environments (such as WebCT, Blackboard or Lotus Learning Space and many others, commercial or developed in-house) provides integrated institutional systems that draw together several elements into a single online framework.

It is not the purpose of this chapter to give detailed explanations of each element in the above list; to do so would take up several books and would miss the point of this discussion. Rather, it is important for us to note the obvious central role that ICT has taken in our educational processes, and to consider the role of educational development in its further implementation. We have given several examples of possibilities above, but observe that a number of conflicts between technology and education can emerge.

Those working in educational development have a professional position and role with respect to the use of ICT that is somewhat different from that of most lecturers in higher education. The educational developer is a lecturer in his or her own right, but also has a major role in support of others; ICT will feature in each of these responsibilities.

ICT AND THE ROLE AS LECTURER

In the role of lecturer (perhaps delivering a training programme for novices to the institution), the educational developer will certainly use many ICT products for programme administration, teaching and research. In this, the decisions (to use or otherwise) are essentially those that will be faced by other lecturers. We each need to make personal evaluations and judgements of the costs and benefits for each ICT option. For example:

- Once the basic skills have been learnt, slick presentations are relatively straightforward when we use ICT-based slide-generating and -presenting software such as PowerPoint. But it may be preferable to value flexibility, in which case a simple flipchart or whiteboard – or even the printing of slides onto acetates and their projection via an OHP – may be more appropriate. As with all approaches to the presentation of information, there is a need to consider the medium as well as the message. It is all too easy when adopting the ICT route to over-use the technical options, with the unfortunate result that a multiplicity of effects and gimmicks distracts rather than enhances the delivery. The focus must remain on student learning.

- Personal Web pages or the institution's virtual learning environment can be used to distribute teaching materials and to offer advice and suggestions. The extent to which any individual does so is likely to be determined by a number of factors. In some institutions, there are corporate or departmental strategies that (for instance) require all modules, units or courses to have an online presence; for others the choice is left entirely to the individual. Whichever strategy is in place, the actual detailed content of online material will reflect the individual lecturer's approach to his or her teaching, within an overall policy about learning and teaching. Formulaic impositions are no more appropriate and acceptable in the virtual seminar room of the ICT environment than they are on the physical campus. Rich use of this information delivery mode depends as much on the integration of the ICT resource with other approaches as it does on the quality of the resource *per se*. This is not a new phenomenon; the mere provision of a 'wonderful' textbook would not guarantee that a course is similarly 'wonderful'.

- For one dimension of ICT in higher education, the element of choice has been reduced. E-mail is *de facto* the principal mode of communication within the academic community at all scales from in-house to internationally. Even though it is widely recognized that e-mail offers the fastest and most convenient mode of communication with colleagues and with students, there is considerable variation within the academic community in the extent to which the possibilities are used. Some people use e-mails just for quick notes to colleagues and research associates, whereas others are happy to receive a draft of a 3,000-word assignment online (probably as an attachment rather in the body of an e-mail) and then will return this to the student with feedback embedded in the original text. High-level individual provision of embedded feedback is extremely time demanding and is not generally an option for mass education undergraduate programmes, but it may be appropriate for higher-level programmes and it is particularly useful when providing dissertation support to graduate students located some distance from the institution. (One of the authors, SF, has used this support method with his MSc and PhD students located at a distance and can vouch for the substantial time requirement. Where in-depth commentary is required on a substantial document (such as a chapter from a graduate dissertation), it can be more cost-effective to eschew the ICT option for feedback and to use the services of a reputable courier company. Many of us prefer the flexibility of reading from and annotating paper rather than screen.)

Although the above paragraphs suggest that a personal choice may exist for the educational developer, we all have to remember that others' priorities may have to take precedence. E-mail is the obvious example; if all messages are being sent by this route then to ignore this ICT method is not realistic. Similarly, institutional priorities may demand the universal adoption of online ICT-based documentation in support of each module, unit, course or programme; in such instances, the educational development team will often be placed in the position of 'early adopters' even if not given the more substantial task of being direct champions for the initiative. As with all lecturers, the educational developer will need to ask a number of key questions:

- What educational capabilities do the ICT resources available offer to me and to my students? Supplementary questions here will add focus by linking the response to clear analysis of both personal and student benefits. If the benefits of an ICT approach are less than those of a similar investment (in terms of time, money or other element) then the ICT approach may not be appropriate.

- Which parts of these capabilities are appropriate for the tasks that I have to undertake? ICT now offers all sorts of options. Many are, and more seem, technologically wonderful. But which add genuine educational substance over and above that which was available previously? ICT opens new options, but luckily does not close the possibilities that were there before. A well-presented lecture with up-to-date substance from a knowledgeable and inspiring lecturer who is able to utilize inter-personal skills fully and generate appropriate student activity will be more educationally effective than a formulaic, pre-set and impersonal ICT approach.

●   What do I have to do to take advantage of these capabilities? This trans-lates almost immediately into questions about who is knowledgeable about the technical capabilities and who is going to do the work. Here institutional strategy can play a significant role; if there is a team charged with the task of moving curriculum content and academic process on to ICT then the individual lecturer serves principally as custodian of the academic content and the learning process, and needs to know only what the ICT can do, not how to do it. But if a more hands-on approach is called for, then the lecturer will need not only to under-stand the possibilities but also to be in a position to implement these. In general, there is a strong advantage if substantial specialist support is available at least in the initial phases of introducing ICT for learning and teaching.

All of the above, taken together, lead to consideration of threshold ICT capabilities for the university lecturer. There is no instant and ready-to-use 'off-the-shelf' model for the required capabilities. Useful models such as the European Computer Driving Licence (ECDL) exist, but these do not meet fully our requirements, having been developed for a wider context. There may be a need for an HE blueprint here, although ECDL provides a valuable underpinning.

ICT AND EDUCATIONAL DEVELOPMENT

A more substantial role for educational developers in the context of ICT is in the support for the wider constituency of higher education staff. Here the education developer may be involved in activities at all stages from initial demonstration of the options, through evaluation, commissioning and implementation, through to provision of ongoing support. In all these phases, the specific roles of, and actual tasks undertaken by, the individual educational developer will depend upon a range of factors such as the following:

●   The institution's strategy with respect to ICT. Where the decision has been taken to promote substantive use of ICT across all disciplines, it generally becomes incumbent for the educational developer to 'walk the talk' in support of the initiative. This does not necessarily mean that the educational developer has to become an ICT expert, rather that it is appropriate for the educational developer to experience the trials and tribulations encountered by other lecturing colleagues who face adding an ICT dimension to their teaching. The educational developer may be called upon to act as champion in support of an ICT-based strategy; again the emphasis must be on the educational capabilities of the system (what it will offer) rather than the technical (how to do it) aspects.

- Membership of the institution's educational development team is important. Where the team includes ICT specialists, the technical aspects can be undertaken by such persons. But there is a clear need to ensure that the technical aspects do not overpower the broader pedagogical matters; the educational developer and the ICT specialist working together to build on the strengths of each will often be the most productive. This 'double act' approach will be familiar from many other aspects of the educational developer's role; for example, few educational developers will be expert in the adaptive technologies that may be used to assist the disabled student, and will therefore work alongside the appropriate specialist. Even here, however, the educational developer will benefit from enhancing his or her own understanding of such adaptive technologies. This will mean taking advantage of the available resources, such as those provided by the UK-based organization TechDis (for further details see TechDis, 2003).

- Educational developers, like other lecturers, do indeed have to operate in an environment where the predominant model is 'do-it-yourself'. We are all expected to become hands-on practitioners, if not experts. However, there is a real possibility that any educational developer with minimal ICT skills could find him- or herself distracted by the technology, and might even feel deskilled or suffer feelings of personal and professional inadequacy. This one aspect of educational practice, ICT, must not overwhelm the broader work of the developer.

- The nature of the programmes offered by educational developers differs from those delivered by other lecturers. To a significant extent, participation in educational development programmes (or events) will be subject to choice made voluntarily by busy people who fit attendance around their own busy schedules. While certain lecturers will participate on a regular basis, others never seem to have the time. The use of an ICT-led approach may offer such persons the benefit common to all open-learning programmes: the chance to participate at a place and time that suit personal requirements, rather than centralized scheduling. This benefit may be even more important for non-voluntary participation in staff development such as accredited programmes for new teaching staff.

- We should remember that most lecturers in our HE institutions completed their own formal studies ahead of the mainstream introduction of ICT approaches. While they may be adopting the new technologies for delivery of material to their students, they may have had no experience of learning in this way. Participation in an ICT-based programme under the auspices of educational development may yield them powerful insights in how to make productive and efficient use of ICT in their own teaching.

CONCLUDING MESSAGE

In this discussion, we have recognized that ICT is playing an ever-increasing role in higher education, and that this is, or shortly will be, the case across all disciplines. Within this increased role for ICT, the specific modes of ICT usage will vary from institution to institution and from lecturer to lecturer. This means that each of us in higher education will need to gain a degree of personal competence with ICT, and furthermore we may be called upon to assist others to build their competence.

However, although ICT is important, it is essential that we remember that it is merely the latest tool – more accurately, set of tools – in the lecturer's portfolio. The use of ICT cannot provide an instant panacea for educational development any more than it is able to do so for any other area of the higher education curriculum. Used appropriately and with professionalism, ICT will yield benefit. If misused, ICT will certainly cause as many difficulties as it resolves.

REFERENCES

Fallows, S J and Bhanot, R (2002) *Educational Development through Information and Communications Technology*, Kogan Page, London

Gosling, D W (1996) What do UK educational development units do? *International Journal for Academic Development*, **1** (1), pp 75–83

Gosling, D W (2001) Educational development units in the UK: what are they doing five years on? *International Journal for Academic Development*, **6** (1), pp 74–90

TechDis (2003) TechDis Web site (accessed December 2002) [Online] http://www.techdis.ac.uk/, TechDis, York

FURTHER READING

The theme of this chapter is developed further in the following two volumes:

Fallows, S J and Bhanot, R (2002) *Educational Development through Information and Communications Technology*, Kogan Page, London

Fallows, S J and Bhanot, R (forthcoming) *Ensuring Quality in ICT-based Higher Education*, Kogan Page, London

8

Working on educational development projects

Rachel Segal

Educational development projects have now emerged as a particular genre of work in higher education. Such projects are typically made possible by both internal and external funding initiatives, of varying scales. All told, the higher education (HE) sector has seen in recent years a substantial rise in the number of fixed-term projects that aim to develop specific aspects of learning and teaching. However, the fixed-term project faces a number of challenges in ensuring that deliverables promised are produced to an appropriately high standard and to deadlines. While tangible outcomes, such as publications, CD ROMs and similar resources, are important for project work in general, *educational development projects* are distinctive in that the process of development itself is often just as important as the promised end products, if not more so.

Educational development work is centred around the concept of change. It will help to clarify the kind(s) of change that the project aims to effect, whether it is designed to impact on resources, practice, procedures or policy. Clear and careful planning can usefully begin with an attempt to define and clarify project aims and objectives. The team will need to be clear about who or what the project is designed to benefit, why this is desirable or important and how it might be achieved. Indeed, it is essential to consider the process by which the desired change is effected, and this is a central focus of this chapter.

We thus initially consider the nature of project work. This provides a helpful point from which to address a range of issues that will directly affect the project's chances of success. The contexts in which the project is carried out must be considered. Risks that might influence the viability of the project must be identified, as must cultural issues that affect participation in development work, the internal communication within the project and sources of support. The actual impact of the project on the target audience for inclusion, however, remains core to the concept of change. It is therefore essential to address the ways in which a project is disseminated, evaluated and continued.

THE NATURE OF PROJECT WORK

Project work offers a number of advantages over rolling, ongoing schemes and initiatives. The first of these is the focus that a project can bring to development work, drawing people together for a common purpose. The intensive short-term nature of project work can be a highly productive means of achieving clearly defined goals, allowing teams to concentrate their collective attention on a very specific area. Indeed, in-house projects can provide 'a focus for interaction, cooperation and discussion and the building of learning communities both within departments and across an institution' (Gibbs, Holmes and Segal, 2002: 6).

The restrictions of short fixed-term projects can be frustrating, not least for the staff employed full time on them. However, such projects allow staff who would otherwise be unable to participate to be involved for manageable periods. For those with a heavy workload, it is often easier to commit to a short-term initiative than to an ongoing programme with no fixed end in sight. In addition, with their shorter timescales, projects can encourage individuals to test the water and may therefore be a less threatening forum for experimentation. All these factors allow a wider range of contributions than might otherwise be made.

In addition, projects can provide staff development opportunities in which stakeholders, including core project team members, taste ways of working collaboratively not only with immediate colleagues but also with colleagues from other departments and institutions. Such alternatives to working in isolation can help colleagues to observe and learn more about a range of approaches that can usefully inform and enhance their own practice. Indeed, larger-scale consortium-based projects hold out prospects for success both locally and across institutions and discipline communities. They allow scope to forge productive links between HE, graduate employers, professional bodies and the wider community.

Finally, it is worth noting that advantages stem from the funding stream that is typically associated with a project. Projects can recognize and support enthusiasts, secure the time of over-busy teachers, orient attention to institutional priorities, build learning communities, allow for staff development, build capacity to change and build infrastructure (Gibbs, Holmes and Segal, 2002). All these outcomes depend at least in part on a sufficient level of funding.

There are, however, some aspects of working with project funding streams that can be problematic. While the process of bidding for funds can be a useful collaborative experience, if the deadline for submission of applications is not too tight, an unsuccessful bid can be extremely demoralizing and can deter colleagues from investing time and energy in future applications or engaging in further work in this area. Developers working with successful projects would be well advised to consider carefully some strategies for minimizing the negative effects of unsuccessful bids, and for harnessing, supporting and further developing the interest that the bidding process may have encouraged. If the original bid generated a strong and committed team, the team may find alternative sources of funds. It is usually possible to undertake a smaller but still useful version of the proposed project with less money!

The short timescale of project work can also cause difficulties. Fixed-term projects usually have rigid budgets, and there is rarely any opportunity to expand the original funding envelope. Careful preparation is thus important, to ensure that your project plan is sensible and achievable within the constraints of time and funding. In addition, projects generally offer only short-term contracts, which can be frustrating at the best of times but, more importantly, can also lead to problems with continuity of personnel. For example, as the end of a fixed-term contract approaches, team members may quite reasonably apply for other jobs, some of which will necessitate their leaving the project before its completion. When a project relies on team working and allocation of specific roles and responsibilities in order to achieve outcomes, this can have a destabilizing effect on the project. Project planning must involve contingency plans, following careful risk assessment, as we will subsequently consider in greater detail, to minimize the negative impact of changes in personnel.

The peculiarities and the regulations of the funding source will, to varying extents, determine or at least inform the nature of any project. External agencies funding learning and teaching development work have guidelines to which projects must adhere. Generally speaking, project work is funded because it addresses a particular set of priorities as identified by the funding body. Addressing those priorities is therefore advantageous, not least because large-scale funding initiatives tend to be founded on high-profile issues that resonate with the academic community. There may, however, be occasions when it is prudent to market the project independently of its funding source. Negative perceptions of the impetus for the initiative or funding stream, eg as rooted in purely bureaucratic government targets that do not command much respect or enthusiasm, can prove a disincentive to participation.

KNOWING YOUR CONTEXT

While generic considerations are important, projects are always carried out within a specific situation. Awareness and understanding of the context in which your project is carried out is thus important, and you and your colleagues need to share a clear understanding of this. In particular, you will need to consider several key questions:

- How will you ascertain the nature of the most immediate needs and concerns of the groups with which you are working, including those of your project colleagues?

- What are the key concerns and needs of the constituency for which the project is designed?

- How will you involve those who hold the levers for policy and procedural change?

- What kind(s) of contributions does the project need?

- How will these contributions be secured?

- What specialist support is available to you?

- How will you keep people on board?

- What motivates your project team?

It is worth addressing such questions in greater detail, while remaining aware that the project environment(s) and concomitant needs will be constantly shifting and changing.

The project team will need to know of whom the stakeholder groups consist. Are they from a particular discipline area, a specific faculty, a certain type of institution? Will they be undergraduates, heads of departments, postgraduate students, students with disabilities, part-time tutors, senior managers, alumni, pro vice-chancellors, new lecturers, students on work placements, curriculum developers, professional bodies, employer organizations, prospective students, graduate recruiters? Whatever the combination of the above, your project team must be clear about the groups with which it is working in order to ascertain how best to interact with those groups and to consider how working relations might be enhanced across those categories.

The next step is a needs analysis for your target audience(s) and your immediate project team (ie the core group of colleagues committed to and responsible for the project's planning, development, dissemination, evaluation and continuation). Consultation via focus groups, e-mail or paper surveys can be a useful means for obtaining a range of information. As contexts and priorities change, so can the needs of stakeholders. It is necessary to ensure that the project builds in communication channels that allow the team to obtain feedback. The frequency and timing of both needs analysis and the obtaining of feedback will be determined by the nature of the project's scale (remit and time) and its aims and objectives.

Once the needs of your stakeholder groups have been identified, you can determine how the set-up of your core team will relate and contribute to the key project outcomes and to the people with whom you will need to work. You will need to ascertain how your core project team will operate in synergy with your stakeholders and on a day-to-day basis. If, for example, your team has decided that it will need to address and work with post-graduate students, the approaches used are likely to be different from those more fitting for an employer organization or a group of senior managers. Priorities and approaches adopted by different stakeholder groups will inevitably differ. These different priorities and approaches in turn will determine the ways in which the project team must operate with a range of contributors and end users. Whether you are choosing the team, have been presented with a set of colleagues or are a member of the team, it will be useful to get a sense of the kinds of competencies and attitudes represented in that team and thus available to the project.

Literature that relates to team building and to learning styles thus will be of use to developers working on projects. In particular, the theories of R M Belbin provide a good starting point for further investigation of the area of effective team building. Two of his texts in particular, *Management Teams: Why they succeed or fail* (1981) and *Team Roles at Work* (1993), are still frequently cited, and there are many other interesting and relevant adaptations of his work. Belbin suggested that there are nine key team roles, based on personality types, that constitute a well-balanced team. The roles do not have to be represented equally but an omission of one of them will result in a less successful team.

Awareness of the capabilities of your project team and its members will help you to consider the ways in which the team can most usefully address the groups with which you are working. While many colleagues working on educational development projects do not see themselves as developers, it may be interesting and useful to consider Ray Land's typology of educational developers' practice (2001). He identified 12: managerial, political strategist, entrepreneurial, romantic, vigilant opportunist, researcher, professional competence, reflective practitioner, internal consultant, modeller–broker, interpretive–hermeneutic and discipline-specific. Reviewing your project team through this typological filter will help you to consider which of the above types of developer would function most effectively in the environments in which your project is based. It is highly likely that the institutional, departmental or particularly the disciplinary context in which the project is working will align with one or more of the above types. This will help you to decide how best to present your project team members to the relevant stakeholder groups.

We should not forget that educational development is a learning process, and that the theories and practices that apply to learning styles may also usefully be adapted and applied to those participating in and contributing to educational development processes. While educational development involves 'working with people to solve their educational problems, to meet their educational challenges', it also usually implies 'client active participation and immediate use of what is learned' (Baume and Baume, 1994, cited in Macdonald and Wisdom, 2002). Pask (1988) defines a learning style as a 'predisposition' to adopt a particular learning strategy. His earlier work led to the identification of two learning styles: a holist and a serialist approach. Honey and Mumford (1982), meanwhile, identify four learning styles: activists, reflectors, theorists and pragmatists.

It will be productive to gain a clear picture of the kinds of factors that motivate your project colleagues to engage with the project. There are a number of ways to do this:

- It is crucially important that a sense of ownership of both the project and the development process is fostered among your wider project team. This will strengthen commitment from contributors, help to keep stakeholders on board and enhance dissemination and implementation of project outcomes.

- Once the project's purpose has been clarified, it makes sense to discuss the specific aims and objectives of the project to allow a common understanding of them.

- Early inclusion is important; getting the right people on board as early as possible will also enhance a sense of ownership and collegiality among the project team.

- A good project manager will clarify the rationale for the work of the project. It is useful to be as transparent as possible about this, in order to set the project in a well-defined context so that individuals can understand where they might fit into the wider picture.

RISK ASSESSMENT

It is evident from the above sections that project work carries with it a number of risks. For example, stakeholders may fail to make an adequate contribution, or problems may occur during an implementation phase.

Furthermore, given the short-term nature of project work, there is less room for error or prevarication than might be permissible in a longer-term initiative. Such factors necessitate risk assessment on the project.

A good starting point is for a project team to work together on a 'SWOT' analysis, an exercise that involves identification of the project's Strengths, Weaknesses, Opportunities and Threats. In general, a risk assessment takes into account the project's aims and objectives; considers the demands of your funding source (eg guidelines, timescales, reporting requirements); and identifies some of the organizational and practical obstacles that your project will need to overcome. Most traditional risk assessment exercises in business look at risk factors that might jeopardize the completion of the project, consider the likelihood of their occurrence and assess the scale of their impact if they were to happen. There is a range of paradigms that can be adopted for this, including force-field analysis and traditional risk assessment charts.

Such exercises will enable you and your colleagues to share concerns about a range of factors that you feel could place the project at risk. For example: your project's success may hinge on the input of expert advice or knowledge from a specific colleague. What will happen to the project if that input suddenly becomes unavailable? He or she may become ill or may leave the project, institution or even the country. One of the most common problems facing short-term projects is personnel changes. Calculating the likelihood and impact of that risk occurring may prompt your team to devise an appropriate contingency plan.

Whatever the nature of your project, a key factor for consideration in educational development is that of securing and retaining appropriate active participation. This should certainly figure in your risk assessment. While in longer-term programmes this kind of information can emerge gradually and slowly, early task-oriented teamwork elicits information quickly, offers a common focus, and provides a tangible start to the collaborative processes involved in a project.

Risk assessment next helps to identify action that can be taken to minimize the impact of those risk factors. Risk factors can be prioritized in relation to their projected impact. This, in turn, is transformed into a list of success factors; that is, actions to be taken that will help to ensure the success of the project. All the above methods are helpful for devising appropriate contingency plans and can be undertaken as a team exercise, which in turn can provide a useful team-building opportunity.

Once aims and objectives have been clarified, the team will need to map them against specific milestones by which progress will be measured. At the same time, the team can negotiate how those milestones will be achieved and monitored and can allocate responsibilities for events, publications, meetings, etc while attaching corresponding deadlines at sensible points within the project's timescale. While most of the final decisions will be the responsibility of the project manager, in consultation with whatever kind of steering, advisory or management group the project has, these initial nego-tiations are an important part of fostering commitment and keeping team members on board. The resulting activity plan will form a core part of the monitoring and evaluation framework for the project.

PARTICIPATION IN DEVELOPMENT WORK

Participation (or not) in development work has been highlighted in the above section as a key source of risk within projects. What factors affect participation? Individual perceptions of the status of educational devel-opment work will have a profound effect on levels of engagement with your project from academic colleagues. A common complaint stems from the perennial research-versus-teaching tension: that is, the view that research is privileged far above learning and teaching in HE. Following this, many academics feel that within their institutional or disciplinary context, their involvement in educational development work will have a detrimental effect on their career and will inevitably detract from research activity and professional status. This perception may be attributable at least in part to the policy and funding context of the HE sector and of many institutions, especially HE institutions identified as research intensive; but changes in sectoral or organizational culture quite clearly cannot be achieved quickly or easily. However, it makes sense to discuss the issue among the project team and devise alternative strategies (and stock responses) to acknowledge and address the problem.

Perception of the way in which institutions encourage and support educational development work is a determining factor for academics' engagement with these projects and processes. At one research-intensive institution, a common concern cited by academics for their resistance to visible involvement in and championing of learning and teaching develop-ments was that it would have a detrimental effect on their career prospects. The institutional response, via a central learning and teaching support unit, was to track the decisions of the university's promotions committee over a two-year period. In a system that allowed an upper limit of 10 points per promotion application, a maximum of 3 of which could be awarded for teaching and 3 for research, it was found that for 40 per cent of the promo-tions applications approved, the points rating for teaching exceeded that given for research. In this instance, the facts contradict the general perception, and approaching half of promotions are given more for teaching than for research. Academics often respond to hard data, and this investigation provided potential ammunition for developers dealing with sceptics. This is an encouraging story, showing a team prioritizing an issue and devising a strategy that responds to concerns expressed by staff. Simultaneously, this work allowed the team to raise the profile of the institutional policy on promotion, showing that it was possible to succeed via engagement in learning and teaching development work. Acknowledgement and recognition of contributions to educational development are important incentives for some staff.

Even allowing for such cultural issues within institutions, it is still important to find ways to engage possible participants in your project. It will help if you can find alternative ways of describing and presenting (ie explaining and marketing) your project to different audiences. This is likely to be most effective if you can match the concerns and difficulties of your target audience(s) with the activities, events and deliverables you intend to generate as part of your project. The team will need to prepare a range of different descriptions (eg press statements, e-mail flyers, promotional articles) of the project, using different modes of expression to address different stakeholder groups, such as students, colleagues within your institution, colleagues from other discipline areas, senior management, professional bodies and graduate recruiters.

It is also worth remembering that academics are invariably hard pressed for time, with heavy and varied workloads. Assuming that the project would benefit from the contribution of a particular group of academics or vice versa, it makes sense to promote your project as an opportunity to develop a potential solution to a particular problem. For example, suppose that 'x-ology' and 'z-osophical studies' are universally under-resourced, so the academic staff are constantly multi-tasking. As a widening participation drive in the institution succeeds in increasing student numbers with no corresponding increase in staff, delivery and monitoring of small-group tutorials in those discipline areas are becoming increasingly problematic. A project that is designed to support postgraduate tutors or to develop a peer support paradigm for undergraduates is likely to appeal. Staff participating in educational development projects that relate to their own practice are highly likely to have readily available, strong and useful opinions to offer. Tapping into those concerns and presenting your project accordingly will help to encourage participation in the project and/or take-up of project outputs at a later stage.

SOURCES OF SUPPORT

In order to allow your project to reach its potential, it is sensible to identify what institutional and external support is available for your work; your resources are, of course, finite and it does not make sense to rely on your team to deliver everything. There is likely to be a wealth of expertise and information on which you can draw, some of which may become apparent via a literature review. In addition, there are likely to be several agencies outside your immediate environment that could enhance your project. For example, a relevant discipline network may well have advice or opportunities for support or networking to offer the project. If you are not an institutional educational developer, your educational development unit, learning and teaching support unit or equivalent may well have resources and expertise that will help. Your institution may have a disability support unit. If so, this could advise you in making your deliverables accessible to a diverse student population or point you to national bodies or initiatives that support work in this area (eg within the United Kingdom, the National Disability Team (NDT)).

Across the HE sector, there is a wealth of experience of engagement in development projects. You and your project team will need to become acquainted with the findings of current or recently completed projects. This will help the team to identify areas of overlap and underdeveloped areas relating to the remit of the project. Within the United Kingdom, for instance, there is the Web site from the National Co-ordination Team (2003), which details projects of all four phases of the Fund for the Development of Learning and Teaching (FDTL) and the three phases of the Teaching and Learning Technology Programme (TLTP). In addition, the Learning and Teaching Support Network Subject Centres and the Generic Centre fund a range of learning and teaching-related projects, activities and research. There is also a wealth of experience in undertaking educational development work, for example in the Staff and Educational Development Association (SEDA).

INTERNAL COMMUNICATION

The quality and frequency of communication by the project team will have a profound effect on the quality and success of project processes. You will need to be careful to establish and maintain appropriate modes of communication both within the immediate project team and into your constituency. What will be the primary channels of regular communication between team members? You may find that the working patterns of some team members (especially if they work part time on the project) make e-mail access difficult, so the telephone is a preferred option for regular communication. Some projects use pro formas for regular reports of progress on an individual or departmental basis. Some prefer to use Web boards, synchronous communications tools or similar electronic means of communication. Within one institution on a single site, or across geographically close sites, it may be preferable to schedule regular face-to-face meetings, perhaps alternating or rotating the venue for the meeting. It works for some projects to have all team members feeding information to a central project manager who will then assimilate that information, disseminate it among the team and use it to inform future planning and internal evaluation.

It is also worth noting that the scale of the project and its time constraints will determine how the project team might best communicate its progress and concerns. This becomes even more of a pressing issue when the development work takes off and starts to include larger numbers and a more diverse group of people (such as a wider project team in other departments and institutions, different stakeholder groups, 'satellite' staff piloting ideas, models, etc). In the case of larger-scale projects involving more than one site or institution, the project manager will need to decide on how the team will keep communication channels open when it includes personnel with different remits, needs and concerns, in different geographical locations and different organizational environments. Communication with the wider project team, over whose working patterns the project has little or no control, will also need to be carefully planned.

It is vital that project communication is two-way, that a project team both listens (and responds) and talks to stakeholders and users of project outputs.

DISSEMINATION

You will need to decide who needs to be aware of your existence and purpose and at what stages in the project's life. Once these people and groups have been identified, the project team will need to decide how they might best be approached and to what ends. What kinds of contributions does the project need in order to succeed, and what reciprocal relationships might be established between the project and stakeholder groups?

Dissemination and collaborative development are thus two strands that can be productively intertwined, especially in the light of the short-term nature of project work. Effective dissemination is about much more than the mechanics of distribution; it is an integral part of a project, from the very beginning, and involves sharing and conversing about both the development work and the project outcomes with the stakeholders and end users. There are many ways in which dissemination can be usefully incorporated into development activities. For example, if the colleagues asked to pilot the developing project outputs are part of your target audience, the development work, if designed and supported properly, automatically incorporates dissemination for awareness, understanding and action. I consider these three forms of dissemination in more detail below.

Tapping into appropriate existing mechanisms for dissemination (eg via publications, Web sites or events stemming from disciplinary networks or from professional bodies) will often be appropriate. Working with a variety of agencies and other projects will bring other benefits as well as cheap and well-targeted distribution. Such collaboration will enhance your knowledge and understanding of context by exposing your team to information and personnel carrying out work elsewhere, helping you to avoid the familiar academic malady of 'reinvention of the wheel'.

As is implied above, there are useful distinctions to be made between different levels and modes of dissemination. Attention to these will facilitate the design of your project's dissemination strategy, as considered in greater detail within Chapter 6.

The three principal levels are self-explanatory. The first of these – dissemination for awareness – flags up the existence of the project and its *raison d'être*. The second – dissemination for understanding – helps stakeholders to see how the project might relate to them and/or their work and experience. The third – dissemination for action – facilitates experimentation in relation to project outcomes, eg piloting of a module or a new approach. I also use a fourth category, dissemination for implementation, which takes the process further and encourages embedding of project outcomes.

EVALUATION

Virtually all projects have to adhere to monitoring, evaluation and reporting regulations, often incorporating financial safeguards. While such regulations are necessary and educational development projects typically demonstrate excellent value for money, evaluation should be about much more than a financially oriented bureaucratic exercise.

Many academics have experience of working on research projects but educational development projects differ in several ways. Such points of difference may include the reliance on collaborative development, a wide range of participation, and a concern for the needs of all potential stakeholders, whether project staff, the wider project team or end users. Additionally, the key benefits of educational development projects tend to be less tangible than a set of deliverables that can be ticked off a checklist. The nature and extent of project impact are often not apparent during the life of the project, and meaningful change often occurs beyond the official life of a project. Meaningful, long-term changes in practice and policy tend to evolve over periods of time and so are difficult or impossible to evaluate during the life of a project. While it is relatively easy to measure the number of deliverables produced, if they are to be viewed as evidence of process, rather than as ends in themselves, their evaluation is more complex.

Furthermore, if process really is so important, how does one track developments; how can project teams capture the essence of a process? We can keep quantitative records, for example of how many people attended project events, how many queries we received, or what kinds of data we gleaned from feedback forms. We can collect qualitative testimonials from end users, developers and participants. We can take care that our evaluation strategies are designed at the outset of the project rather than retrospectively, and include answers to questions such as 'what contribution will this project make?', 'what do we want to achieve?', 'what are we evaluating and why?', 'are the project modes of operation appropriate for their purpose?', 'are we achieving what we need to achieve?', 'how can we improve such and such?', 'what constitutes success in this project', 'how will we gauge the success of this project?'.

The evaluation approaches adopted in any development project will be determined by a range of factors, including scale of project (such as the budget, timescale, number of people, departments and institutions involved), aims and objectives, discipline or theme areas. Whatever the outline of your project, a common success factor is the use of regular internal evaluation methods – ways of monitoring and seeking feedback from the team and beyond, in relation to project activities, events, processes and outputs. Teams should ensure that the project's feedback mechanisms are accessible to a diverse range of stakeholders. For example, part-time and peripatetic staff may not be on-site to pick up a feedback pro forma, so the team will need to bear this in mind when setting the deadline for its return, or find an alternative. Staff without regular e-mail access might find a paper-based version more convenient or stakeholders with dyslexia might prefer to participate in a verbal focus group. The best projects do not just obtain a range of feedback, they also act upon the feedback they receive and use it in their regular cycle of re-evaluation and planning of their work. Opportunities for reflection on the appropriateness of project processes and the quality of the work being done should not be underestimated. Where possible, try to build in regular time to reassess whether what you are doing and the way in which you are doing it make sense in light of the project's unanticipated outcomes and what you have learnt collectively about the context in which you have been operating.

It is also the case that external evaluators can often provide more objective overviews of projects and can act throughout as project advisers. Other than enhanced objectivity, the advantage of an external evaluator is that he or she can make important comments or suggestions that a team member within an institution might feel unable to express, for reasons of institutional sensitivity. It makes sense to bring in the external evaluator at an early stage so that he or she can comment on the status quo before the project work has begun, in order to gauge the impact of the project when the time comes to write a reflective evaluative report. The monitoring and evaluation of educational development are considered in much more detail in Chapter 5.

CONTINUATION

As has already been mentioned, the impact of a project is not always apparent until after the official end date, sometimes long after. Unless you are happy for your project outputs to sit uninterrupted on a colleague's shelf, your team will need to ensure that the dissemination strategy not only hits the first two levels, of awareness and understanding, but also provides the kind of information and support necessary for dissemination for both action and implementation. What will happen to tangible project deliverables when there is no longer a project officer on the end of the phone?

This is perhaps where your by now extended project network, discipline network or professional body can help, perhaps by promoting project outcomes, maintaining your project Web site, keeping a list of consultants, or distributing materials. If dedicated continuation funding is not available, there may well be support available from a range of sources. If your aim was to develop a new model for delivery of a particular module, to promote diversity in the curriculum, or encourage the adoption of a specific approach to peer tutoring within your institution, continuation is implicit in a successful project and can be seen in the form of the practice of others. Evidence of ongoing and evolving impact also resides in the unmeasurable enhancement of individual contributors' personal development by virtue of their involvement in the project.

CONCLUSION

Educational development projects are by their very nature fixed term, involving limited periods of activity, with tight budgets, specific deliverables and outcomes and many challenges to overcome. Despite the constraints of this genre of work, positive development is achievable via careful planning and preparation and with the energy and commitment of a good project manager and a strong project team. It is through the richness and complexity of broadly based collaborative and inclusive development practices that educational development projects can and do support and effect meaningful change in higher education.

REFERENCES

Baume, C and Baume, D (1994) Staff and educational development: a discussion paper, *Staff and Educational Development Association (SEDA) Newsletter*, (2) (March), pp 6–9

Belbin, R M (1981) *Management Teams: Why they succeed or fail*, Butterworth Heinemann, Oxford

Belbin, R M (1993) *Team Roles at Work*, Butterworth Heinemann, Oxford

Gibbs, G, Holmes, A and Segal, R (2002) *Funding Innovation and Disseminating New Teaching Practices*, National Co-ordination Team for the Teaching Quality Enhancement Fund, Open University, Milton Keynes

Honey, P and Mumford, A (1982) *Manual of Learning Style*, P Honey, London

Land, R (2001) Agency, context and change in academic development, *International Journal for Academic Development*, **6** (1), pp 4–20

Macdonald, R and Wisdom, J (eds) (2002) *Academic and Educational Development: Research, evaluation and changing practice in higher education*, Kogan Page, London

National Co-ordination Team (2003) Web site (accessed 21 January 2003) [Online] http://www.ncteam.ac.uk

Pask, G (1988) Learning strategies, teaching strategies and conceptual or learning styles, in *Perspectives on Individual Differences, Learning Strategies and Learning Styles*, ed R Schmeck, pp 83–100, Plenum Press, London (accessed 21 January 2003) [Online] http://www.ipat.com/Pdf/teammanual/appendixb.pdf

FURTHER READING

Baume, C, Martin, P and Yorke, M (eds) (2002) *Managing Educational Development Projects: Effective management for maximum impact*, Kogan Page, London

Kennett, P (1999) Partnerships and the supermarket approach to project management, in *Proceedings of the Fourth International Conference on Language and Development*, October 1999, Hanoi

9

Development in the disciplines

Caroline Baillie

INTRODUCTION

This chapter is intended for those who work within discipline-specific educational development. You might work within a department or faculty, full or part time (where you might also work as an academic part time), or perhaps as part of a co-ordinated team across a university or a national network such as the Learning and Teaching Support Network (LTSN) in the United Kingdom. You might also work within an educational development unit or directly for the director of learning in your institution, but have the remit to develop within particular disciplines rather than across the whole university. The trend to move towards working within disciplines is fairly recent, and brings with it a range of interesting opportunities and challenges. Here we will look at the various issues that might occur, and I will offer a way of looking at these to help you to select the most appropriate alternative for your own context.

One of the most important things to recognize is that each discipline-based educational developer is unique. You will find that your job will in some ways differ from those of others. Over the past 20 years or so, the backgrounds, experience and roles of educational developers have changed and diversified. Educational development is shifting back towards the disciplines. The case for this shift is made eloquently by Jenkins (1996). These changes, and the new positions in which many developers see themselves, are the foci of this chapter.

TRENDS IN EDUCATIONAL DEVELOPMENT: MOVING BACK TO THE FUTURE

In the United Kingdom over the past 20 years, we have seen some definite shifts in attitude to development in UK higher education. Stefani refers to some of these shifts in Chapter 1 of this book. In this section, we see how the discipline-specific nature of development has emerged.

1. Staff and educational development in the 1980s (or academic development in Australasia) arose from a group of enthusiasts who saw that higher education (HE) was not as effective as it should have been. These are the first generation referred to in Stefani's chapter. Many of the developers from this era left their teaching posts and created new capabilities in facilitating lecturers in understanding and better supporting the learning of their students. Much of the knowledge on student learning emanated from Sweden (Marton and Hounsell, 1984). It was important at this time for the developers to work from a solid base of knowledge about learning and its facilitation. They created development centres, and staff and educational development started to gain credibility as a discipline of its own. Some very useful publications on teaching, learning and assessment were created at this time. They offered generic advice (eg Gibbs, Habeshaw and Habeshaw, 1984; Habeshaw, Habeshaw and Gibbs, 1987; Jaques, 1984). As with feminism, a period of building strength on their own, away from departments, was necessary at this time. Many of the early developers came from a strong teaching background, and were less involved with research.

2. In the early 1990s, the second generation of developers as described by Stefani were lecturers in other disciplines, often with research profiles. We also started to see more educational research being conducted, as the developers moved their academic work into another area, development. However, in most cases the developers at this time still saw the need to drop their original discipline focus and moved into generic centres for educational development. A variety of positions were created, some academic (with a teaching and research profile) and others administrative (with a staff development–personnel profile). Texts such as Ramsden (1992) were often drawn on at this stage to help lecturers reflect on the need to build educational developments on a strong pedagogic research base.

3. During the late 1990s, universities within the United Kingdom started to become more interested in learning and teaching, owing largely to the efforts of the above groups of developers, especially those that had by now moved on into informing policy. All UK institutions were asked to create a learning and teaching strategy, and many new training courses were developed for lecturing staff. More educational developers were required, and many more joined the profession, training on the job.

4. Some institutions at this time were beginning to think about discipline-specific educational development (eg Hazel and Baillie, 1998; Moore and Exley, 1994). For example, Imperial College London developed a strategy of employing a co-ordinator in each department, and part-time educational developers who were also academics in different departments. These posts were not common in UK higher education at this time, and

those involved were considered unable to make their mind up about their career! The way we decided to work was to create a network of enthusiasts who would support each other. Ideally, they would have the central support of a core group. This core group could supply educational know-how and pedagogic research, and help with the 'translation' of generic educational know-how to particular disciplinary settings. Furthermore, they could identify departmental needs.

The start of the new millennium has shown a marked change in educational development, for two reasons. The first is that academics graduating from university training courses on teaching, and working on educational projects, were becoming more interested in teaching and learning as a scholarly pursuit. They were happy to do this as part of their job at the same time as maintaining their disciplinary work. Disciplinary educational development started to take hold, especially in the United Kingdom. The second reason, as far as the United Kingdom was concerned, was that the disciplinary strand of the funding council's Teaching Quality Enhancement Find (TQEF) had been created and we were starting to see the results of the first Fund for the Development of Teaching and Learning (FDTL) and Teaching and Learning Technology Programme (TLTP) projects. Finally, the LTSN was created and provided the mechanism and support for much necessary discipline-based educational development. Hence we saw the emergence of part-time academic educational developers who could better understand the disciplinary needs of their students (eg Garratt, Overton and Threlfall, 1999).

5. The final breed of educational developer today is the career educational developer. They come from two main sources. Some have come the long road from lecturer to part-time and then full-time developer. Others have become developers via, within the United Kingdom, project management, for example on LTSN and FDTL projects. The former group of developers have lectured undergraduates and researched their discipline. The latter may also have taught and carried out research, typically as graduate teaching assistants and PhD students, or may not. As discussed by Stefani in Chapter 1, it is through the emergence of these developers that we start to see the potential for a profession. But whatever their background, they increasingly have a theoretical stance on the subject as well as practical experience as educational developers, facilitating workshops and training courses. Their academic subject is educational development.

DISCIPLINE-BASED EDUCATIONAL DEVELOPMENT

From whichever background you emerge, you will need to think about why what you are doing is important so that you can help others understand your role better! There are many factors that create the need to work from within the discipline. These are some I have considered and you will find more:

1. There is a certain amount of 'tacit' knowledge (Polanyi, 1966) that we learn when we are part of a culture or 'tribe' (Becher, 1989). We know how to behave and how to think without being told. We just assume our students will pick this up, if we do the sorts of things that practitioners do or if we tell them the things that they should know. However, this tacit knowing is the most difficult part of an education and induction into a discipline. If you are part of the disciplinary tribe then you will inherently understand some of the student needs within that discipline. It is, of course, better that academic staff and students begin to reflect on this tacit knowledge and share it once they have discovered it. But this will take some time. If you are not part of the tribe yourself, you can do some very good work by trying to help those within the tribe to reflect on their own ways of thinking. It will be harder for you to understand their ways of thinking, but easier for you to make the tacit knowledge explicit as an outsider because for you it is not assumed knowledge.

2. If you research in the discipline itself, or have done so, especially if you are in a technical area, you will find that your discipline uses different methodologies and ways of thinking as compared with the discipline of education. This does not mean that in order to research in educational development, you need to adopt the currently accepted pedagogic research patterns. Your way of knowing and conceptions of knowledge will vary according to your discipline as well as your culture (Fulop, 2000), and hence your way of facilitating the development of knowledge will differ. It will be far easier to interest your colleagues if your approach to research in teaching, learning and development has strong links with their own way of thinking. The University of Learning (Bowden and Marton, 1998) provides a framework in which the links between research and learning through knowledge development can be enhanced (see also Baillie, Emanuelsson and Marton, 2001). One suggestion is to create PhD studentships in which the student researchers create knowledge and study their own knowledge-building process.

3. Professional skills development is of immediate relevance in vocational disciplines. Links with professional, real-life case studies and project work can be employed in some disciplines, and your understanding of the needs and approaches to the development of the skills needed by the profession will be very important. You may find that your own research-related contacts can become involved in educational projects. The industrial partner can act as a great motivator to your colleagues, stressing the importance of the need for professional skills and attitude development in students. The need for practical and theoretical learning and the relation

between the two will be more relevant to some subject areas than others and the approaches to educational development necessarily different. For example, problem-based learning started in medical areas with the obvious need to help students start with the problem and end with a knowledgeable solution. It has not been so easy to develop this approach in more conceptual and less problem-oriented areas, even though it is still possible.

4. Different subjects and departments have different problems. Some have too few students and some too many. Technical disciplines have problems with student numbers, whereas fashion design and drama are swamped with applicants. In some disciplines, therefore, students will already be keen to learn and your task is to help them learn better. In other disciplines, it may be your main task to help them see the point of learning anything!

The way you will need to work and deal with these issues will depend largely on your own background and the way you choose to work, as well as on the needs of your community. In the following section, we work through a series of possible roles and contexts that you might find yourself in. It has drawn largely on my own experience at Imperial College London and the LTSN, and as such has a technical flavour to it. However, much of the thinking will apply more generally. Suggestions have been given as food for thought, and these will need to be translated into each new context in order to be successful. Underlying the thought process of how to undertake discipline-based educational development is how to be creative, to be responsive to the needs of the community you are working with and how to communicate and negotiate with the members of that community. The most important part of any creative idea is the communication of that idea. I hope that these suggestions will start to help you to generate ideas of your own, as well as ways of implementing them that will be sustainable.

WORKING FROM WITHIN THE DISCIPLINE

Based in a department or faculty

If you work with a department and do not work with or for the centre for educational development, or whatever it is called, within your institution, this centre is your first port of call. Find out what support the centre for educational development offers. This support may include training courses, workshops, publications and individual support. The centre can support you in your job as well as your community. Some further important areas to consider are described below and are shown in Figure 9.1.

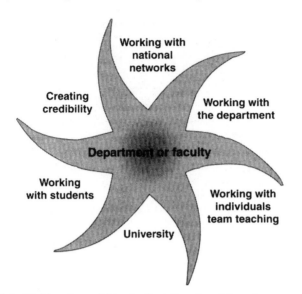

Figure 9.1 *Working from within the discipline: based in a department or faculty*

Creating credibility
Your credibility in educational development is as important as in the subject area. If you work within a department that you have trained in as a student or as a beginning lecturer then you will need to establish your credentials in educational development. Even if you have been working in the department for a long time, it might be difficult for your colleagues to understand that you know more than them about educational development and that you can help them. Some suggestions that may help areas follows:

- As soon as you have the opportunity, offer to give a talk. You can relate what you will do to current pedagogic practice. The department staff will get to understand that you have a scholarly appreciation of the area.

- Try some 'quick wins'. These are strategies that you know (from other educational developers) will work; that is, they will have a welcome and positive impact on the department's staff and students. It is best to get some ideas from others through your educational development unit or through the Staff and Educational Development Association (SEDA). Often things that don't cost any money or staff time but that students like will work wonders. There are such things, but you do need to be creative. Peer tutoring, if you gain acceptance from the teaching staff, is one example; the Department of Materials at Imperial College London has found great success with this programme (Baillie and Grimes, 1999).

- Ask the staff what they would like from you, rather than telling them or assuming you know. Then you can tailor what you do to meet their needs.

If you come from educational development and not from the discipline, you will need to establish your ability to work with the subject matter (even if you have a degree in the subject).

It becomes important for you to gain some sense of understanding of this new 'tribe'. Imagine that you have gone to live in a new country. You may not like the way things are done, or you may not understand why they are done that way, but there will be reasons why things are done as they are, and you need to find what the reason is before you suggest any alternatives. Asking questions is the way to go. As mentioned above, it is easier for you to discover the tacit knowledge underpinning local practice than it is for someone who has been trained in that way of thinking all his or her working life. However, you will need to be very focused and learn to listen for the signs and symbols, the language and hidden meaning of the discipline. Interviews and focus groups with staff and students about their needs would be a good starting point.

Working with the department
When you are based within a department or a faculty, you have an important position on the inside, which you can make the most of if you are strategic. It is important to understand what influences the curriculum. Apart from policies from outside the department, these influences may come from an industrial advisory panel, internal teaching committees, a head of teaching or year courses, course teams, etc. Some suggestions that may help are as follows:

- Find out which committees and panels at department or faculty level involve themselves with teaching, and which could or should, even if they currently do not. Ask to join the committees.

- Find out if the faculty or department has a teaching and learning strategy, and discover what are the most important aspects that affect your position and your effectiveness.

- If possible, either with the internal teaching committee or with a selected group of individuals (who will need to include the head of teaching, senior tutor, year advisers, etc as well as student representatives), hold a discussion about what the aims are for your position.

- Create a strategic plan (if one does not already exist) for educational development for the department. This will clearly involve others.

Include the resources needed if you are to fulfil this plan. If one exists already, examine it for its realism and its resource implications. Offer an amended version if necessary.

- Professional advisory panels often offer advice about curriculum content. With some small encouragement, these advisers can also offer some good support on skills development.

Working with individual staff

Apart from influencing policy at the department level, you will work with individual teaching and learning enthusiasts. These people will provide much motivational input to you, and in turn need to be supported. You will need to help individual lecturers to work with the constraints that they may have to face in introducing innovations, as well as advancing rather than impeding their careers. This will not be easy. As well as supporting them directly, you can put them in touch with others in the university or in other universities who are facing the same issues or have done so before. Innovative teaching and an academic interest in teaching can now count towards professional membership of the Institute of Learning and Teaching in Higher Education, as well as for promotional panels. In order to gain evidence of success of innovations, the lecturers will need to be made aware of evaluation methods that may be used to collect data that show how the innovation supports student learning. Some of the currently used evaluation systems in place in the department may not actually be valid for new teaching and learning methods. Evaluations need to be demonstrably rigorous if they are to be taken seriously within the department.

Team teaching is also a possibility. You could offer to work with an individual, and discuss the planning of a curriculum and assessment. You could also even share a lecture with that individual. If he or she is nervous about getting student interaction going, you can show how it can be done. Sometimes it is easier to have a go with buzz groups (discussion in pairs) and so on once you have seen them in action and you see how to gain control again.

Working with students

There are many possibilities for working directly with students. You can work together with the student representatives on various committees, or create other mechanisms for helping the students improve their own learning environment. Some suggestions that have worked well are the following:

- Train the student representatives. A good approach is a weekend training course. Bradford University takes the reps away for the weekend and trains them in teamwork and educational awareness. The UK Centre for Materials Education (UKCME), following Bradford's example, now runs a course for all materials departments reps on an annual basis. We also train students in communication skills, especially presenting in committee meetings, and also in how to collect and represent opinions so that they can better represent their fellow students' views at staff–student liaison committee meetings.

- Work with the student union. Imperial College London has recently created an Education Development Sabbatical Officer, which is a great boost to the work that students can do in raising awareness about their rights to a better education.

Linking to university and national policy
One very important early task is to connect to the university policy on education. This includes the teaching and learning strategy and the human resources strategy, as well as, within the United Kingdom, external funding council initiatives and directives, and who within the university may be working with these. Your educational development unit can support you in this and give you the right material and contacts. You can then base what you do within the goals of the university.

Working within national networks

Most of the educational development work done to date has been at a local university level. As far as the United Kingdom is concerned, within the Teaching Quality Enhancement Fund disciplinary strand, FDTL, TLTP and LTSN centres have developed national networks. They have mostly had to draw upon local strategies that were created as cross-disciplinary approaches and extend these to a larger scale within a disciplinary context. Some important aspects for reflection are shown in Figure 9.2. Furthermore, some examples of schemes that you might be able to use within your department follow. You should check out the latest details on their Web sites:

- teaching development grants – small sums of money to support developments in departments and/or by individuals;

- booklets that offer support to discipline-based staff and speak their language;

- workshops that you can recommend staff to attend.

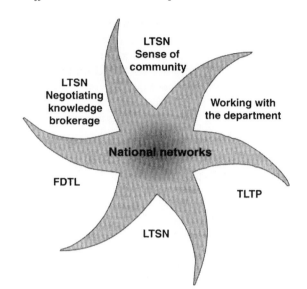

Figure 9.2 *Working from within the discipline: with national networks (UK example given). LTSN = Learning and Teaching Support Network; FDTL = Fund for the Development of Teaching and Learning; TLTP = Teaching and Learning Technology Programme*

Building a sense of community

The task of building a sense of community concerns the less tangible 'how' questions relating to the success of educational developments. Often it appears that a strategy works in one context but not in another. There are many and plentiful evaluation reports available for various educational projects, but little cross-referencing to draw out general conclusions about the effectiveness of educational development. It is to be hoped that many chapters in this book and its companion volume will help you. A working group within the LTSN has been looking at how we build a 'sense of community' within a distributed network, bearing in mind that it is not so easy to get people together to have those important informal coffee, lunch and drink sessions (Mannis and Baillie, 2001).

Negotiating knowledge

The sometimes controversial term 'brokerage' has been used within the LTSN to help people understand the ways in which we try to share good ideas about teaching and learning. I prefer the term 'negotiating' knowledge (Baillie, 2003), as this implies more of a discussion and mutual understanding. A working group of the LTSN has explored the multiple ways in which we 'broker' knowledge, and what seems to work and why. Toolkits of the approaches used to broker knowledge, and the reflections of the success of the various initiatives such as workshops, newsletters, publications and grant schemes, are reviewed on the Generic Centre Web site, http://www.ltsn.ac.uk/genericcentre/ (accessed March 2003).

Working groups
Working groups are set up, as mentioned above, through the LTSN. Another example is the Maths Team led by LTSN Maths, Stats and OR Network (Baillie and Moore, 2002), which involves academics and educational developers working nationally to disseminate effective strategies for helping remedial maths students. These groups are always willing to take on new enthusiasts.

Working part time as a consultant academic

Most of the suggestions given above hold for any context that you work within. However, if you are working part time as a developer, while still continuing to work as a discipline-based academic, some additional ways that you might consider using are given in Figure 9.3 and detailed below.

Balancing research/teaching and educational development
We already split ourselves into several parts when we undertake teaching, research, administration and professional community service. And now we set

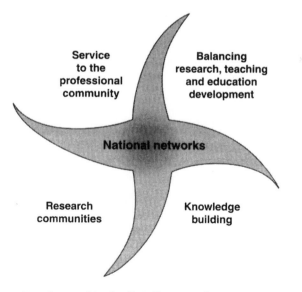

Figure 9.3 *Working from within the discipline: part time*

ourselves another role, as developer! We start to think about writing up what we do as well, and our working lives become even more full. Now, we women have of course always been able to multi-task, but we know that for men it is harder, and we will offer all the support we can! But it is worth thinking about how the various projects that you take on will affect your career. All of us involved in educational development have very colourful careers, and there is no straightforward solution. However, it is my belief that adaptability and creative multi-tasking is the way of the future – not streamlining.

Knowledge building as an approach to bridging the research–teaching gap
I have been engaged in work together with Ference Marton, Shirley Booth and others (Baillie, 2003; Bowden and Marton, 1998; Ingerman and Booth, 2003 forthcoming) where we consider the links between the approaches that researchers take towards knowledge development (knowledge that is new for the world) and those that students take (knowledge that is new for them). I find that lecturers talk about the knowledge that they teach very differently from the same knowledge concepts if they are researching them. In teaching, it is as if the concept has one meaning only. In research, they know full well that there are multiple conceptions. This is an exciting area of research that has firm foundations within pedagogy and yet draws on the thinking of researchers in the disciplines. It can be an important area of development as well as a mechanism for gaining the attention of researchers who may be interested in knowledge but less in teaching.

Working with research communities
If you continue to research in your discipline area, there are lots of ways in which you can engage with your research community and disseminate ideas about teaching and learning. You are part of the family, and are accepted in this way. Suggestions are:

- Go to your normal annual conference and, over coffee, wine and dinner, ask your friends and colleagues what their issues are regarding teaching.
- Submit an abstract and give a talk at this conference about teaching and learning in the area.
- Try to submit a paper about knowledge development in your disciplinary area within the technical journals. The knowledge development process is just as valid a topic for scholarly activity in your discipline as the knowledge content.
- Visit your old mates in departments where you did your undergraduate degree or your PhD. Visit research buddies. You will be welcomed as a friend. You can always discuss teaching in an informal way over coffee.

You could offer to give a talk at their seminar series; they are always looking for speakers.

Service to the professional community

If you are a member of an editorial board, you can help to shape the criteria for acceptable publications and ensure that pedagogic research is welcomed. Ultimately you could do the same for research grant applications if you are on a review board. You are one of the gatekeepers of the knowledge that is allowed to be created and written about!

If you are appointed as an external examiner because of your expertise in a certain disciplinary area, you can have a substantial impact on the education within the departments that you are examining. You can seek advice from previous examiners about what they are usually asked to do. However, you can ask to examine any aspect of the curriculum and make recommendations. It is an enormously important role which you can gain help for from your centre for educational development.

WORKING ACROSS DISCIPLINES

You might work from within an educational development unit or for a director of learning or similar and be asked to develop ways of engaging with departments or individuals at a more disciplinary level. Some interesting approaches are shown in Figure 9.4 and discussed below.

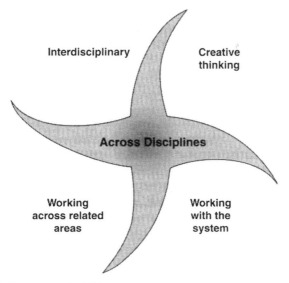

Figure 9.4 *Working across disciplines*

Working with the system rather than against it

An interesting approach at Imperial College London has been to develop a very intensive workshop at a department level that runs annually for each department. New lecturers are asked to come along and present thoughts on what they will teach, how they will teach it and how they will assess and evaluate it. They then receive questions from the others. A discussion ensues for up to one hour. The head of teaching should also be there and can offer guidance on departmental issues and regulations. Facilitating the discussion between colleagues at this level is very beneficial, and this discussion serves many purposes. The subject content itself and how it can be learnt by the students is addressed. Often the head of teaching in turn learns more about what is actually happening in his or her own department. Cross-fertilization among courses can occur.

Working across related areas

Group together subjects that have similar concerns, eg recruitment or practical skills development, and run courses and workshops with a particular focus. Involve outside professionals and employers if possible.

Find out what FDTL projects (or equivalent in your country) have been or are running and whether or not the FDTL might be interested in your joining their project. The Keynote Project led by Nottingham Trent University is an example of a project aimed at helping to develop key skills in students of Materials, Art and Design programmes. The project became very relevant to Materials Science and Engineering students as well, and many different departments joined in.

Interdisciplinarity

Workshops run by the European Union-funded 'Composites on Tour' project (Baillie, 2002) developed the visual thinking processes of Engineering students while enhancing Design students' knowledge about composite materials. Together students created incredible designs in two days. Sheffield Hallam Materials students and Robert Gordon Electrical Engineering students have joined together using videoconferencing processes to work together on projects (Bramhall and Fraser, 2002). Interdisciplinary approaches such as this can be encouraged between departments within a university, or between universities. They help students to reflect on their own learning by experiencing a very different perspective (Bowden and Marton, 1998).

Creative thinking

Students profit from thinking creatively about their learning as well as being more creative in the content of their studies. Creative thinking can be enhanced by 'juxtaposing' two very different thought patterns, as might be found in different disciplines. This idea has enhanced workshops on creative thinking that employ techniques such as TRIZ (the Russian abbreviation for Theory of Inventive Problem Solving) and Synectics (a creative problem-solving methodology) (Dewulf and Baillie, 1999). Much expertise exists in this area, and advice can be sought on ways of enhancing creative thinking in students and running multi-departmental workshops for undergraduate students and PhD students (Baillie and Longman, 2002) and staff.

SUMMARY

This chapter has explored the growing area of discipline-based educational development. It has drawn largely on my own experience (and the scholarly literature) and offers some suggestions for ways of thinking about developments in different contexts. The ideas are intended to guide thinking in the generation of the most effective strategies for plans that will work, that will be sustainable even after you have left, and for gaining acceptance of these plans. It is imperative that we work together on these initiatives and support each other. There are many of us around to offer support and guidance, and who believe in the ultimate aim of enhancing student learning in higher education.

REFERENCES

Baillie, C (2002) Enhancing creativity in engineering students, *Engineering Science and Education Journal*, **11** (5), pp 185–93

Baillie, C (2003) Negotiating scientific knowledge, to appear in *Negotiated Universals*, Campus Press, Berlin

Baillie, C, Emanuelsson, J and Marton, F (2001) Building knowledge about the interface in composite materials, *Materials Research Innovations*, **3** (6), pp 365–70

Baillie, C A and Grimes, R (1999) Peer tutoring in crystallography, *European Journal of Engineering Education*, **24** (2), p 173

Baillie, C and Longman, J (2002) Creative PhDs [Online, accessed January 2003] www.materials.ac.uk

Baillie, C and Moore, I (2002) *Effective Learning and Teaching in Engineering*, Kogan Page, London

Becher, T (1989) *Academic Tribes and Territories*, Society for Research into Higher Education and Open University Press, Milton Keynes

Bowden, J and Marton, F (1998) *The University of Learning*, Kogan Page, London

Bramhall, M and Fraser, M (2002) *Teaching Development Grant Report*, UK Centre for Materials Education, Liverpool

Dewulf, S and Baillie, C (1999) *CASE: Creativity in Art, Science and Engineering*, Department for Education and Employment, London

Fulop, M (2000) Epistemological beliefs of knowledge: a cross-cultural comparison, Private communication

Garratt, J, Overton, T and Threlfall, T (1999) *A Question of Chemistry: Creative problems for curious chemists*, Boston, Longman

Gibbs, G, Habeshaw, S and Habeshaw, T (1984) *53 Interesting Things to Do in Your Lectures*, Technical and Educational Services, Bristol

Habeshaw, S, Habeshaw, T and Gibbs, G (1987) *53 Interesting Things to Do in Your Seminars and Tutorials*, Technical and Educational Services, Bristol

Hazel, E and Baillie, C (1998) *Improving Laboratory Teaching*, Higher Education Research and Development Society Australia Gold Guide, Sydney, Australia

Ingerman, A and Booth, S (2003 forthcoming) Expounding on physics: a phenomenographic study of physicists talking of their physics, to appear in *International Journal of Science Education*

Jaques, D (1984) *Learning in Groups*, Croom Helm, London

Jenkins, A (1996) Discipline-based educational development, *International Journal for Academic Development*, 1 (1), pp 50–62

Mannis, A and Baillie, C (2001) Creative communities, paper presented at Staff and Educational Development Association Conference, November 2001, Manchester

Marton, F and Hounsell, D (1984) *The Experience of Learning*, Scottish Academic Press, Edinburgh

Moore, I and Exley, K (eds) (1994) *Alternative Approaches to Teaching Engineering*, 2 vols, Engineering Professors' Council with the UK Universities' and Colleges' Staff Development Agency, Sheffield

Polanyi, M (1983) *The Tacit Dimension*, Transaction Publishers, Gloucester, MA

Ramsden, P (1992) *Learning to Teach in Higher Education*, Routledge, London

10

Working creatively with national agendas

Diana Eastcott and Neill Thew

INTRODUCTION: NATIONAL AGENDAS

In this chapter, we introduce some of the main agendas in higher education
(HE) today and ways of working with these. We are concerned here with
those agendas that relate directly to teaching and learning, and to the
quality of students' educational experiences. The focus is primarily on the
issues that directly affect developers working within the United Kingdom,
but developers working in other countries will undoubtedly recognize
similar issues in their own work and experience.

Globally, HE is expanding rapidly, but even in this wider context, its
growth in the United Kingdom over the past decade has been extraordinary. Part of the reason for this is the increasingly widely held political
given that any individual who achieves at least an undergraduate degree
will thereby attain significant personal economic gain, which in turn
benefits the democratic and economic well-being of the nation (see Wolf,
2002). Whatever the merits or otherwise of this argument, two of its end
results have been an increasing recognition of the importance of teaching
and learning in HE and the identification of a pressing need to rethink the
curriculum and its delivery. This recognition has led to an ongoing period
of considerable change – its opponents might say 'turmoil' – in which the
emphasis in HE is gradually shifting away from being supply driven and
towards being demand driven; away from instructional delivery (centred on
the teacher and on stable bodies of information) and towards the acquisition of learning (centred on students and on their development of
conceptual understanding and skills); away from a focus on knowledge and
specialization, and towards one based on an ability to perform well in a
wide range of settings and to integrate knowledge and skills. We both
welcome these changes, but acknowledge that they are highly contested

and that HE is likely to face some turbulent years as these changes work through the system. (For further analyses of the current situation in HE, and its likely short- to medium-term development, see Cuthbert, 2002; Jarvis, 2001; Middlehurst, 2002; Ramsden, 1998; Tierney, 1999.)

The current HE teaching and learning agendas in the United Kingdom, then, are best understood within these contexts. Seen in this light, the current emphases on widening participation, improving student retention, equality of opportunity, support for students with disabilities, lifelong learning, and skills and employability are not random, passing fads, but have as their linking themes the drive to increase educational opportunity, and to improve student learning and achievement.

The stance we take throughout the chapter is that staff and educational developers can and should use such national agendas to create positive change and to help move their institutions forward. We suggest that we need to pay particular attention now to linking these different initiatives coherently, because such linkage gives us the opportunity to put teaching and learning centre stage and to enable improvements to be made strategically. We illustrate our position through reflecting on two contrasting case studies. We finish with some further reflections on our own encounters with national initiatives. We aim, by the end of the chapter, to leave you feeling informed, and committed to taking advantage of the personal and institutional opportunities afforded by the current HE scene both in the United Kingdom and more widely.

As developers, locating our work within these agendas brings many opportunities – not least the possibility of accessing external funding. But to begin with, certainly, the shifting mass of acronyms, initiatives, bodies and funding streams is daunting. We remember that as we began our careers in educational development, we sometimes felt like a character in Margaret Atwood's novel *Cat's Eye*: she sees on the snow a spilled tin of alphabet spaghetti and finds herself facing a horrid jumble of meaningless, muddled orange letters. Readers are offered a resource to help with the acronym jungle: the glossary at the end of the book incorporates a checklist of some of the most significant bodies and initiatives currently on the educational development map within the United Kingdom – comparable bodies and initiatives will exist to varying extents in other countries. This map is a changing one, but most of the bodies represented here should be around for some time, even if the initiatives and funding streams change. In any case, getting into the information loop is always the hardest part; once you are in, tracking the changes is much easier. From most of the bodies we list, developers within the United Kingdom might expect to be able to access:

- funding;
- information;

- shared ideas about good practice;

- opportunities to network;

- opportunities to ask questions;

- opportunities for professional development and/or accreditation;

- resources;

- case studies of educational change and/or practice, which are often useful levers to use to help motivate change in your own institution.

If you are a new, or a relatively new, developer, you may initially react to some of the material and the case studies we present below by feeling that they represent a strategic level of work that currently lies beyond your own remit or sphere of influence. We have two responses to this. First, we hope that you find the material interesting and valuable in and of itself, and that it usefully helps explain the wider context within which you are undoubtedly already working. Second, and more importantly, a good working knowledge of national initiatives, and of your own institution's policy stance with regard to these, is of enormous benefit to your ability to be effective. If, through keeping an eye on the wider strategic picture within your own institution, you can demonstrate that your work can help it to achieve, for example, its goals for teaching and learning, widening participation or disability, then you are much more likely to be able to gain support and resources. You are also in a significantly better position to achieve lasting impact and success. It is worth thinking about your own current work and projects as you read the rest of this chapter. Ask yourself: what can I learn from these ideas and case studies that will help me achieve the change I want? The two case studies represent different aspects of a response to that question: one presents some strategies for embedding lasting change and the other for bringing a relatively small-scale project into the mainstream.

INTRODUCTION TO THE CASE STUDIES

We have chosen to use two case studies as the main focus for this chapter on working creatively with national agendas. Our aim in using the case study approach is to enable you to make sense of staff and educational development through the experience of the authors. Both case studies demonstrate strategies and tactics for using national initiatives as levers for educational change. In our choice of case studies, we provide two deliberately contrasting examples. One is from an 'old', pre-1992 university, the other from a 'new', post-1992 university. One is a study of top-down strategic change and development, the other an example of a bottom-up development, perceived by some as marginal, being main-streamed to impact across the university. For readers unfamiliar with the UK university sector, 1992 was the year in which it became possible for the former polytechnics to become universities.

As we explained in the opening section of this chapter, there have been a large number of recent development initiatives in HE, many of which have attracted specific funding. It is becoming increasingly clear that if we are to work effectively with these initiatives, then we need to consider carefully how we link them. By and large, the sector has not yet been very effective at linking initiatives strategically. In part, this has been due to the fact that these initiatives and funding streams have been introduced in a rolling programme over the past three years or so. It is only now, as universities are being asked to produce revised versions of earlier strategies, that clearer links are being made. We would argue that the most effective model is to see the learning and teaching strategy as the 'senior partner', and to consider how the other strategies can help support it. Ultimately, all of the strategies are intended to help universities improve their provision for larger and more diverse student groups, within rapidly changing educa-tional, social and employment contexts. By keeping the improvement of learning and of the student experience at the heart of what we do, ways of aligning strategies flow naturally.

CASE STUDY 1, UNIVERSITY OF CENTRAL ENGLAND IN BIRMINGHAM: LINKING INITIATIVES COHERENTLY WITHIN AN INSTITUTION, WITH THE AIM OF PUTTING LEARNING AND TEACHING CENTRE STAGE

This case study provides an example of positioning learning and teaching strategically within a university through the effective channelling of national agendas by staff and educational developers within the institution.

The starting point for the learning and teaching strategy at the University of Central England in Birmingham (UCE) is the 'Educational Character and Mission Statement' of the university. The mission focuses on national agendas, in particular through seven core values:

- quality;
- employability;
- community, including widening participation and ensuring fair access to HE;

- learning and teaching, where progression and retention are key measures of the university's effectiveness, and excellence in teaching is both encouraged and rewarded;
- lifelong learning, to meet the changing professional needs of individuals and the economy;
- research, scholarship and development;
- partnership, including working closely with franchise partners and other educational institutions.

This mission is supported through three university-wide strategies:

- the Learning and Teaching Strategy;
- the Widening Participation Strategy;
- the Rewarding and Developing Staff Strategy.

These three strategies are interlinked, and it is in the activities of the Learning and Teaching Strategy in particular that aspects of all three can be found. Indeed, as Figure 10.1 illustrates, the Learning and Teaching Strategy is centrally placed in that it is the focus of articulation for work with both students and staff.

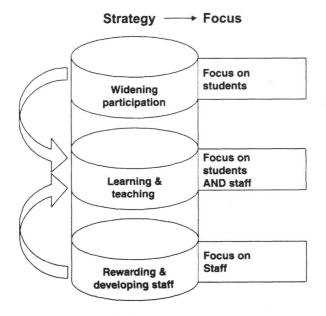

Figure 10.1 *The centrality of the Learning and Teaching Strategy*

UCE has allocated the majority of its Higher Education Funding Council for England (HEFCE) Teaching Quality Enhancement Fund (TQEF) funding to support innovation projects within faculties. This is an example of working creatively with national agendas to ensure that the funding of developments is oriented to the strategic goals of the Learning and Teaching Strategy, which in turn are derived from the university mission and its focus on national issues. In this way, educational change is brought about by linking learning and teaching developments, motivated by individual enthusiasms, to top-down strategic planning for change. Individuals and teams within faculties bid competitively for funding from the TQEF budget against criteria that address national priorities. In the first round of institutional TQEF funding, 1999–2002, 18 projects were undertaken. For example, one of the goals of the Learning and Teaching Strategy, 'to encourage innovations linked to the employability of UCE graduates', is targeted by a Linked Teaching project in pre-registration nursing. It is an approach to the development of skills that involves a recently qualified practising nurse and a UCE physiologist jointly preparing and delivering teaching sessions to pre-registration students. The principal aim is to develop the ability of students to apply physiological knowledge to aspects of their nursing practice (see also HEFCE, 2001: case study 15, p 26).

As Figure 10.2 illustrates, a number of teaching and learning developments managed by the Staff and Student Development Department (SSDD)

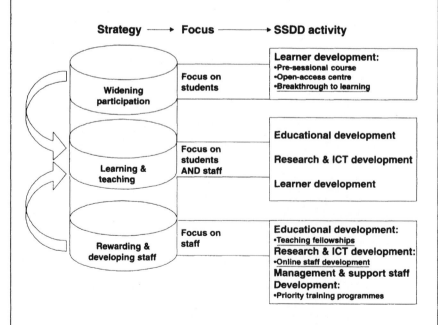

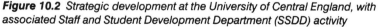

Figure 10.2 *Strategic development at the University of Central England, with associated Staff and Student Development Department (SSDD) activity*

arise from the co-ordinated and planned use of a range of national initiatives and the linking of Widening Participation, Learning and Teaching, and Rewarding and Developing Staff Strategies. The example of Linked Teaching in pre-registration nurse education was provided to show how project funding in faculties is linked to national agendas. The three developments underlined in Figure 10.2 and described below are examples of university-wide educational change.

The Teaching Fellowships project realizes in practice the statement in the University Educational Character and Mission Statement, 'Excellence in teaching and the promotion of independent learning take priority. The university encourages and rewards excellence in teaching.' It provides a mechanism for Rewarding and Developing Staff. Twenty-eight members of academic staff across the university have been appointed as teaching fellows during the first three years of TQEF funding. Good teaching linked to leadership of innovation within the faculty were the main criteria for the appointment of fellows. Evaluation of the scheme to date demonstrates that the academic leadership role has been enthusiastically adopted by the majority of teaching fellows, including taking part in workshop presentations and providing examples of good practice on the university's Postgraduate Certificate in Teaching and Learning. A number of fellowship holders have published and presented academic papers on their developments, acting as key agents of change in raising staff perceptions of learning and teaching as a scholarly activity.

The Online Professional Development programme, run by the SSDD, works with national initiatives on electronic learning environments to provide programmes aimed at academic middle management, course directors and staff with academic course responsibilities. The programmes will enable staff to experience problem-based learning in an electronic learning environment.

The Breakthrough to Learning Project provides an excellent example of synergy between the Widening Participation agenda and the Learning and Teaching agenda. One of the goals of the UCE Learning and Teaching Strategy is to reach out to the community by helping potential university students to develop their skills in the use of academic English. Breakthrough to Learning provides over 300 students in six local sixth forms and eight colleges of further education with a well-tested self-access bridging programme designed to develop academic English, especially in relation to writing skills. The rationale for the project is based on research into the linguistic features of academic language. 'It aims to empower students by equipping them with academic writing skills and teaches them how to move from conversational language to the abstract forms used in academic subjects. It can also help to boost students' confidence by giving them tasks in which they can achieve success' (Mortiboys, 2002). This university-wide development meets the objectives of the Widening Participation Strategy by providing a focus on raising aspirations, preparing non-traditional students for entry, and being 'active in reaching out to all parts of the community and acting as a major force in the struggle against social exclusion' (University of Central England, 2002).

The priority for learning and teaching initiatives at UCE for the next three years of TQEF funding is embedding good practice in the context of links with other relevant strategies. From the point of view of educational development, the aim is to gain further credibility for learning and teaching and to strengthen the role of faculty-based staff as change agents.

The strategy of the SSDD will therefore be to pay particular attention to the work of two faculties in order to develop two case studies of embedding good practice in learning and teaching. The faculties chosen are Health and Community Care and the Business School.

The Faculty of Health and Community Care project, entitled 'Fostering Innovation and Embedding Change in Learning and Teaching', has an action plan that is supported by both senior management and successful innovators who were funded through the last round of TQEF. The aim is to move beyond individual projects to make wider-reaching changes in learning and teaching across the faculty in line with university priorities. Senior management have demonstrated support by meeting the majority of the staff costs for the projects proposed. There is an important link with the UCE Estates Strategy, as the new building programme for the faculty will be taking place alongside the learning and teaching developments, providing the opportunity to create the appropriate learning spaces. The strategic focus for the project is improving student retention.

The next UCE case study will be in the Business School, where much progress towards embedding good practice has already taken place and has been published as a case study in the HEFCE publication *Successful Student Diversity* (HEFCE, 2002: case study 14). An important principle in the revised strategy is the use of a large project team to embed developments and to gain critical mass to provide a positive environment for change and innovation.

CASE STUDY 2, UNIVERSITY OF SUSSEX: CREATING LINKS BETWEEN THE WIDENING PARTICIPATION, DISABILITY, AND LEARNING AND TEACHING STRATEGIES

This case study shows how what might initially have been conceived of as a very localized, even marginal, project (a curriculum review to identify the needs of students with disabilities and particular learning needs) was turned into an opportunity to create positive institutional change. With this project, our primary strategic aim in the Teaching and Learning Development Unit was to demonstrate the benefits of ensuring that the university's Widening Participation, Disability, and Learning and Teaching Strategies, and funding, were constructively aligned. Our secondary aim was to ensure that participation, retention and disability issues not only are seen as aspects of student support but also have a real impact on curriculum design/delivery/evaluation and on teaching/learning/assessment. The primary focus of the case study presented here is assessment. A fuller version of this case study is to be found in HEFCE (2002: case study 22).

The case

Part of the money coming into the university under the Disabilities stream has been used to fund a part-time worker, for a year in the first instance, based in the Teaching and Learning Development Unit. Her project was to lead a curriculum review, identifying the kinds of barriers the curriculum erects that impede the progress and success of different kinds of students. The primary focus was on students with disabilities and special learning needs. However, as the project progressed, it became increasingly clear that some of the key issues identified affect many students. These include, for example, timetabling, assessment loads and diets, and over-reliance on the seminar as the primary teaching and learning mode. Therefore, the project's findings have a great deal to offer us as we attempt to improve the curriculum to meet the needs of an increasingly diverse student body.

Activities

The project worker spent the first term identifying good practice elsewhere in the sector, and interviewing a large number of key players at the university. During the second term, there was a very wide-ranging exercise in consultation/awareness-raising, mainly with academic faculty and students. The third term was spent producing Web-based guidelines and support materials. Crucially, these materials will include a guide for committees in approving new curricula, and its principles will also become part of the university's curriculum approvals process.

One of the project's first interim recommendations was that the university needed to look again at its assessment regulations because these had been identified as a major infrastructural block to progress in developing a more fully accessible curriculum. The project reached this point just as the university's revised Learning and Teaching Strategy was being drawn up. This also takes assessment as one of its focal points. Linking these initiatives has enabled assessment to be pushed to the top of the university's policy agenda. A working group, whose remit includes the requirement to address the needs of disabled students, has been set up to look at developing our assessment strategy. This group has already recommended that:

- Assessment regulations should be expressed in terms of principles instead of in terms of (restrictive) assessment modes. For example, final-year students should be able to demonstrate an in-depth engagement with an area of study, and a percentage of assessed work should be produced under secure conditions where we can be reasonably certain that the work is that of the candidate. This is much more helpful than the previous regulation, which required all final-year students to write at least one dissertation and sit at least one examination.

- In order to help meet the needs of disabled students, colleagues will need to make a specific case that a particular teaching or assessment mode is essential to the achievement of the learning outcomes or to the intellectual integrity of the course if these modes substantially disadvantage certain students. The normal expectation will be that there should be flexible and negotiable ways of delivering and (in particular) assessing outcomes.

Reflections

The way we have tried to steer this project to maximize its impact has been unashamedly opportunistic. The fullest potential of the project became apparent only as it progressed, and we have had to remain flexible throughout. Some of its early successes have been:

- to make concrete links between university strategies and initiatives – the project was funded through Disability money; has been explicitly linked to the Learning and Teaching Strategy; and its outputs in changing assessment regulations should impact positively on student retention;

- to bring a perceived marginal activity right into the mainstream – a project set up to look at disabled students resulted in an overhaul of university assessment regulations;

- to identify institutional, infrastructural blocks to educational development and seek to overcome these;

- to engage with the university at its legislative level, helping to ensure that the curriculum approvals and monitoring process itself becomes a lever for positive educational change, by redesigning it so that it itself embodies a model of constructive alignment between learning outcomes, teaching modes and assessment practices designed to be as responsive as possible to the varied needs of our students;

- keeping sight of developing student learning as the heart of what we do.

Next steps

Like UCE, Sussex is now moving into a second phase of Teaching and Learning Strategy: we are trying to embed educational change by addressing three priority areas – fostering innovation and development, improving student support, and enhancing equality – at an institutional and infrastructure level, rather than at the level of discrete projects only.

CONCLUSIONS

It is clearly very useful to us as developers to have access to the resources, examples of good practice and networks that the national initiatives provide. However, these need to be deployed with extreme sensitivity within our own institutions, as any sense that the changes we are trying to foster have been imposed on academic colleagues from the outside will generally undermine our efforts. We suspect that colleagues at 'old' universities are more prone to sensitivities in this area, as there is often a (mistaken) impression that the drives for educational change – to focus on learning and on the quality of our students' experience – are solely a 'new'-university agenda. So, excessively zealous approaches from us, constantly and uncritically invoking the importance of national initiatives, are unlikely to be productive, no matter how excellent the initiative in question. Our job as developers is to make use of these initiatives for change while remaining sensitive to the range of individual and institutional attitudes towards them.

It is also important to work to enable colleagues to take ownership of national initiatives for themselves. Colleagues' reactions may range from the highly proactive to the resistant. Part of the subtle complexity of our role, therefore, concerns making judgements not only about which national agendas to pursue when, but which faculty colleagues to work with in pursuing these initiatives for the benefit of our students.

There is another way, however, in which the national agendas have been very important to us: getting involved with them has been very significant in our own professional development. For a (relatively) new educational developer, or for a member of academic faculty, perhaps taking on a split role as lecturer and developer, getting plugged into a network of colleagues outside your own institution is vital. The Staff and Educational Development Association is very helpful. For subject or discipline specialists within the United Kingdom, a further route is to explore the Learning and Teaching Support Network (LTSN) subject centre relevant to your area, as already indicated in Chapter 9. For educational or staff developers, we would urge you to consider developing a particular area of specialist expertise alongside your role as a generalist. An in-depth knowledge of widening participation, or disability issues, or changes to assessment, will certainly stand you in good stead as you seek to develop your career over the next few years.

REFERENCES

Cuthbert, R (2002) The impact of national developments on institutional practice, in *The Effective Academic*, ed S Ketteridge, S Marshall and H Fry, pp 32–48, Kogan Page, London

HEFCE (2001) *Strategies for Learning and Teaching in Higher Education: A guide to good practice*, HEFCE, London (accessed December 2002) [Online] http://www.hefce.ac.uk/pubs/hefce/2001/ 01_37.htm

HEFCE (2002) *Successful Student Diversity: Case studies of practice in learning and teaching and widening participation*, HEFCE, London (accessed December 2002) [Online] http://www. hefce.ac.uk/pubs/hefce/2002/02_48.htm

Jarvis, P (2001) *Universities and Corporate Universities: The higher learning industry in global society*, Kogan Page, London

Middlehurst, R (2002) The international context for UK higher education, in *The Effective Academic*, ed S Ketteridge, S Marshall and H Fry, pp 13–31, Kogan Page, London

Mortiboys, A (2002) Retention as a measure of university effectiveness, *Exchange*, **1**, pp 14–16

Ramsden, P (1998) *Learning to Lead in Higher Education*, Routledge, London

Tierney, W G (1999) *Building the Responsive Campus: Creating high performance colleges and universities*, Sage, Thousand Oaks, CA

University of Central England (UCE) (2002) *Educational Character and Mission of the University*, UCE, Birmingham (accessed December 2002) [Online] www.ssdd.uce.ac.uk/Strategy/charactermission.htm

Wolf, A (2002) *Does Education Matter? Myths about education and economic growth*, Penguin, London

FURTHER READING

Higher Education Funding Council for England (HEFCE) (2001) *Strategies for Widening Participation in Higher Education: A guide to good practice*, HEFCE, London (accessed December 2002) [Online] http://www.hefce.ac.uk/pubs/hefce/2001/01_36.htm

HEFCE (2001) *Analysis of Initial Strategic Statements for Widening Participation: Report by Action on Access*, HEFCE, London [Online] http://www.hefce.ac.uk/pubs/hefce/2001/01_36a.htm

HEFCE (2001) *Analysis of Strategies for Learning and Teaching: Research report by Professor Graham Gibbs*, HEFCE, London (accessed December 2002) [Online] http://www.hefce.ac.uk/pubs/ hefce/2001/01_37a.htm

HEFCE (2001) *Supply and Demand in Higher Education*, HEFCE, London (accessed December 2002) [Online] http://www.hefce.ac.uk/pubs/hefce/2001/01_62.htm

11

Being an agent of change

Val Roche

INTRODUCTION

This chapter assumes the role of developers as agents of transformative change through organizational learning. It is written primarily for developers new to the role as enablers of change who operate from a client-driven agenda in which the client is all university staff, not only academics, as well as the overall organization (Knight and Wilcox, 1998; Roche, 1999; Roche, 2001).

With a focus on practical application, the chapter uses a systems perspective to introduce concepts, strategies and techniques to support organizational learning. It illustrates how developers can apply a systemic framework in designing programmes for transformative change. While acknowledging other important perspectives for change, such as action learning (Revans, 1982), self-management (Pedler, Burgoyne and Boydell, 1988) and appreciative inquiry (Cooperrider, 1990), it assumes that a systemic framework underscores these approaches. A systematic approach takes account of the organization's ecology – specifically, inter-relationships between contextual factors, for instance people, events, history and values – to inform holistic programme design. Major implications of this approach for university developers are discussed.

THE CONTEXT OF CHANGE

In the past 20 years, universities across the world have been working progressively through a process of transformation to reinvent and extend themselves, from being solely seats of scholarship and higher learning to also becoming competitive business enterprises in global lifelong education.

Many would argue that such change has brought undoubted benefits to universities, such as financial efficiencies and student-centred thinking. But this radical shift in aspirations has not been without its costs. International research indicates that higher stress levels, anxiety, depression and heart disease are indications of a staff malaise brought about by role conflict, overload, and ambiguity associated with unrelenting change (Kahn *et al*, 1981; Roche, 1999). In the interests of organizational survival, therefore, the pressure is on for universities to become adaptable 'learning organizations' made up of networked communities of staff well able to embrace change. Through a process of cultural transformation, effective developers assist staff to align their personal aspirations and strengths with organizational goals and collectively engage in change. There are exciting opportunities for developers in universities to undertake pivotal roles as agents of change using organizational learning strategies that will assist staff to bridge the education–business divide.

EMBRACING THE CHALLENGES

Given the shifts, it is becoming increasingly clear that developers in higher education (HE) require a more complex overarching methodology to inform their practice as catalysts/consultants for organizational learning (Marshall, 1998; Roche, 2001; Roche *et al*, 2002; Weeks, 1994; Zuber-Skerritt, 1992). Systems thinking provides this firm foundation (Senge, 1990). The metaphor of an iceberg is a convenient way for thinking about an organizational learning framework premised on systems thinking.

The tip of the iceberg, that which we see above the waterline, is the product of organizational learning: transformative change. Below the waterline are techniques, strategies and fundamental principles of organizational learning. Hence nine-tenths of the iceberg – unseen by the traveller – are those critical elements of organizational learning that inform preparation, implementation and review of transformative change cycles. The elements include systems thinking, as well as strategies and techniques encapsulated within constructivism, action learning and critical inquiry frameworks. Thus systems thinking is a useful meta-methodology for delineating the scope and focus for professional development programmes in universities, and for designing strategies to achieve transformation. In turn, participative approaches involving self-management, action learning teams, reflective practice, networked groups and critical inquiry are well-researched tactics for successful organizational learning that complement systems thinking.

By integrating systems thinking into their practice, developers are more likely to gain the support of university managers and staff to undertake a consultant role that is essential for their future long-term survival. Significantly, there has been minimal work published explicitly on the integration of systems thinking in the design of development programmes for HE, possibly because the field has been dominated by learning traditions that, while very important, are insufficient to facilitate organizational transformation. This being the case, the chapter provides an introduction to systems ideas and shows by practical example how core concepts can be integrated with key learning methodologies within a structured framework. The reader is further referred to a range of literature for details about other methodologies, such as constructivist, action learning and self-management.

KEYS TO TRANSFORMATIVE CHANGE: AN ORGANIZATIONAL LEARNING FRAMEWORK

Let me first define transformative change. In the context of this chapter, transformative change is radical change that impacts on culture and practices in an organization and involves individual and collective organizational learning. From the literature about transformative change and my own experience over several decades, there are ten essential keys to successful change. Developers need to be aware of these if they choose to take on the challenge of organizational transformation. The keys include the following:

- Innovators and leaders need to have a long-term view about change.

- Change must be driven and owned by committed people with diverse input coming from inside and outside the organization.

- A supportive organizational culture is needed, in which process is as important as outcomes and key stakeholders are meaningfully sustained through all stages of the change process (education, resources).

- The change process is a collaborative, co-operative, shared learning experience where a 'learning web' – network – forms that utilizes and builds on the strengths and assets of the whole organizational system.

- Leaders/managers need to know and understand the constituency (university system, needs, dreams, culture, history).

- Change comes from seeing possibilities, creating opportunities from mistakes and unexpected experiences (often negative ones).

- Change is a pro-active, incremental and co-ordinated process that facilitates bottom-up stakeholder engagement from the start of the change process – all stages.

- There must be sponsor(s) – champions with whom the university staff can identify. Sponsors are powerful; they can advocate for the system, open doors to smooth the process, access resources (people, funding, technology) across the local and wider HE system.

- The change readiness period must be taken seriously, so that transitional stages such as denial, resistance and exploration are accepted as normal reactions to change.

- Necessary resources are provided to support all stages of the change.

A SYSTEMS THINKING BLUEPRINT FOR PROGRAMME DESIGN IN ORGANIZATIONAL LEARNING

Systems thinking has been used in many social science disciplines for analysing, designing and evaluating change over the past 40–50 years. Interestingly, in university professional development circles it is only recently that systems concepts have become part of the dialogue. So what is systems thinking, and what do systems practitioners do?

In his popular book about learning organizations, Senge (1990) refers to systems thinking as the fifth discipline that is critical for supporting a process of change. According to Senge, 'Systems thinking is a discipline for seeing wholes. It is a framework for seeing interrelationships... for seeing patterns of change... It is a set of principles... it is also a set of specific tools and techniques' (1990: 68). There are four systems principles that are fundamental in programme development for organizational learning and transformative change. These are:

- holism;
- interdependence;
- congruence;
- reciprocity.

First let us consider holism: By embracing a systems approach to intervention, practitioners assume that the organization is a multilevel whole made up of inter-related parts within a series of nested sub-systems. University sub-systems can be identified at four levels: the intra-personal (individual), inter-personal (group), wider organizational (faculty, executive) and extra-organizational (community, society) levels. Although an intervention may span only one level of a university system, nevertheless factors in the total system that could be contributing to local issues should be taken into account in the design of programmes to ensure their integrity. By way of illustration: a developer aims to assist collaboration between a faculty's academic and technical staff in designing electronic curricula. The imperative for change at this level is brought much more sharply into focus as factors in the wider societal and organizational levels are taken into account, such as deregulation, increased competition, accessibility of programmes through electronic technology, and diversity of student needs. Inclusive strategies for change, involving key stakeholders in the design of professional development programmes and their role delineation, would follow from the principle of holism.

The second principle is interdependence. While operating from a systemic foundation, a developer is likely to ask questions about interdependence; that is, about the quality, frequency and types of interaction, relationships and inter-relationships between variables (people, events, structures, environments) within the context of change. In addition, the relationship between different roles, specific responsibilities, and activities can be investigated. The better the quality and extent of interdependence between people, roles and activities across a system in networks and teams, the more opportunity for organizational learning through synergy.

Third is congruence. According to the congruence concept, an organism continually strives to find the best fit between itself and its surroundings. Therefore, using a systemic perspective, the degree of fit (congruence) between people, services and the organization in terms of values, goals, abilities and needs would also be taken into account in programme design. Development programmes are therefore constructed to achieve a *good fit* between such factors and the strategic intent of the whole organization. For example, a systems analysis of academic stress would assume that the problem occurs and is maintained when there is a poor fit between the role undertaken by actors and the requirements of the situation. In this example, professional development programmes would consequently target employee roles and assist people to clarify and modify their roles in order to improve the goodness of fit.

The fourth and final principle is reciprocity. The reciprocity principle assumes a flow-on effect of change in one part of the system across different levels of the system, similar to ripples in a pond caused by dropping a pebble in the water. In using this principle, practitioners believe that development is mediated by appropriate environmental supports, and that the impact of learning in different parts of the organizational learning system incrementally leads to development across the whole system. Likewise, reciprocity highlights the effect of changes in one part of a system on another. It is assumed that these changes can be in both negative and positive directions. For instance, administrative or academic staff can feel powerless to overcome conflicts in their work if a front-line manager uses an autocratic and punitive style. A feeling of powerlessness in one staff member can spread to other staff in the immediate work environment and have an overall effect on lowering staff morale.

In the following practical 'how to' section, these overarching principles and strategies are illustrated in a critical inquiry framework. Developers can use the framework in several ways: for example, to scope, determine the primary target, and negotiate respective roles of participants in an organizational learning programme.

TRANSLATING SYSTEMS IDEAS INTO PRACTICE: A FRAMEWORK FOR PROGRAMME DESIGN

This section introduces key questions and techniques on which developers can draw to design programmes premised on systems thinking, and utilizing well-proven methods derived from action learning (Revans, 1982) and constructivist (Kelly, 1963) traditions. Irrespective of the context, and with slight modification, any groups engaging in a transformative change process can use the framework for scoping, preparing and planning an intervention. In designing programmes, developers are urged to take time, and, with key stakeholders, use the framework to analyse carefully their organizational system. It is important to resist the urgency syndrome and reject the allure of quick-fix solutions or superficial planning. While these are sometimes attractive, simple and hastily designed programmes or packages are unlikely to achieve long-term transformation because they are incomplete, or were designed for other contexts with different sets of actors and circumstances.

Instead, this inquiry explores the organizational context and provides a foundation for change. Developers can use the framework in devising strategies to safeguard self, team and organizational learning. Examples of questions, related strategies and tools are shown in Table 11.1. The rest of the chapter seeks to explore how these strategies and tools can be used within a framework of inquiry.

Inquiry 1: Stakeholder analysis stage 1 – Who are the people?

As indicated in Table 11.1, the question 'Who are the people?' provides an important starting point for exploring the context and likely target of change. This inquiry involves a stakeholder analysis. Stakeholders are those people who are, or are likely to be, impacted in some way by a proposed change. A stakeholder analysis can be conducted in two stages. Stage 1 of the analysis explores the organizational context: levels of the system, key variables, stakeholders. Stage 2 of the investigation examines needs and expectations to be

Table 11.1 *A reflective framework and strategies to scope programmes for professional development and transformative change*

Areas of inquiry	Questions premised on systems principles	Strategy, technique
1. Who are the people?	Understanding constituency, linkages and participation: key stakeholders – people, groups, networks, power sources	Stakeholder analysis Ecological map
2. What are stakeholder values, aspirations and needs: – for organizational learning? – of professional development roles?	Needs and expectations of stakeholders for organizational learning? Needs and expectations of stakeholders about professional development roles/programmes for organizational learning?	Role, programme design and clarification for organizational learning
3. Degree of fit between expectations and current situation?	Degree of fit between programmes, professional development roles and ideal, needs of constituents?	Repertory grid and gap analysis
4. What do people interpret as the issues and needs requiring attention?	What are the major issues, targets/priorities for change and future local ideal situation?	Mental models and envisioning a better way: rich pictures, vision statements, storytelling
5. Requirements or givens requiring transformative change? 6. What is a vision for the future? 7. Where is the leverage for change?	What's worked well in the past? What opportunities, assets, drivers do we have? What are the forces for and against change; pockets of resistance?	Force-field analysis, asset audit
8. What has been learnt from the exploration for programme design, and/or change direction?	Do the current programmes fit with people's needs and the organizational values, priorities and practices? If not, what needs to change? What is the team's shared vision for change? What's working well in the current situation that we can take forward into the future? What's the leverage for change? How will we achieve a good fit between individual, group and organizational goals?	Rich picture or vision statement mental model Structured reflection – SAID process (considered later)
9. Starting point for enabling transformative change?	How will we create ownership? How will we build in participation, safeguard representation?	Representative steering group
10. Who should be involved in leading/steering the change?	How will we build networks for individual and team learning across situations? What's the purpose of a steering group?	Secondary stakeholder analysis and role clarification of group

Source: Adapted from Roche (1999)

addressed by the transformative change programme. Note that issues considered in Chapter 2 will be relevant for this stage of the investigation.

A useful tool in stage 1 of the stakeholder analysis is an ecological map. In an ecological map, the organization is represented as a circular entity like a Russian nested doll within which there are several smaller circles and different 'nests' representing levels of the system that are inter-related. Within each level are stakeholders – individual people, groups – who use the services of, or work in, the system. There are no set rules for the number of layers and the amount of detail put into an ecological map; it depends on how the developer wants to use it in scoping and targeting the change domain. However, it is important to identify key variables: groups who can drive and/or inhibit change.

Dick (1996) identifies four categories of stakeholders. Using these categories in the area of learning management systems (LMS) technology for remote students, these could be:

- direct – those likely to be directly involved in or impacted by a programme, for example lecturing staff's need to learn how to use LMS, such as Blackboard and WebCT;
- indirect – groups who have an interest in seeing that the LMS is used, for instance students in remote locations and information and communications technology (ICT) offices in the university;
- experts – people who have expertise, knowledge in an area related to the topic of concern, for instance graphic artists and programmers;
- activists – those who feel strongly about the concern and will champion a cause, such as the deputy vice-chancellor, ICT staff, the student union.

Start by drawing an ecological map of the system:

- Working outwards from the centre, identify different levels in the organizational system that are related to the issue at stake.
- Identify key stakeholders and influential factors in each level.

Reflect on the following:

- What are the potential links/relationships between people, environmental variables to forge change?
- Consider groups likely to be supportive or resistant to the change.
- Identify power sources and estimate their strength in relation to the focal issues.

Figure 11.1 provides an example of an ecological map detailing sub-systems, stakeholders and influential factors in effective professional development programmes for transformative change. Key groups and factors are denoted by an asterisk.

Inquiry 2: Stakeholder analysis stage 2 – What are stakeholder values, aspirations and needs, and what is the fit between expectations and the current situation?

As shown in Table 11.1, in this stage of the exploration, and using information from Inquiry 1 above, the developer examines the fit between clients, stakeholders' expectations, needs and aspirations, as well as the requirements of the situation and current services provided to support change. The aim of the activity is to identify instances of 'poor fit' or gaps, and work towards their resolution. This stage is important to indicate scope, gaps, and likely targets of a development programme. In this area, constructivist techniques can be very useful because they enable people to share personal assumptions and ideas about a topic and sketch out core attributes about a future ideal state.

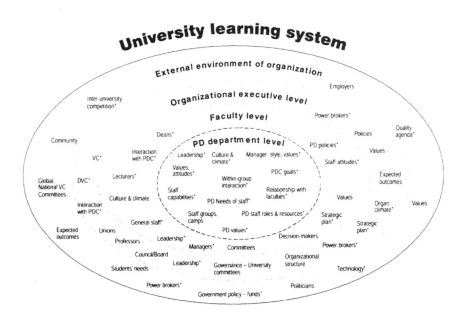

Figure 11.1 *An ecological map showing stakeholders and key influential factors on developer roles, structure and programmes. PD = professional development; PDC = professional development centre*

A constructivist technique derived from Personal Construct Theory (Kelly, 1963) is the repertory grid. The technique is an established research and development tool. It uses structured individual or group interviews in which the participant constructs a verbal portrait detailing effective and ineffective attributes concerning a subject under examination. Research studies demonstrate the value of the grid for individual professional development, group role clarification, team development, planning, research, teaching and learning (Kreber, 1999; Pope, 1993; Roche, 1999; Roche, 2001; Roche *et al*, 2002; Zuber-Skerritt, 1991).

The basic components of a grid are constructs and elements. Constructs help people organize their perceptions of the world. Elements are examples of areas of the subject under study. For example, in Roche *et al*'s (2002) study, participants compared different types of development programmes, such as workshops, self-directed learning, project teams, to identify key attributes of effective programmes for transformational change.

The person elicits the grid by proceeding through a series of predetermined triadic comparisons of elements resulting in the production of bipolar constructs that describe attributes of the topic under study. To elicit the bipolar construct, participants are asked, in comparing three elements, which two are similar, in what ways, and how the third element is different. In this way, opposing construct poles are drawn out of the comparison. Constructs are subsequently rated in terms of their alignment with the elements and, in the final stages of analysis, can be clustered according to the degree of numerical relationships between them. For example, it is possible to detail attributes (constructs) closest to effectiveness and use these as a guide in role and/or programme clarification. Detailed information about Personal Construct Theory and the repertory grid is provided in Roche (1999).

Table 11.2 shows the kind of information that a repertory grid workshop exercise can generate for future learning discussions between stakeholders (Roche *et al*, 2002). Data generated in this study (Table 11.2) contributed to the design of future professional development programmes using the three dimensions identified by the group: scope (capacity building and capability enhancing), target (general, academic, managerial staff) and principles (adult learning, systems – organizational learning).

Overall, the repertory grid assists people to generate collective meaning. This is particularly important in academic environments, which are well known for their isolationist cultures. Together with the stakeholder analysis, a grid provides the basis for understanding the present and envisioning a future world that is explored in the following sub-section.

Table 11.2 *Academic, general and professional development staff constructs detailing attributes of effective professional development support*

	Effective constructs	Ineffective constructs
Construct clusters in the target *dimension*		
Cluster 1: Individual based	• More formal • General useful knowledge • Other people present information • Timely/individual	• More flexibility in what you learn • More structured one-off event • Decide what you want to learn • Directed limited engagement
Cluster 2: Team based	• Context situation driven • Ownership of programme by group • Problem based/ organizational improvement	• Fixed topic/predetermined • Ownership outside group • Skill based/self-determined
Construct clusters in the scope *dimension*		
Cluster 3: Formal lower-order learning	• Task orientated • Team based • Structured	• Development of individual • Individual centred • May not be strategic
Cluster 4: Contextual – multitask – higher-order learning	• Group/applied • Meets group goals/ objectives • Job/task specific • Applied/practical/focused	• Individual • Meets individual needs • Risk of not being relevant • Group-based theory/ 'talk not do'
Construct theory in the **principles** *direction* Cluster 5: Principles of effective support	• Supports adult learning theory • Human interaction • There is a 'product' • Content focused	• Usually one to one • Self-focused • Supports process • Interactive by nature

Source: Roche *et al* (2002)

Inquiry 3: What do people interpret as the development issues requiring attention and what is their vision for the future?

Table 11.1 indicates the key questions in this stage of the reflective inquiry, which are 'What are the major issues, targets/priorities for change?' and 'What is a vision of a future ideal situation?' Rich pictures are a powerful constructivist technique for investigating these concerns. Originating from a branch of systems thinking – Soft Systems Methodology (Checkland, 1989) – rich pictures can be used in a variety of ways for planning individual, team and group learning. Rich pictures are pictorial interpretations of issues to be addressed, visions of a future ideal situation. An example of a rich picture of 'the University of the Future' is shown in Figure 11.2, and an accompanying explanation appears in the following case study. Other examples and explanations of rich picture drawing can be found in Checkland (1989).

RICH PICTURE EXPLANATION: THE UNIVERSITY OF THE FUTURE

The University of the Future is likely to be a multinational conglomerate that is privately owned, pragmatic, and a continually evolving entity. It will have a global student population and meet the needs of students located on Earth, other planets and space stations. The university will be made up of collaborative autonomous satellite companies located in continents across the world, each with its particular niche and speciality.

The University of the Future will operate as a knowledge and e-technology broker. It will also have massive interplanetary real estate interests for income generation. However, it will operate with limited physical facilities and have a simple infrastructure with regional satellite headquarters maintaining the university's human face to the public. The university will depend on integrated information and communications technology for its total operation, as well as revenue raising. It will accumulate substantial earnings by leasing real estate, technology, equipment and staff to community groups, government and businesses across the world for their day-to-day business operation, enhanced communication, knowledge creation and dissemination.

Staff numbers will decline, so that the University of the Future will have a very lean and multiskilled workforce serving a student population of millions. Most academic, general and technical staff will be private contractors. Contractors will work together in collaborative temporary self-managing task teams as communities of practice. This small body of international staff will telecommute, and work within a project management structure, as opposed to being located in teaching disciplines or permanent support functions. Many academics will be educational information technology specialists, instructional designers, while others will undertake assignments as organizational coaches, mentors, and research consultants to outside companies.

Students of the university will connect to a virtual campus and form learning sets with peers across the world. According to his or her enrolment profile, a student may be connected to different sets simultaneously. Paper-based books will become museum exhibits. Most, if not all, of learning and teaching will be electronically mediated by videoconferences, satellite broadcasts, and asynchronous and synchronous conferencing. There will be limited face-to-face conferences according to the needs and wishes of the customer. For example, instead of annual examinations, student teams will be invited to present their work at virtual or face-to-face conferences. All other work will be marked electronically by administrative staff using prepared templates.

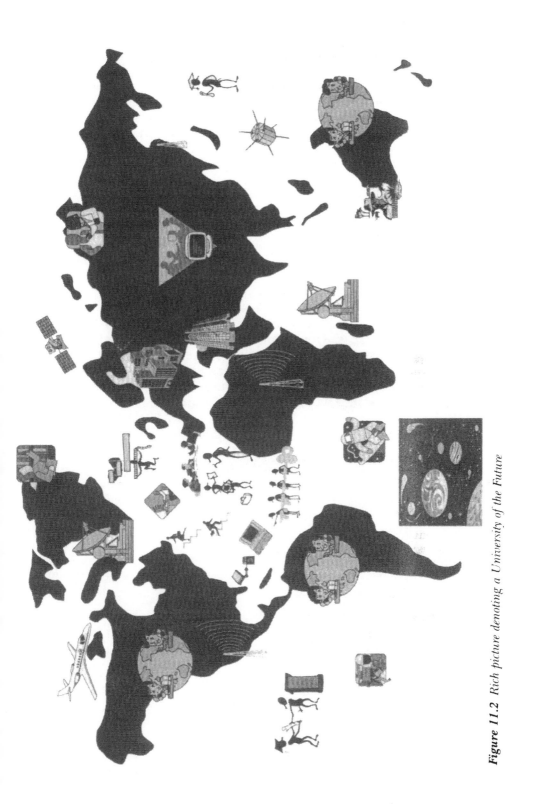

Figure 11.2 *Rich picture denoting a University of the Future*

Rich picture drawing during a workshop can be good fun, particularly when people become fully engaged in the activity. The procedure energizes a group to be creative and co-operative as they explore the influence of key issues, such as values and culture, in an area of investigation. The activity also assists people to share mental models to determine future direction. Also, at the final stage a rich picture can be distilled into a 40-word statement about the 'problem' at issue and a possible future vision of what success will look like if it is addressed. However, participants can disengage from a rich picture activity if they are habitually reliant on linear thinking and the written word. Therefore, this technique should be used with caution if the facilitator does not know the audience or omits to give people a choice of engaging in the picture drawing or more common methods like brainstorming.

Drawing a rich picture
There are no fixed rules for drawing a rich picture. It depends on the key questions being asked about an issue or target for change or a successful future state. A picture can target the whole or only parts of the organizational system. Information obtained in an earlier stakeholder analysis can be depicted in the drawing. To identify targets for change and/or to envisage the future, the following aspects could be included in a picture:

- people – individuals and different stakeholder groups likely to be affected by the change;

- language/symbols that express relationships, attitudes, culture;

- problems – challenges to be addressed/overcome at the centre of the change issue within and between groups, and in the context;

- barriers to change that include any of the above attributes;

- activities, situations that work well currently, and/or have done so in the past: strengths, assets that can be incorporated into a future vision and offer leverage for change;

- other important features that capture the essence of the system in organizational structures, buildings, facilities, campuses and/or in the community.

It can be useful to show important linkages between different parts of the picture, and to draw a line around the major target(s) for change. The picture is then interpreted, and shared in a group. Often a written explanation is recorded.

At this point in the reflective investigation, change agents are well placed to summarize and reflect on the meaning of data for programme design using information gathered through stakeholder analysis, repertory grid and rich pictures. Consequently, three further stages in this inquiry first consider leverage for change; second, reach a conclusion about the scope and target for change; and finally, determine how best to enable key stakeholder participation in programme development and implementation.

Inquiry 4: Where is the leverage for change?

A preliminary vision statement is critical for identifying a target or targets for change. So too is the realistic scoping of a change effort. Scoping involves defining the boundaries of an intervention. In doing so, the change agent is well advised to take into account potential forces that could support or negate the desired change within an organizational context, combined with an audit of strengths that will help to drive any transformation.

A combined force-field analysis and asset audit assists the change agent to identify leverage and assets for, as well as energy against, a proposed change to determine the potential viability of an emerging agenda. Interestingly, examples of force-field analyses can be found in many organizational behaviour references, for instance Cummings and Worley (1997), while strategies for developing asset audits can be located in the community-building literature, including Kretzmann and McKnight (1993).

Two major questions are:

- What opportunities, assets, drivers do we have for the envisioned change?

- What are forces for and against the envisioned change; what are the pockets of resistance?

Positive and negative energy and assets across the organizational system are determined in order to make clear key factors that need to be taken into account in scoping change and reworking a preliminary vision. These include forces:

- within the person – intra-personal;

- between people in an immediate working group, between departments, faculties – inter-personal;

- overarching organizational factors – wider organizational (including structures, resources, culture);

- between the organization and the community, society at large – extra-organizational.

Table 11.3 illustrates the use of this technique. The example taken is a staff development section that needs to design flexible development programmes spanning all staff in the university system as well as spanning radical change at team and individual levels.

Should an investigation reveal that resistance factors outweigh leverage factors, and this be reinforced by other sources, a considered response in the next stage of the reflective framework may well be to modify the scope of change and build in activities that target resistance, for example influential lobbyists against change. In the above example, a priority target, and an essential precondition for systemic intervention, could well be assisting developers to make a paradigm shift from being learning experts to being catalysts of change. This would be an intervention in its own right. Consequently, in the penultimate stage of the investigation programme, designers bring together information from all sources and reflect on learnings that can be used for concluding the scoping of a programme.

Inquiry 5: What has been learnt for programme design and/or change direction from the exploration?

The SAID process (Hogan, 1995) is useful for critically thinking about linkages behind all the sources of data and their relationship to the local

Table 11.3 *Asset audit, drivers and resistance factors in the design of flexible development programmes, within an organizational system*

Factors at different levels of the system	Drivers (+)	Resistance (–)	Assets
Intra-personal	Strong commitment to change	Developers' role – focused on curriculum development rather than on organizational learning	Skills in facilitation
Inter-personal	Need to develop faculty-based development services	Developers located outside faculties – no insider knowledge; no credibility as change agents	Outsider status enables objectivity – conflict mediation
Wider organizational	Executive commitment to set aside funding	Gap between espoused theory and practice	Resources, policies
Extra-organizational	Diversity customer needs for flexibility	Community does not understand degree of cultural shift, costs to make changes	LMS technology available

change agenda. Further reflection can be used for reflection on action, as well as planning and other purposes, as explored in Chapter 12. SAID is a mnemonic for the four stages of an experiential learning cycle as follows:

- S – Situation recall (eg of the people, activity, images) and a reflective observation of the event or activities to do with a focal issue.

- A – Affective domain, recording feelings and emotions about the event/situation.

- I – Interpretation or theorizing about the meaning of the event/situation. *What does the experience mean?*

- D – Decisions about future action: the final stage of reflection and recording of new knowledge. This stage leads to active experimentation based on the increased understanding.

I use the SAID process extensively in my work to debrief on experiences and to guide and improve performance in organizational learning programmes, as well as workshop facilitation. For example, in Roche (1999), journal entries record critical encounters with programme participants and university committees in an organizational learning programme: the SMART project – Self Management and Reflective Practice in Teaching and Learning. Journal reflections enabled me to consider events in terms of future required actions for both individuals and the SMART programme as a whole.

In partnership with key stakeholders, this structured reflection process is likely to lead into the final stage of the critical inquiry that centres on enabling participative organizational learning interventions for transformative change.

Inquiry 6: Enabling participative organizational learning interventions for transformative change

As is pointed out in earlier sections of the chapter, sustainable change goes hand in hand with stakeholder participation and ownership, and in terms of starting the process of change and maintaining momentum this means:

- A change management steering group has been formed, and has worked out its role and responsibilities in the overall change management process.

- The change management steering group is representative and includes people from the key stakeholder groups.

Within a transformational leadership paradigm, which is critical for organizational learning, the change agent facilitates and builds a vision with key stakeholders who can steer the process. In addition, the steering group provides a body of trusted people who can collectively critically reflect with the developer and influence the wider context in the desired direction.

Successful steering groups are a safeguard to achieving coherence or a good fit between what is designed to support change and the requirements of the situation. In this way, they promote interdependence and through their advocacy and modelling role they foster reciprocity so that goodwill about the programme and practices promoting change gradually become embedded in the wider organizational system.

For example, in the SMART project (Roche, 1999) the advisory (steering) group was formed in stage 1 of the project and had cross-university representation of both general and academic staff. Members elected a chairperson whose role was to call, chair and record meetings of the group. The chair also reported to the project sponsor, the university's Teaching and Learning Committee, and, with the co-ordinator, was jointly responsible for administration of the project's budget. The advisory group met frequently in stage 1 of the project to plan programme parameters and methods. It also was an important support network for the co-ordinator during the two-year period.

Rose and Buckley (1999) present a useful model for building a steering group and/or other self-directed teams. I have adapted this in the formation of a leadership steering group in the early stages of a complex change process, and for team development in an organization that was undergoing massive change. The framework is shown in Figure 11.3.

Key questions therefore in this starting point for change are:

- Who should be involved in leading/steering the change group membership?
- What is the role of the group and members within the group?
- How will we build in participation, safeguard representation?
- What is the purpose of a steering group?
- What resources can we mobilize to start to move on this change?

This section has completed an explanation of the key areas for deliberation in identifying the target, scope and boundaries of an inclusive organizational learning programme for transformative change. The inquiry opens the door for future collective action that incrementally builds to individual and organizational transformation. *Change is not a 'quick fix' process* that emanates from the latest management fad or package. Learning is a partnership. It requires

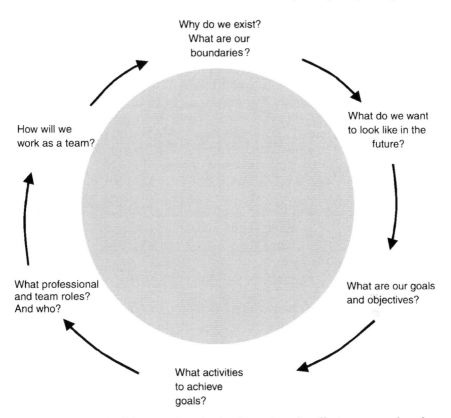

Figure 11.3 *A cyclical framework and critical questions for effective teamwork and transition*

Source: Adapted from Rose and Buckley (1999)

courage, authenticity and steadfastness to a goal, empathy, integrity and a willingness to take risks. The structured inquiry goes hand in hand with these values and provides a road map for the early stages of the journey.

THE JOURNEY AHEAD

Unquestionably, organizational learning projects have the potential to be powerful catalysts for transformative change, especially when they are played out in contexts open to change, and they utilize systemic principles, together with complementary strategies derived from action learning, constructivist and self-management traditions. This chapter has presented a comprehensive framework that developers can use to start a process of participatory change leading to organizational learning. With minimal adaptation, the framework applies across a range of organizational contexts.

At the outset of the chapter, it was pointed out that systems thinking is a complex, emergent meta-methodology in academic staff development, traditionally dominated by pedagogic concerns to the exclusion of forays into organizational learning. Nevertheless, by force of circumstances, a persuasive argument can now be made for the urgent integration of systems thinking into everyday professional development practice.

Without a doubt, systemic practice means a much more demanding role for developers who accept the challenge to be agents of change in a much wider domain compared to a learning specialist role. Although a potentially hazardous journey for many, this route also offers many exciting opportunities for growth where challenges are accepted as part of the learning process in the overall transformation.

ENDNOTE

This chapter provides a practical introduction and guide to systems practice in transformative change. While the simplistic interpretation of complex concepts could be criticized by some, I make no apology. Instead, my goal has been to make the complex simple and accessible. My interpretation tries to avoid elitism and minimizes the unintelligible jargon often associated with systemic explications. My account of systems thinking attempts to provide a coherent approach that the neophyte can utilize when seeking to initiate transformative change. I hope this chapter emancipates you to join with others to confront the challenge of change.

REFERENCES

Checkland, P (1989) An application of soft systems methodology, in *Rational Analysis for a Problematic World*, ed E. Rosenhead, pp 101–20, John Wiley, Chichester

Cooperrider, D (1990) *Appreciative Management and Leadership: The powers of positive thought and action in organizations*, Jossey-Bass, San Francisco

Cummings, T and Worley, C (1997) *Organizational Development and Change*, Southwestern College Publishing, Cincinnati, OH

Dick, B (1996) *Stakeholders and Participation* (accessed December 2002) [Online] areol-r-l@scu.edu.au

Hogan, C (1995) Creative and reflective journal processes, *The Learning Organization*, **2**, 4–17

Kahn, R L, Wolfe, D M, Quinn, R P, Snoek, J D and Rosenthal, R A (1981) *Organizational Stress: Studies in role conflict and role ambiguity*, Robert E. Kreiger, Malabar, FL

Kelly, G (1963) *A Theory of Personality*, W W Norton, New York

Knight, P and Wilcox, S (1998) Effectiveness and ethics in educational development: changing contexts, changing notions, *International Journal for Academic Development*, **3**, pp 97–106

Kreber, C (1999) A course-based approach to the development of teacher-scholarship: a case study, *Teaching in Higher Education*, **4**, pp 309–25

Kretzmann, J and McKnight, J (1993) *Building Communities from the Inside Out: A path toward finding and mobilizing a community's assets*, ACTA Publications, Chicago

Marshall, S L (1998) Professional development and quality in higher education institutions of the 21st century, *Australian Journal of Education*, **42** (3), pp 321–34

Pedler, M, Burgoyne, J and Boydell, T (1988) *Applying Self-development in Organizations*, Prentice-Hall, New York

Pope, M (1993) Anticipating teachers' thinking, in *Research on Teacher Thinking*, ed C Day, J Calderhead and P Denicolo, pp 19–33, Falmer Press, London

Revans, R (1982) *The Origins and Growth of Action Learning*, Chartwell-Bratt, Bromley

Roche, V (1999) Self-managed organisational transformation: a case study of roles in higher education, unpublished PhD thesis, School of Social and Workplace Development, Southern Cross University, Lismore, NSW

Roche, V (2001) Professional development models and transformative change, *International Journal for Academic Development*, **6** (2), pp 121–29

Roche, V, Towers, S, Gunson, C, D'Abrew, N and McLain, L (2002) Developers and transformative change, submitted for publication

Rose, E and Buckley, S (1999) *Self-directed Work Teams*, American Society for Training and Development (ASTD), Alexandria, VA

Senge, P (1990) *The Fifth Discipline*, Random House, Sydney

Weeks, P (1994) Facilitating a reflective, collaborative teaching development project in higher education: reflections on the experience, unpublished PhD thesis, School of Curriculum and Professional Studies, Faculty of Education, Queensland University of Technology, Brisbane, Queensland

Zuber-Skerritt, O (1991) Eliciting personal constructs of research, teaching, and/or professional development, *Qualitative Studies in Education*, **4**, pp 333–40

Zuber-Skerritt, O (1992) *Action Research in Higher Education: Examples and reflections*, Kogan Page, London

12

Learning from experience

John Cowan

INTRODUCTION

My message with regard to the title of this chapter could have been presented very briefly. For all that I really wish to suggest to you is that people do not learn much from experience on its own; rather do they learn from what they *take* from that experience. I would then further argue that they can be assisted in this 'taking' process if they are consciously prompted, by themselves or by a teacher or a peer who facilitates their development, to question themselves about how they do things, how well they do them and how they might do them more effectively next time.

So what, you may well ask, is in all the following pages that might be of use to you in assisting both your own learning as a developer and the learning of staff and students? It's a good question, and deserves an answer before you decide to go any further. I offer:

- First, an outline of the views that I hold in relation to the development from experience of personal and professional capabilities – because I hope it will assist you, by knowing where I am coming from, to make your judgements about the suggestions I present in this chapter.

- Next, three examples to illustrate and amplify some of the beliefs I have declared and outlined.

- From that, an analysis of the approach that (I believe) features in each of these examples.

- Then a three-in-one example, within which I maintain that various categories of 'learners' were developing relevant capabilities in a similar manner. I will try here to show that development arises from much the same process, and so should follow much the same approach, whether the developing learner is a student, a teacher on a staff development programme, or someone engaged in delivering staff development.

- At this point, I will relate these various examples to the commonly quoted constructivist model (Kolb, 1984). I will then expand this to what I believe to be a more appropriate *socio*-constructivist one (Cowan, 2002), wherein the important contributions made by interactions between peers to learning and development are more explicitly recognized – and planned for.

- After that, I freely admit that I will digress somewhat, to ride a hobby horse. I will advance the argument, illustrated by yet another example, that conscious and evaluated 'active experimentation' is both a valuable and (currently) a somewhat neglected component of these two models of personal and professional development.

- Finally, I include two afterthoughts, offering you food for further thinking about the whole business of developing capabilities through experience.

WHAT DO I JUDGE IMPORTANT FOR PURPOSEFUL DEVELOPMENT THROUGH EXPERIENCE?

My contribution in this chapter derives from, or has led to, a number of convictions that I hold about the development of personal and professional capabilities by students and by their teachers. I hope it will be helpful to you if I table these views frankly, at the outset, so that you can check them out as you read what follows.

- I define teaching as the purposeful creation of situations from which motivated learners should not be able to escape without learning or developing (Cowan, 1998). My qualification regarding motivation is a carefully considered caveat. As a teacher, I am wholeheartedly committed to do all that I can to motivate those who learn with me; but I cannot guarantee that by such efforts I will succeed with those who are determinedly unwilling to learn, for whatever reason.

- I see staff development activity as just another form of 'teaching and learning', in terms of that definition.

- My approach to supporting learning is to help my students, my colleagues and myself to become action researchers (Cowan, 1987) of our own practices, in the belief that we will thereby enhance our learning and development.

- I believe that we first learn about concepts from examples (Skemp, 1982); and that meaningful theorizing and formalizing come later. I am therefore committed to explaining, in the present context as elsewhere, through the use, initially, of examples.

EXAMPLES ILLUSTRATING THE ABOVE OPINIONS

Please consider for yourself the extent to which my examples are in line with the views I have just summarized. In the first example, for instance, I will describe (through an example, of course!) what it can mean for a student learner to become an action researcher of his own practices.

Example 1

About 20 years ago, Andrew was a research subject in a small study I was carrying out into problem solving in Applied Mechanics (Cowan, 1983). I was getting him to talk out his thoughts aloud (Cowan, 1980) as he tackled several problems of the type he was meeting in the course of his engineering studies. One day I met him in the corridor. He buttonholed me eagerly, because he had had a thought that he wanted to tell me about. 'These problems in Applied Mechanics are really Applied Maths, aren't they?' he asked – and I agreed. 'Well, I've been thinking about how I decide what to do first in problems in *Applied* Maths, and comparing that with how I decide what to do first in the problems they give us in *Pure* Maths, which the Maths department teaches us. And it's quite different. In Applied Maths, we... *(he detailed his approach succinctly)*... whereas in Pure Maths, we have to... *(and again he detailed crisply)*.'

Andrew had learnt a restricted amount about problem solving in mathematics from his past experiences at school, and in his first term at university; he learnt a lot from the experiences of a brief period in my research study, when he was constantly prompted to record how he did things; and when he had subsequently chosen to think and question himself, about why he opted for each approach.

That week I lost a research subject – and recruited a junior colleague in the process of action-researching our practices when we are tackling mathematical problems. I noted that he, like many whom I encouraged thereafter to follow in his self-analytical footsteps, moved up the mathematics class in ranking order – and that in a subject which I did not teach!

My second example is again about encouraging someone to become an action researcher of his own practices. In this case, the learner was a teacher, and my 'staff development' for him was a form of teaching on my part.

Example 2

I met a young man on a train a few years ago. We were travelling home from a conference that we had both attended. He told me that he was trying to get his students to think critically and creatively in their project work. It was not going too well for them, or for him. He questioned me about my work with learning journals, which I had described during part of my conference presentation. He speculated about the usefulness of getting his own students to do something similar. Bluntly I asked him why he did not begin with himself – keeping a thoughtful record of what he was planning, and why; of what he *expected* to ensue; of what *did* happen – especially in terms of critical incidents; and of what all of that suggested to him, for the following week.

He went on to do just that, for a year. Each week he sent his journal and analysis of critical incidents to me for Rogerian comments (Rogers, 1983). I had rashly agreed that, as his 'critical friend', I was to display unconditional positive regard for his aims and methods, empathy with his struggles, and congruence when that could be exercised without appearing to suggest or instruct (Rogers, 1967). Over that year, he reported a marked decline in negative reactions from his students, noted that plans on his part more often translated into reality, and recorded significant improvement in the students' project work (S Jones, private communication, 2001).

He had not learnt much simply from the accumulated experiences of the past semesters; he did learn a lot from the experiences of a year in which he was constantly prompted to question himself about how he did things – and why; and about how well that had worked out; and about how he might do better next time.

My final example for the moment relates to my own learning from experience.

Example 3

As a staff developer, I recently ran a series of workshops for teachers in one particular university, which sought to support applications by experienced staff for membership of the Institute for Learning and Teaching in Higher Education (ILTHE). The first workshop was rated highly on the 'happiness sheets'. Nevertheless, I found scope for improvement, as always, when I thought back. I felt some disappointment with some of the questions that had arisen – because I thought, or hoped, that I had already covered them adequately in my brief inputs. When prospective applicants sent their draft applications to me for my comments and helpful suggestions, I noted a tendency to describe rather than, as I had advocated (or *thought* I had advocated), to explain decisions and choices, in relation to a rationale. When I identified features with which I was dissatisfied, I pushed myself to plan directly for changes that should lessen these negative features the next time.

Over a sequence of some six such workshops, continually refined as I have described, the proportion of attenders who went on to make acceptable applications to ILTHE increased. Moreover, I judged the quality, relevance and usefulness to other participants of the questioning during the workshop to have improved, and I received fewer and fewer drafts for comment that were in need of major surgery or rethinking.

Helping experienced colleagues to prepare a critical and analytical review of their practices was a particular type of workshop outcome, one that I had not really had to address previously. I didn't learn much from the mere experience of preparing and delivering that very first workshop. I learnt by consciously pushing myself during the event, and with the help of a colleague, to identify critical incidents that might be associated with both successes and failures – and by actively seeking out and iteratively experimenting thereafter with possible ways of bringing about improvement.

Comment

I hope you will have noticed that I have been devious in my choice of examples. I have shown action-researching in practice. And I have also been trying to show that the same principles and practices about learning from experience can apply to the learning and development of students, of teachers and of staff developers themselves.

WHAT IS THE UNDERLYING APPROACH, THEN?

I find that it is effective in developing what I like to call capabilities if I try to plan an activity in which all participants will:

- if possible, actively seek out and consider optional approaches to the task – to 'doing it', whatever 'it' is;

- then 'do it' in a real-life situation, following their carefully defined and chosen option;

- arrange to gather, or better still have gathered, relevant data describing that experience;

- interrogate those data, looking for patterns, surprises, anomalies, successes and weaknesses;

- assemble the best possible analysis of what these data convey;

- probably also judge how well the doer did the task, judged against clear and predetermined criteria; and hence where and how there may be scope or need for improvement;

- consciously plan that next time round the participants will actively experiment with their revised method, again collecting data so that they can in due course review its effectiveness;

- think, analyse and summarize in everyday vocabulary, however colloquial, that is meaningful to the persons concerned.

ILLUSTRATING THAT APPROACH, WITH THREE EXAMPLES IN ONE

This compound example, which seeks to illustrate the approach outlined in the above section, relates to the development of process analysis in the Basic Technology Year at Aalborg University in Denmark, in 1993. The Basic Technology Year at that time was centred upon classical project orientation. The main activity for these first-year students was group-working on a problem that each group chose and specified, from within a problem area that the teachers had decided. Some basic instruction in core topics was provided; otherwise any instruction relevant to particular project topics was negotiated – and provided only if it did not directly address the challenge of the chosen project.

At the end of the semester, groups presented both their project report and a process analysis relating to the way they had handled the project process. There was an oral examination by internal and external panel members. My involvement was sought because the course leader judged that if the process analyses were suitably and effectively restructured along the lines of an approach that I had taken in Britain (Cowan, 1995), they would have the potential to contribute more than hitherto to the students' learning and development.

A small group of teachers agreed to explore such an approach with me; and a group of about 25 student volunteers also agreed to assist us. The activity took place in the gap between first and second semesters, in a large guest house on the Danish coast, free of other visitors. Three Scots facilitated the entire event – two of whom, as it happened, had had no previous experience of this type of staff development.

It was accepted without discussion that:

- Tasks that formed a part of the process analysis were not described. Instead, they were demonstrated (in English) for a context (Science, in Scotland) that was not quite that of the participants. However, the demonstrations were sufficiently understandable for participants to grasp what *they* were then being asked to do, in Danish and for their own context (Technology, in Denmark).

- All working by Danes with other Danes was to be in their own language – which meant that they often had to choose a vocabulary that came naturally and meaningfully to them.

- There were no opening inputs other than of the suggested structure for the programme. Facilitation was planned to arrange that participants simply drew upon their own recent and directly relevant experiences, to construct their own learning and development accordingly.

- Theories and models were input only *after* participants had had the opportunity to think back over their experiences, and to generalize. They were then able to compare their generalizations with the theory advanced.

The event lasted overall for a week; but participants arrived and departed at different times within that week. First came the Scots facilitators and their Danish opposite number. Together, over 24 hours, they finalized the detail of events and timings. Then came the Danish teachers. They were taken by the facilitators through a sequence in which they were to identify what was being asked *of them* in project orientation; how *they* went about that assortment of demands upon *them*; how they judged their effectiveness in their use of the relevant capabilities; what judgement they then reached; and where they saw scope and suggestions for improvement therein.

In the various workshop activities – whether for teachers or students – no one was told what to do. They were *shown* what to do, although in an example taken from a different context from their own; and they were then invited to repeat the activity they had seen, in relation to their own context and experiences. Tasks for the Danish teachers were exemplified in this way by the trio of Scots facilitators. The Danish facilitator chaired the event.

The three Scots worked as one who questioned, one who responded, and one who recorded on a flipchart what was unearthed. The questioner, for example, might open the sequence of enquiries described in the previous paragraph by asking the respondent to detail what abilities and activities are required of a British supervisor of Science project students. This situation, although one that the Danes could comprehend, was markedly dissimilar to their own work in project orientation with their Danish students of Technology. So, when the demonstration was concluded, with the summary that the recorder had been assembling displayed (in English, of course) on the flipcharts, the Danish facilitator only had to ask, 'Is it like that for us, in the Basic Education Year?' to be given in response a firm (Danish) 'No!' 'Well, then, please work in trios as the Scots have done, and assemble in Danish lists of the abilities and activities that are important for supervisors in *our* context.'

Consideration, in a similar way, of what each supervising activity demanded, in detail, followed on thereafter, first with the Scottish example, and then with the Danish version – each leading into general analyses and self-evaluations. After each trio had concluded their questioning and recording, they naturally wanted to see what the others had produced. Often they found an item here and there that was in accord with their own experience, but that they had not themselves identified, but now wished to add to their lists. The end results were strengthened by this peer interaction.

Now the students arrived. Danish teachers took Danish students through the similar sequence. In trios, Danish teachers would ask, answer and record what *they* had to do in the course of project supervision. They would then ask students, working in similar manner, to unearth what *they* had to do – as project students. Again there were no inputs other than the demonstrations to show the students the type of analysis and the form of closing self-evaluation expected of them. No hints were offered about what that analysis and evaluation might contain. As in the programme for the teachers, trios freely interacted with their peers after the conclusion of each stage of the programme, strengthening their understanding of the processes in which project work had engaged them by sharing perceptions and analyses with peers.

The event moved towards a conclusion. First, it being the month of January (and at the request of the *Danish* facilitator), all took part in a memorable Burns Night in the full Scottish tradition, greatly assisted by the arrival of a charismatic Scot who was the Danish facilitator's partner. Haggis, bashed neeps and champit tatties (ie chopped turnip and mashed potatoes) were consumed with ample libations of the national drink, and the traditional toasts and recitations were made before the evening broke into Scottish country dancing. These elements, I need hardly explain, were certainly not *necessary* features in the total programme I am describing. But I thought them significant, for a reason that I am about to mention.

On the morrow, before the students departed, Danish and Scots facilitators helped the students to review and unpack their feelings, experiences and learning during what had been for them almost a three-day event. Reactions were positive, and expectations for improved performance in the next semester were optimistic. Perhaps this was due to the immediate euphoria of having done something different, perhaps it was a result of having been invited specially to participate, or perhaps it was due to the lingering effects of the festivities of the previous evening.

The students departed. The teachers, facilitated by their course leader, carried out their own review and unpacking, informed but not directed by the many observations of a factual nature that the Scots had made, recorded and summarized during the all-Danish events involving the students and their teachers. This was in the spirit of illuminative evaluation (Parlett and Hamilton, 1972), to which concept the teachers had been introduced. The teachers' reaction to the event was positive. But in their final judgement, they were acutely and realistically conscious that they would be unlikely to persuade their colleagues to undertake such a process analysis, let alone the other ongoing activity during the semester which they had learnt the Scots would also advocate.

While the teachers unpacked their experiences, so too did the Scots trio – identifying what had been the critical incidents during the five previous days, what could be taken from these – and generally what *they* had learnt in respect of both their roles and their programme. Thus all three groupings finished by focusing on the question of what they might do 'next time', so that their next use of the relevant capabilities would be an improvement on their use in the activity that had just been completed.

Mindful of the possible optimism in the students' immediate reaction, the planners returned to the students five months later, at the end of their second semester of project orientation. They asked for more considered and consolidated feedback. They were told, 'Yes, we've thought and talked about this, and we are quite clear what we want to say to you. It is that you must *never* do that again!' The students were thanked for their frankness, although the facilitators admitted to disappointment and asked why such a strong conclusion had been reached. The students explained, 'Because we had *so* much advantage over the other 375 students. You must *never* do that again, unless you do it for *all* of the students in the class.' So it was that this pilot became a standard practice in the following year, somewhat streamlined in timing, and without the residential experience or the Burns Night celebration. In the event, it was to be almost 10 years before the full curriculum shift ensued (Kolmos and Kofoed, 2002).

THE CONSTRUCTIVIST MODEL – AND A SOCIO-CONSTRUCTIVIST MODIFICATION

The underlying model for the pilot was explained to students and teachers *after* they had followed it. It was the classic diagram attributed to Kolb (1984) (see Figures 12.1a and 12.1b). Students, teachers – and two inexperienced staff developers – began from a simple declaration of a suggested programme that they were invited to follow, having agreed to suspend any disbelief until after that active experimentation with it.

All participants (including the staff developers) followed a facilitated structure of carefully chosen tasks, framed around questions chosen to assist them to extract meaningful development from their experiences. Students and teachers began their travels around the cycle by dwelling upon their recent experiences – on the first semester project (students) and during several recent semesters (teachers) – as shown in Figure 12.1a. In contrast, the two inexperienced staff developers and the Danish facilitator began from a thorough briefing on the underlying model, and how it should influence the sequence of structured activities for the development of capabilities in which they would engage, as shown in Figure 12.1b. In

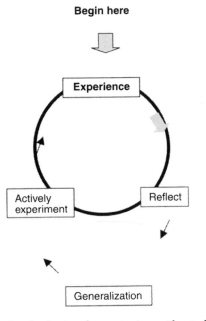

Figure 12.1a Kolb cycle – beginning from experience (the students and the Danish teachers)

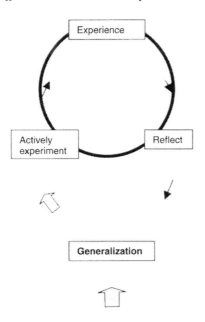

Figure 12.1b *Kolb cycle – beginning from a (given) generalization (the two inexperienced staff developers)*

both cases, though, this is a *constructivist* model, in that learners constructed meaning and learning from their experiences.

They also related their analyses to their memories of prior experiences and to the reactions of their fellows, before reaching their personal generalizations about how to do this kind of thing next time, with more effect than on the present occasion.

In each layer in my example, I hope you can discern these features:

- All participants, whether students, teachers and staff developers, were following similar types of programme, with their own development and relevant capabilities in mind.

- The 'teaching' effort centred on capabilities that participants themselves identified.

- The 'teachers' firmly set, prompted and facilitated the structure – but made few inputs about rationale or the theoretical model.

- Attention was given separately to the various elements of the process. These were:
  - the describing of recent past experience;
  - the questioning of that experience;
  - the analysis of the outcomes of that questioning;
  - the formulation of possibly new or revised generalizations arising therefrom;
  - the conscious planning of how these generalizations might be tested out in the next new but similar experience.

- The 'teachers' posed what appeared to be pertinent questions where these were not being asked and considered by participants – and pointed out non-sequiturs in participants' reasoning, as well as omissions in their lines of argument.

As my use of similar such activities has progressed over the years (Cowan, 1998), I have come to see that it is more purposeful to expand the classic Kolb diagram, perhaps to Figure 12.2 (Cowan, 2002). This still models the structuring provided by the facilitation of the tutors, but further acknowledges the constructive interactions and inputs that can be derived from the contributions of peers. The enriched model is a strongly *socio-constructivist* one, as Vygotsky would perhaps present it (Wertsch, 1985). The learning, meaning and development that emerge depend heavily on interactions with others as well as upon the learner's experiences and personal thinking. The model thus incorporates and encourages both the intramental thinking (dialogue with oneself) that is the characteristic of the Kolb cycle when it is followed almost in isolation; and the intermental thinking and dialogue with others that is a feature when interaction with peers features strongly.

IS SUFFICIENT ATTENTION GIVEN TO ACTIVE EXPERIMENTATION?

In the past two decades, we have seen a strong emphasis on what is called reflection (Weedon and Cowan, 2003 forthcoming), based upon all that Schon has written on that topic (eg 1987, 1991). Mostly, it takes the learners from particular experiences to transferable generalizations. I suggest that regrettably little attention is generally given to the reverse activity, which Kolb titled 'active experimentation'. I believe that we can all gain a lot more from our experiences if we devote conscious thought and effort to active experimentation. Please allow me to illustrate this with yet another example.

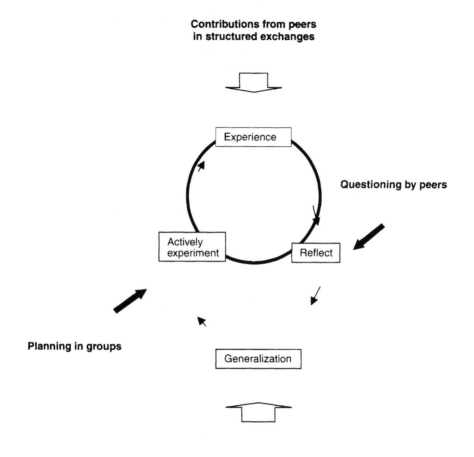

Figure 12.2 *The elements of socio-constructivism (contributions to intramental thinking)*

In the Open University, there have always been acute challenges for those responsible for tutorial support of learners, where a small number of students are spread across a large geographic area, and holding a tutorial in one convenient location is not a viable option. In such cases, tutorial groups have been brought together for many years through the use of telephone conference calls, in which perhaps six or eight students meet on one call with their tutor. Many tutors are highly regarded by students and colleagues for the quality and effectiveness of the support that they provide in such circumstances.

I found that there was, in 1992, general agreement about what constitutes 'good practice' in such tutorial work (George, 1983). It occurred to me that these generalizations might rudely be classed as 'folk wisdom' – for there was no evidence to justify them. Without doubting such well-established guidelines, I planned to seek evidence of their effectiveness by actively experimenting with the approach as practised. I brought together eight of the most respected and experienced conference-call tutors in Scotland for an inquiry in which they would capture evidence of the outcomes of 'good practice' for their students' learning.

The method was simple and non-confrontational. Tutors were to work in pairs, with a partner from another discipline. The pairs changed regularly. When a conference-call tutorial was to be given, the teaching tutor recruited two students who would be willing to receive a call from the enquiring tutor within ten minutes or so of the tutorial. They were told that the enquirer would be asking them:

1. What was the most significant learning for you as a result of that call?

2. What was it that the tutor did that made the call effective for you?

3. Were there any parts of the call that you found ineffective for you?

4. May I pass on this information to your tutor?

The last of these questions was invariably answered affirmatively; but it was felt important to offer that let-out clause.

The enquiring tutor contacted the two volunteer students as arranged, and then called the teaching tutor, who had meanwhile been considering his or her own answers to these questions – asked in respect of what the teaching tutor took to have been the students' learning and their learning experiences. The teaching tutor declared his or her impressions before hearing what the students had reported. The pair might then discuss the findings, and any possible mismatches between the tutor's perceptions and the students' reporting, which were often marked and deemed important by the tutor. Within a short time, usually less than a week, the roles were reversed, and the enquirers became the tutors on their own courses, with the first tutors now doing the enquiring.

Some four months into the inquiry, I arranged a conference call for the octet plus myself, to review progress. After 40 minutes of busy conversation, one of my colleagues commented that I had not been saying anything, which was unlike me. I responded that I had been thinking – because it seemed that the project had been a total failure. 'What do you mean?' more than one exclaimed indignantly. 'We've just been reporting all that we've learnt from this, and taken from it. Every single one of us has already found several ways to improve, and we've all been consulting with our students to see what we are all getting from such changes.' 'Well,' I replied, 'I had *hoped* that you would be taking snapshots of best practice and what that achieves for student learning. Instead you are telling me that as a result of finding out the nature of the learning, and of the learning experience for your students, you have learnt, and experimented, and developed your practice.'

I had my tongue in my cheek, of course. Although the outcomes, which were marked changes in practice, were surprising in their magnitude (Lee, 1997), I had indeed expected that it would be worthwhile to test out the assumptions that underlay accepted generalizations. Since that study, the Open University has widened the scope of that pilot, to involve a greater range of tutors, and in settings beyond the telephone conference call (George, 2001). Always, the result of engaging in active experimentation and assembling of findings (eg George and Cowan, 1997) has been along the lines of what was to become a frequently heard reaction: 'I would never have imagined that. I'm glad I know. I know now what I want to do about it.'

What point do I hope you will take from this anecdote? Much the same point as that with which I started in my very first example about Andrew – except that now it applies to many teachers and their students, as well as to a single student. I am suggesting that it is when we, teachers *and* learners, become action researchers of our own practices, and when we think about what our findings tell us for the enhancement of learning and teaching, that effective development is most likely to ensue. I am also suggesting that this happens most effectively when teachers and learners join together to engage in action-researching the nature of the experience in which they both participate – an experience in which one is rather more of a teacher, and one rather more of a learner.

DIFFERENTIATING TYPES OF REFLECTION

Reflection is a vague term. It has been used in so different many contexts in the past 20 years, to describe so many different types of thought, that I do not find it a very helpful term – and so have avoided its use in this chapter, until quoting Kolb in the previous section. My main reason for avoiding the term is because I feel it is too often applied to fundamentally different types of self-questioning.

Thus, I find it helpful, for myself and my students, to present reflection first as asking questions of oneself, and trying to find the answers. With that starting point, I suggest that it is unfortunate and limiting that 'reflection', as Schon described and popularized it, has become restricted to its application within the Kolb cycle. Schon himself has pointed out that there can be both reflection-*in*-action and reflection-*on*-action. In the model (Figure 12.3) that I have followed in designing activities for my students (Cowan, 1987, 1998), I have introduced a third type of reflection, or of question asking, namely, reflection-*for*-action. This is that self-questioning that yields a list of aspirations or needs or hopes for a development experience that lies immediately ahead.

Do these distinctions matter? I suggest that they do. For the types of questions we pose of ourselves should differ in these three types of reflection. When we reflect *for* action, we should be first of all mulling over the nature of our present capabilities, and then asking ourselves, 'What am I looking for now, in terms of my development?' In contrast, a closing reflection-*on*-action is a review in which we look back over a recent developmental experience and pick out what we can take forwards from that into our next experiences. We are asking ourselves, 'What have I learnt from that which should be useful to me in the future?'

In between these, we have the reflection-*in*-action, where, prompted perhaps by serendipity or structure, we pause briefly to ask ourselves, 'What is happening here? Is it significant? If so, in what way?'

Reflection-on-action, as occurred towards the end of the Aalborg residential event, was initially analytical and then became evaluative. As it became evaluative, it at times identified learning on which the learners felt able to depend, and also other items that went on to their next shopping list for development. I submit that it is important to distinguish between being analytical, as we so often are called upon to be in the Kolb cycle, and being evaluative, as we are before we begin on further development, and

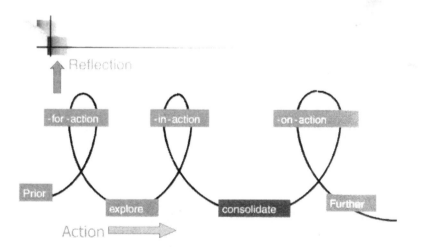

Figure 12.3 *The Cowan loopy diagram*

after we hope it is satisfactorily concluded. Consequently, I find myself designing and delivering quite different activities for my students, and for myself, according to which type of reflection I am seeking to promote at a given point in time. Might such a distinction help you to design and plan for reflection more effectively? – I wonder.

AN AFTERTHOUGHT

Consider, for example, the not-so-simple task of designing an activity to facilitate reflection-for-action. This can be complicated by the way in which learning needs are internalized by the aspiring learners.

I want to learn how to use the 'Draw' function more powerfully on PowerPoint, and I don't mind telling you or anyone else; just ask me. It's a readily *declared* need, as far as I am concerned.

On the other hand, I'm a bit ashamed of the fact that I can't do much for myself in assembling Web pages. If you want to know my need, you'll need to arrange safety, if not anonymity, for me, so that I will be secure from laughter or scorn when I make it known. It's a known, but so far *undeclared*, need for me.

I wish I could improve my capability to handle silences and lack of response in workshop-style activities. I can't put my finger on what it is that I need or want, but I feel that if I once met it, I would know it was for me. I'm a bit like Tigger (Milne, 1928) searching for the perfect breakfast; I *know* the right thing for me must be there, but I haven't pinpointed yet what it is. If you want to help me to get it on your list of learning needs during any reflecting-for-action, then you'll probably have to plan to arrange for me to explore options until I find the right one for me. It is still *undefined* as far as I am concerned.

I have many needs of which I am unaware – so I cannot give you an example. My friends and colleagues could probably tell you what should go on my reflection-for-action list. But if you want *me* to recognize them, and engage with them, you'll need to challenge me in such a way that they emerge for me, without my feeling confronted and threatened. They are *unrecognized* needs, for me (at least until now).

Four ways of regarding learning needs, and four types of facilitative activity to edge them on to any reflection-for-action list.

CONCLUSION

I hope I have persuaded you to endorse, or at least consider further, my conviction that people don't learn much from experience alone. Rather, they learn from what they *take* from that experience. I also hope that I have persuaded you that they can be assisted in such development if they are consciously prompted, by themselves or a facilitator, to question themselves about how they do things, how well they do them, and how they might do them more effectively next time. If so, I encourage you to ponder over this argument, and my afterthoughts, and work out, perhaps through active experimentation, what that may have to offer you and your students – especially as you facilitate your own development from experience, in the company of others.

FOR YOUR FURTHER READING, AS SOURCES OF ALTERNATIVE VIEWS AND SUGGESTIONS...

... I would recommend, first and foremost, Jenny Moon's splendid, scholarly, highly readable and extremely useful book on reflection in learning and personal development. It is rich in thought, ideas and references; I often return to it; I never re-read it without finding something new for me to think about, and to do something about.

On a different tack altogether, you will have noted that I have found that it is when we search purposefully to discover the nature of our students' actual learning and of their learning experiences with us that we are prompted to see need for change and development, and to find ways of bringing that about. The key source here is a text by Angelo and Cross describing what the North Americans call Classroom Assessment Techniques, which on this side of the Atlantic we would probably call methods for formative evaluation and of data collecting with our own students.

You may well find that learning from experience is much more effective if it is not a solitary activity. Even if you don't go to the lengths of setting up an action learning set, the features of that approach contain many elements that are powerfully constructive. I would spend time reading McGill and Beaty, not least for their splendid amplification of what such as Carl Rogers meant by empathy, congruence and unconditional positive regard. They expand helpfully on what place these qualities can have in our teaching and development, and how they can be brought about. On the other hand, if you want a direct practical guide to action learning sets, in which you and your peers can help each other to learn from experience, I'd start with Weinstein.

A book that troubles me, in the most positive sense of that word, is Brookfield's thoughtful consideration of challenging adults to explore alternative ways of thinking and acting. I find it worth reading slowly and thoughtfully.

Finally, I hope it may be permissible to mention my own little book on becoming an innovative university teacher, which has a chapter in particular concentrating on how we as teachers can learn from and within experience.

SUGGESTED READING

Angelo, T A and Cross, K P (1993) *Classroom Assessment Techniques*, 2nd edn, Jossey-Bass, San Francisco

Brookfield, S D (1997) *Developing Critical Thinkers*, Open University Press, Milton Keynes

Cowan, J (1998) *On Becoming an Innovative University Teacher*, Open University Press, Milton Keynes

McGill, I and Beaty, L (2001) *Action Learning*, rev 2nd edn, Kogan Page, London

Moon, J (1999) *Reflection in Learning and Professional Development*, Kogan Page, London

Weinstein, K (1999) *Action Learning*, 2nd edn, Gower, Aldershot

REFERENCES

Cowan, J (1980) Improving the recorded protocol, *Programmed Learning and Educational Technology*, **17** (3), pp 160–63

Cowan, J (1983) How engineers understand, *Engineering Education*, **13** (4), pp 301–04

Cowan, J (1987) Education for capability in engineering education, thesis for the degree of DEng, Heriot-Watt University, Edinburgh

Cowan, J (1995) Research into student learning – Yes, but by whom? in *Teaching Science for Technology at Tertiary Level*, ed S Törnkvist, pp 51–59, Royal Swedish Academy of Engineering Sciences, Stockholm

Cowan, J (1998) *On Becoming an Innovative University Teacher*, Open University Press, Milton Keynes

Cowan, J (2002) The impact of pedagogy on skills development in higher education (HE), Keynote address, Hertfordshire Integrated Learning Project (HILP) Project Conference, University of Hertfordshire, July 2002

George, J W (1983) *On the Line: Counselling and teaching by telephone*, Open University Press, Milton Keynes

George, J W (2001) Higher education learning development: final report, internal paper, Open University, Edinburgh

George, J W and Cowan, J (1997) *Tutoring by Phone: Staff guide*, The Robert Gordon University, Aberdeen

Kolb, D A (1984) *Experiential Learning: Experience as a source of learning and development*, Prentice Hall, Englewood Cliffs, NJ

Kolmos, A and Kofoed, L (2002) Developing process competencies in co-operation, learning and project management, *Proceedings of International Consortium for Educational Development (ICED) Conference*, Perth, Australia

Lee, M (1997) *R11 Telephone Tuition Project*, Open University in Scotland Project Report, Open University, Edinburgh

Milne, A A (1928) *The House at Pooh Corner*, Methuen, London

Parlett, M and Hamilton, D (1972) Evaluation as illumination: a new approach to the study of innovative programs, Occasional Paper 9, University of Edinburgh Centre for Research in the Educational Sciences

Rogers, C R (1967) *On Becoming a Person*, Constable, London

Rogers, C R (1983) *Freedom to Learn for the 80's*, Merrill, Columbus, OH

Schon, D A (1987) *Educating the Reflective Practitioner*, Jossey-Bass, San Francisco

Schon, D A (ed) (1991) *The Reflective Turn*, Teachers College Press, Columbia University, New York

Skemp, R R (1982) *The Psychology of Learning Mathematics*, Penguin Books, Harmondsworth

Weedon, E M and Cowan, J (2003 forthcoming) The Kolb cycle: has its use changed in 10 years? Report of discussion seminar at Conference on Improving Student Learning: Theory and Practice – 10 Years On, Brussels, Oxford Centre for Staff and Learning Development, Oxford

Wertsch, J V (1985) *Vygotsky and the Social Formation of Mind*, Harvard University Press, Cambridge, MA

13

Developing professional expertise in staff and educational development

Peter Kahn

INTRODUCTION

The higher education sector is now marked by rapid and complex change. Indeed, Barnett (1997) claims that the sector is characterized by what he calls super-complexity, in which unpredictable transformation occurs on a frequent basis. Staff and educational developers seek to help shape this change, particularly as far as learning and teaching are concerned. They also help others to variously lead, undertake and cope with change, as explored in Chapter 11. Developers clearly require extensive and growing professional expertise if they are to carry out these tasks effectively.

How then might a staff and educational developer gain and maintain the requisite expertise? Indeed, what is the requisite expertise? After all, the expertise that is required may vary significantly depending on the context in which the developer works. Furthermore, for any one developer, this context may change several times over the period of his or her career, as new jobs are taken on or as institutions are restructured. As higher education (HE) continues to transform itself, developers are also likely to be confronted by previously unimagined institutional cultures and by the need to acquire new sets of skills. In this environment, career progression is far from straightforward. All this suggests that developers will need to take a close look at the initial and continuing growth of their professional expertise.

This chapter explores the nature of the requisite expertise, which for any given developer will vary with his or her own unique context. This context includes at least the individual developer's role, the discipline(s) in which he or she undertakes development work and the nature of the unit and institution in which he or she is located. Hence it is important to consider factors that influence the choice of which expertise to develop. The chapter goes on to consider the specific elements of such a development programme. However, before looking more closely at the nature of the expertise that developers require, we first of all consider the existing experience that individuals typically bring with them as they embark upon a career in staff and educational development. Such analysis also serves to provide a more secure basis on which to analyse the expertise that needs to be developed.

EMBARKING ON DEVELOPMENT PRACTICE

In one sense, staff and educational development may be termed a tertiary profession, in that staff and educational developers probably have a primary discipline or profession; the field in which they gained their initial qualification; and then in many cases a further profession, that of academic or lecturer. In another sense, staff and educational developers may be seen as being in a secondary profession, in that the clients with whom developers work are themselves highly specialized professionals. Not only is it the case that the clients are experts in a specific body of knowledge, and in many cases with national and international reputations, but their professional practice also involves passing on this knowledge to others. This clearly affects the nature of the professional expertise that is required of developers, as we will consider in due course. It also influences the way in which someone embarks upon work as a developer. On one level, staff and educational development can usefully be seen as a subset of academic practice. In this case, a typical career path would be to gain expertise as an academic and then to specialize within the subset of that practice that is focused on enhancement, as sketched above. Isaacs (1997) points out that staff often transfer into development work following recognition for their excellence as teachers. This is evidently the route taken by Alan Jenkins, as he outlines in his case study below. For instance, an excellent teacher might engage in an enhancement role on a part-time basis, while still retaining his or her academic identity and position within an academic department. Alternatively, the teacher may move to a central unit and work on the enhancement of practice across a variety of subjects.

However, the situation is yet more complex. It is possible to be an expert in a specific area of academic practice without having personal experience of other areas of practice. And indeed it is to a certain extent possible to gain a significant body of this expertise in fields other than academic work.

This is particularly the case for expertise in teaching and learning, perhaps with the experience gained in secondary or further education, as Sue Clayton outlines in the second of the two case studies below. Webb (1996) points out that staff typically move into a development role after experience as a teacher. The study by Fraser (1999) confirms that teaching typically forms the initial career path for developers. It is thus possible to focus one's development work on a specific area of academic practice without having specialist expertise in other areas of that practice. It is of course also possible to possess expert knowledge of a given academic discipline without actually working as an academic. Such knowledge will be particularly relevant where a developer is working with a specific disciplinary community, as evident in Chapter 9.

It is also worth emphasizing that work that involves enhancing a specialist practice will also draw on skills that will not necessarily be developed by simply engaging in the practice itself. The work of training established professionals, for instance, demands facilitation skills, which may be developed in training other professionals. Specialist skills can, for instance, be developed in the more technical aspects of learning technology. These technical skills may subsequently be applied to assist academics in making use of the technology, or indeed in developing new learning technologies. Staff may therefore transfer into development work following relevant experience in many other fields.

Finally, it is also possible for someone to embark upon a career as a developer right from the outset of their career, as Isaacs (1997) also identifies. Project-based work, for instance, provides evident scope for recent graduates effectively to begin an apprenticeship as a developer. Furthermore, certain forms of development practice involve direct working with students, and this type of work is often suited to recent graduates. We see this most clearly where recent graduates or PhDs join educational development projects, as considered in Chapter 8, or organizations.

In each of these above cases, however, the transition to work as an educational developer requires the development of further expertise. Isaacs (1997) points out that further expertise is required for the two categories that he identified: moving into development work following recognition for one's excellence as a teacher, and becoming a developer at the beginning of one's career. It is thus essential that new developers, and those who are responsible for assisting their development, can identify gaps in their professional expertise and clearly understand the nature of the specialist expertise that is required of development work.

CASE STUDY: CHANGING CONTINENTS (BY ALAN JENKINS, WESTMINSTER INSTITUTE, OXFORD BROOKES UNIVERSITY)

To me, as someone who long taught and researched geography, a love of distinctive places and moving from one place to another is second nature. I know the rush of excitement of the strange – but also that loss of 'moorings', and the questioning of what this place has to offer. That analogy serves as advance organizer for my advice to you, from my experience of moving into educational development.

To give you a sense of where I am writing from; some 12 years ago I moved into the then Oxford Centre for Staff Development at Oxford Brookes University; at first half time, keeping my moorings in geography, and soon full time. I now work from what is the School of Education, with a university-wide responsibility for linking teaching and research in the disciplines and for supporting pedagogic research. I recognize that you are in a different place and in effect a different time to me, so here are pointers from my experience:

- Expect, enjoy and learn from your new environment. People here have learnt much about working with staff to improve teaching.

- Know that you are on a steep learning curve. I was (I think!) an excellent teacher, and could convey to other teachers what *I* did and why. But that is very different from working with staff with *their* concerns and needs.

- Hold on to your connection to your discipline. It gives you an authority with staff in all disciplines. You have done their job. But to be effective, you will have to both learn a new discipline (educational development, and perhaps also educational research); and value disciplines very different from your 'parent' discipline.

- Know you are moving into a political minefield. While in your past role the antics of senior management were sometimes an issue of concern, in this new continent you are immediately affected by changes in senior management and their actions. Sometimes these management changes are for good; sometimes you may feel that you have been restructured to Pluto!

- One continent you may want to, or be required to, visit or inhabit is the Land of Staff Development. Indeed, that land may be close to your parent discipline, or a place you think has much to offer. For myself, when my unit was required to go there and I found that things like sabbaticals, time and money for research and keeping national links with geography were not part of the territory, I had to waste much time in being awkward and then jumping ship. If, when you change continents, you are committed to research and to connecting to your parent discipline, get that commitment and connection clearly defined in your role.

- Take heart – you will work in a different time to me. The creation of the subject centre network in the United Kingdom, and parallel discipline-based initiatives elsewhere, means that the Land of Educational Development is being reconfigured to be more clearly discipline based. If you decide to go that way, you can help it go further.

Continents do drift! And I wish you good speed in going *your* way.

Suggested reading

Healey, M and Jenkins, A (2003) Educational development through the disciplines, in *The Scholarship of Academic Development*, ed R Macdonald and H Eggins, pp 47–57, Open University Press and the Society for Research into Higher Education, Buckingham
Jenkins, A (1996) The go-between: strategies for success and recipes for failure, in *Different Approaches: Theory and practice in higher education*, ed S Leong and D Fitzpatrick, pp 3–7, Higher Education and Research Development Association of Australasia, Perth
Jenkins, A (1996) Discipline-based educational development, *International Journal for Academic Development*, **1** (1), pp 50–62
Jenkins, A (1997) Twenty-one volumes on: is teaching valued in geography in higher education? *Journal of Geography in Higher Education*, **21** (1), pp 5–14

CHARACTERIZING THE REQUISITE EXPERTISE

How, then, can we characterize the professional expertise required of a developer in order to devise an appropriate programme of professional development for any given individual? Given the complexity of the field, it is no surprise that a number of authors have identified various areas of necessary expertise, as summarized in Table 13.1.

A consensus, however, does emerge from these authors that developers require extensive specialist expertise (as suggested below), even if new developers will not always achieve the standard set by Kapp *et al* (1996). In relation to the professionals with whom developers work – academics – it is worth observing that most of this expertise is shared with the academics themselves. In addition, expertise is required that specifically focuses on the skills needed for enhancing academic practice. The balance between shared practice with academics and expertise that focuses on enhancement will, however, vary for any given developer, as we now consider.

Table 13.1 *Suggested areas of expertise for developers*

Author(s)	Professional expertise
O'Leary (1997)	Ability to tailor one's practice to a hectic and competitive climate; interpersonal skills; facilitative skills; skills in networking and co-ordinating
Andresen (1996)	Unique insights into learning and teaching; knowledge of the theory and the practice of higher education; understanding of educational settings and how to solve educational problems; ability to evaluate teaching; ability to facilitate discussion on the practice of teachers and students; knowledge of academic culture
Isaacs (1997)	Understanding of adult learning; knowledge of practice and research in higher education; ability to critically reflect on one's practice; process skills in facilitating the activities of others; relevant technical expertise, such as use of learning technology or specific learning methods; research expertise
Lueddeke (1997: 19)	Expertise in the following areas: learning and motivation theory; evaluation; change management; problem solving; project management; group process; curriculum; learning technology; the context of practice; interpersonal communications; lifelong learning
Kapp *et al* (1996)	At least three to five years' experience of teaching a variety of students; experience of delivering workshops and courses; leadership skills; research experience; PhD; communication skills; problem-solving skills; personal qualities such as enthusiasm, empathy and flexibility

Shared practice

Where there is a common form of life and experience, there is greater scope for the developer to understand how to enhance academic practice. Here, the typical emphasis will be on the development of teaching and learning. Webb (1996: 104) thus suggests, 'The teaching commitment of a developer may thus be seen as a necessary but not sufficient condition for the maintenance of credibility derived from a common form of life.' This commitment to teaching is relatively easy to maintain where the developer focuses on working with staff from a specific academic discipline. The challenge is greater where a developer is based in a central unit, although maintenance of relevant and current experience of one or more disciplines remains important for the developer.

A closely related issue for the developer is how to establish and maintain credibility with academics. Much of this credibility stems from participation in a shared community of practice. In addition to maintaining contact with students, credibility within the academic community stems largely from a research profile. Certainly the complexity of the practice of academic development suggests that research-based solutions will increasingly be required, as suggested by Brew (2001). The requirement to demonstrate to university teachers and to senior management the effectiveness of academic development also suggests that an emphasis on research will provide an important element to successful academic development careers in the future. And more broadly than teaching, the challenge of maintaining one's currency in a subject is also worth addressing.

Participation in such shared practice provides a particular challenge for staff who embark more directly upon a career in staff and educational development or who transfer into the academic world from other contexts. While this lack of shared experience may not count against someone initially, as the developer seeks to take on further responsibility, concern about credibility is likely to come increasingly to the fore.

Expertise for enhancement

However, there is also a body of development expertise that goes beyond this shared practice with the academic community. This is a recognition that developers are primarily engaged not in what is normally thought of as academic practice – teaching, research and the like – but rather in the enhancement of academic practice. One added complexity, although it can also help resolve the problem, is that this enhancement must be done in a properly academic, scholarly, research-based way. The categorization by O'Leary (see Table 13.1) in particular recognizes that change places considerable demands on staff, and that in order to facilitate this change, significant interpersonal skills are needed. Webb (1996: 36) also points out the importance of understanding people in this role. The client here is, however, another professional rather than a lay person – a professional whose role often carries higher prestige within an institution than that of the professional developer. This may provide particular challenges to the developer, as is for example evident in some compulsory course for new lecturers that requires highly developed inter-personal skills to manage.

It is further important to establish early on a limited number of areas of specialist expertise within development work itself. The range of areas in which one can specialize is of course vast. Any area of academic practice can become a specialist area of expertise, as can many of the various development methods evident within this text. Such expertise is often needed if one is to lead specific projects rather than simply act as a member of a team. It also helps in establishing a national profile, an important commodity during career transitions. This will come about in part through relevant experience and through other development opportunities considered later in this chapter. However, it is still important to choose carefully the opportunities that are taken if the expertise is to be acquired. We see here the need for a personal development programme that addresses such issues.

TOWARDS A PERSONAL PROGRAMME

Webb observes in his now classic text on staff development (1996) that the term 'development' can itself be contested. Indeed, significant choice remains as to the directions that our work takes us with academic staff. The same point may be made for the development of developers themselves, as is also evident in the next chapter. Indeed, such a wide choice is evident in both the goals and the means employed to achieve those goals. Furthermore, given both the variety of work that is open to a developer and the tendency for a career to span several institutions, the individual needs to take responsibility for his or her own development.

It is worth emphasizing that the ability to take such responsibility is likely to come into its own at career transitions. It is a basic principle of personnel work that staff are not given increased salary or grading simply because they have acquired additional expertise. Given the demands that are placed on developers, it can be tempting to ignore opportunities for their own development. However, as new job openings arise, especially at career transitions, it is essential to have demonstrated that one has achieved the relevant expertise. Within a job, unless specific measurable outcomes can be clearly pointed to, then alternative demonstrations of expertise are necessary.

Career management skills are thus worth adding to the list of areas of expertise needed by a developer. Literature on career planning is of assistance here (see, for instance, Blaxter, Hughes and Tight, 1998). The initial emphasis here is on identifying what one actually wants to achieve through a career, on identifying one's career goals. Long-term goals may be more difficult to identify given the rapid rate of change within the sector, but shorter- or more medium-term goals are well worth considering. Such goal setting typically needs to be followed up by action planning if these goals are to be realized. Of course, institutional support is important, particularly where an employer is funding any development opportunities. In this regard, assistance may be provided through regular institutional appraisal for one's current work, although it is worth observing that this is still carried out within an institutional context, in which it may be difficult to look beyond the institution.

For example, it might be the case that a new developer decides as a medium-term goal to secure employment on a permanent basis. Short-term goals will then include identifying forms of development work that attract permanent contracts and gaining relevant experience and qualifications. Within many countries, for instance, a staple body of work now exists in the shape of courses of initial professional development for new academics. Capacity here is likely to grow, as students and funding bodies demand appropriately qualified teaching staff. This might suggest an area of expertise that is worth a new developer acquiring.

It is, however, true that any personal set of goals will be constrained by the institutional setting in which the developer is employed. Isaacs (1997: 11) notes that a personal development programme will depend on the nature of one's actual work, and this in turn is set in part at least by the institution. Research-led universities, for instance, may place greater value than many more teaching-led universities on developers' possessing a PhD. As already noted, the location of the unit in which one works is also an important consideration. In his case study on pages 215–16, Jenkins notes a basic difference between working with a unit located within a personnel section and a unit located within an academic department. The emphasis on forms of shared practice with academics will typically be less evident within a human resources or personnel function. While it may be possible to tailor from a base in a personnel section a personal development programme that focuses on this academic expertise, clearly it may be more difficult to do so, or may be so perceived by clients.

The complexity of development work does, however, often leave scope for the individual developer to focus on specific areas of work, particularly as he or she gains responsibility within an institution. The challenge is often to make a case for development in certain areas, perhaps in the light of one of the many national initiatives. If staff and educational development is to form a profession, then such scope for personal initiative is essential. Indeed, Eraut (1994), in addition to identifying the specialist knowledge base that is an essential element of a profession, also notes the need for autonomy and service. According to this analysis, it is impossible to separate the development of professional expertise from wider professional identity.

A GUIDE TO DEVELOPMENT OPPORTUNITIES

The challenge, however, remains for you to devise a programme of appropriate professional development. There is evidently no single qualification that will provide all the necessary expertise, although the Fellowship Schemes of the Staff and Educational Development Association (SEDA) give a reasonably convincing account of the main professional requirements and the underpinning values (Staff and Educational Development Association, 1997). The model of a development programme proposed in this chapter incorporates three elements: formal qualifications, professional experience and professional interactions. These elements are outlined in Table 13.2, and to varying extents all figure in the profile of her personal development that Clayton outlines in the case study on pages 223–24.

Before we look at each of these elements in turn, it is worth noting that each element needs to incorporate reflective analysis. While this is particularly true for experience, as Cowan so persuasively argues in Chapter 12, it is also the case that understanding and skills gained in more formal qualifications need to be explicitly linked with practice. Reflective practice is as

Table 13.2 *Summary of major development opportunities*

Qualifications
Postgraduate qualifications
Postgraduate Certificate in Teaching and Learning in Higher Education; MEd; PhD; professional doctorate in education; qualifications within an academic discipline

Professional qualifications
Fellowship or Associate Fellowship of SEDA (UK based); membership of the Chartered Institute of Personnel and Development (CIPD) (within the UK)

Professional experience
Temporary arrangements
Exchanges; sabbaticals; fellowships; secondments

Developing new initiatives
Funded development projects; research into one's own practice or into the practice of others; publications related to development practice or research in educational development

Extension of one's experience
Teaching students; project management; management; involvement in course for new lecturers; policy work; consultancy

---

Professional interactions
Participation in professional bodies or networks
Involvement in such organizations as SEDA, Institute for Learning and Teaching in Higher Education (ILTHE), Society for Research into Higher Education, Learning and Teaching Support Network (LTSN) (all UK based); American Society for Training and Development Association, Professional and Organizational Development Network in Higher Education (US based); Society for Teaching and Learning in Higher Education (based in Canada); Higher Education Research and Development Society of Australasia; professional groupings that relate to special interests and subject associations; attendance at conferences, participation in committee work. (For a full list, see the section on Networks in the Appendix.)

Other professional interactions
Collaborative projects with colleagues in other institutions; mentoring from a senior colleague or peer

---

Source: After Blaxter, Hughes and Tight (1998)

important as formal academic study and specific skills development. Eraut notes that acquiring knowledge and putting it to use are not separate processes, but the same process (1994: 25). As he notes, 'The process of using knowledge transforms that knowledge so that it is no longer the same knowledge.' Eraut argues that it is essential to make sense of knowledge within specific contexts, adapting one's knowledge and the implications for action. Any programme of professional education needs to respect this account of professional knowledge. Further learning needs to occur if knowledge that has been learnt in an academic context is to be applied in a professional context.

Qualifications are an important aspect of any development programme, especially in the early stages of a career when one is establishing credibility. While additional qualifications may seem a luxury within an existing job, they become essential during career transitions and for certain jobs. Gaining a Master's degree in Higher Education is, for instance, likely to be important if one seeks to lead a programme of professional development for university staff that is set at Master's level. The SEDA Fellowship and Associate Fellowship are again worth noting, providing a specialist education and qualification in staff and educational development. They are based around an individual's professional practice, with the candidate preparing a portfolio of evidence that is assessed against agreed standards. This portfolio incorporates evidence against specific competencies, while also requiring candidates both to evidence their commitment to a number of professional values and to show particular expertise in specialist areas of development work. At the same time, the schemes require extensive reflection on this evidence, so that links are explicitly made between the practice of the candidate and competencies, values and areas of specialist expertise.

We now turn more briefly to the importance of professional experience in a development programme. In particular, the development of new initiatives and the extension of one's own experience provide evident scope for learning. When one initiates a new development, additional responsibility often follows. There is also greater scope to engage in development towards the goals that one has set for oneself. Similarly, writing for publication is an important form of experience that can be developed. Newer developers are sometimes in awe at the publishing record of more experienced developers. But a good idea and the motivation to see it through, perhaps in collaboration with a more experienced developer, are as important as experience.

Finally, it is important for any individual's development programme to include relevant professional interactions, such as becoming active in a professional body or organization. Mintz (1997) identifies the importance of joining a community of others engaged in practice to provide guidance for practice. Taylor (1997) also focuses on the need to emphasize partnership in professional education. One needs to find this community of developers with which to share one's experience. Ideas for new initiatives are not developed in a vacuum. In addition to maintaining currency through reading journals and books, professional interactions provide access to new ideas that is crucial within this field. Partner institutions are also needed to secure funding, and this is far easier where professional interactions are strongest. Such a community is rarely found simply through being a member of a large professional body. The need is to collaborate with other members on specific tasks, through committee membership or sharing practice within specific areas. Mentoring from a senior colleague is also likely to be of significant benefit, particularly if one seeks to take on greater responsibility. Not only can mentoring make a key difference to levels of confidence, it can also help the developer to identify gaps in his or her expertise that need addressing.

CASE STUDY: A CIRCUITOUS ROUTE (BY SUE CLAYTON, UNIVERSITY OF SUSSEX)

It is often the case that staff developers arrive in their roles through circuitous routes. In my own case, the journey took in three educational sectors – and a few 'gap years' pursuing spurious interests in the performing arts world – which actually has something to transfer in terms of the 'show must go on' ethos that I carry around!

My experience represents a transition over a 15-year period from an academic role, and contract, as a history teacher in secondary education, to becoming a curriculum developer and professional developer in further education (also on academic contracts) and now a staff developer in higher education (on an 'administrative faculty' contract). I think the different contractual experiences are significant because, if you allow them to constrain you, they determine differences in how the development roles are perceived, organized, recognized and rewarded, all of which impact on the opportunities to develop expertise – particularly in the area of research. As a Staff Developer focusing mainly on teaching and learning programmes, but based in a staff development unit located in the Human Resources (HR) Division, I have had to find ingenious ways to develop my expertise and interests across institutional structures. In that sense, I think all staff developers develop an innate and outward-looking resourcefulness.

Institutional locations have an impact on the development of expertise. Much expertise can be about negotiating one's way into developments concerning communication strategies at critical stages – and often tailored to particular people – usually well before they hit a committee paper. None of these essential qualities is expressed in job descriptions or is the subject of staff development programmes!

My main area of interest is in the development of teaching and learning through curriculum and staff development, and so I have taken on that side of the Staff Development Unit's work. Being an experiential learner, I have always taken an activity-based approach to my own development. In that sense, my experiences of promoting curriculum/institutional innovation through action research and curriculum development projects have been the methods I most value, as a staff developer and a self-developer. I also find networking the most beneficial route to my own development. So the first things I would seek out, and create if they do not exist, would be the internal and external networks and stakeholders to collaborate with. Working and learning with others is crucial for me.

Qualifications? The Chartered Institute of Personnel and Development (CIPD) route has never seemed relevant to my particular interests, as I have no aspirations to become a Director of Personnel. I hold a first degree and a Postgraduate Certificate in Education with Qualified Teacher status, and the rest is long experience – and that does count for a lot in terms of confidence. If I were to look for further qualifications, and were a tad younger, I would most certainly look for a postgraduate degree. I do feel recognition by a professional body would be useful, eg a SEDA Fellowship and membership of the Institute for Learning and Teaching in Higher Education (ILTHE) – both of which I intend to do but never get round to! That my expertise is accepted without either a doctorate or membership of a professional body is heart-warming, but a little scary nonetheless. I compensate for this by presenting at conferences and getting involved in at least one research project a year.

So, what is my expertise? This mainly involves enabling others to fulfil their potential within a variety of contexts. You really have to be interested in people to do this and I'm not sure there is training for that! However, skills in influencing others are key, and there are training needs around managing development across institutional structures and boundaries of influence, where developers often get involved in very strategic matters but have no direct management responsibility.

My experience as a teaching professional is central, even though most of this so far has been outside higher education. I would not have progressed into staff development by any other route – those generic teaching skills I have found transferable, and very useful. Of course, in a university there is an imperative to be engaged in and promote peda-gogical research. This is difficult when administrative contracts do not allow specific time to do this – but I have sought out opportunities to get involved in collaborative projects and engage in active contact with profes-sional organizations such as SEDA, the ILTHE and the Learning and Teaching Support Network (LTSN). No one directed me to these organiza-tions when I arrived in higher education; I just imagined something like them must exist, and thank goodness they did. Possibly developing my skills further in a national rather than institutional context is where I might next consider putting my energies; learning by doing is again my preferred route. However, I have more than my hands full with institutional develop-ments at the moment!

CONCLUSION

The development of professional expertise requires a clearly thought-out programme that matches the individual needs of the developer concerned. Your programme should probably pay more attention to your goals, to the particular expertise that you want to develop, than to the particular ways in which you will achieve these development goals. Why? Because opportunities – projects, events, jobs even – may arise quickly, and it is important to know which to seize and which to ignore. The best way to decide which development opportunities to embrace is to know what expertise you seek to develop. While chance may allow someone to embark upon a career within development work, more systematic approaches are needed for a rounded expertise.

The more explicit that your programme becomes, the greater the chance that you will carry out that programme. For instance, it is clearly possible for an individual developer to devise and conduct such a programme on his or her own initiative. It is, however, worth exploring the options to involve others in this process. While the institution itself has an interest in fostering the development of developers, there is also a strong case for mentoring and collaboration with peers.

The pace of change now occurring within higher education has given rise to a profession that seeks to shape the nature of this change. With the development and maintenance of the necessary expertise, developers will be well placed to ensure that an improved education results for students, as well as an interesting life for the developer him- or herself.

REFERENCES

Andresen, L (1996) The work of academic development: occupational identity, standards of practice, and the virtues of association, *International Journal for Academic Development*, **1** (1), pp 38–49

Barnett, R (1997) *Higher Education: A critical business*, Society for Research in Higher Education and Open University Press, Buckingham

Blaxter, L, Hughes, C and Tight, M (1998) *The Academic Career Handbook*, Open University Press, Buckingham

Brew, A (2001) *The Nature of Research: Inquiry in academic contexts*, Routledge Falmer, London

Eraut, M (1994) *Developing professional knowledge and competence*, Falmer Press, London

Fraser, K (1999) Australian academic developers: entry into the profession and our own professional development, *International Journal for Academic Development*, **4** (2), pp 89–101

Isaacs, G (1997) Developing the developers: some ethical dilemmas in changing times, *International Journal for Academic Development*, **2** (2), pp 6–12

Kapp, C, Healy, M, Nellisen, C, Mihevc, B, de Winter, H C and Watt, H (1996) Developing faculty developers: some issues when recruiting faculty developers and ensuring the professional growth of current faculty developers, *Journal of Staff, Program and Organisational Development*, **13** (4), pp 229–39

Lueddeke, G (1997) Emerging learning environments in higher education: implications for institutional change and academic developers, *International Journal for Academic Development*, **2** (2), pp 13–21

Mintz, J A (1997) Professionalization of academic developers: looking through a North American lens, *International Journal for Academic Development*, **2** (2), pp 22–27

O'Leary, J (1997) Staff development in a climate of economic rationalism: a profile of the academic developer, *International Journal for Academic Development*, **2** (2), pp 72–82

Staff and Educational Development Association (SEDA) (1997) *SEDA Fellowship Schemes*, SEDA, Birmingham

Taylor, I (1997) *Developing Learning in Professional Education*, SRHE and OUP, Buckingham

Webb, G (1996) *Understanding Staff Development*, SRHE and OUP, Buckingham

14

Personal and professional development: strategies for coping and for growth

Neill Thew

INTRODUCTION

This chapter is about moving out from underneath what Eliot[1] in *The Hollow Men* calls the Shadow – the Shadow of stress; of disempowerment; of feeling, and indeed being, unsupported; of wanting change but not having the means to achieve it; of over-work, over-commitment and a lack of balance in our lives; of losing sight of our values and aspirations in the hurly-burly business and detail of everyday professional life. One of the sad ironies I have often noticed about us staff and educational developers as a group is that while we spend our working lives helping other colleagues to grow, develop and move forwards, we often do so at the cost of ignoring our own needs for development, supportive growth and nurture.

THREE CASE HISTORIES

I will begin by sharing three vignettes that I am certain will resonate with many readers. These are all situations I have encountered over the past 12 months alone. All these stories are, of course, true – although in some of them I have combined the facts of two or three different situations into one story. Moreover, before you imagine that I work in the most pressured institution in the United Kingdom, I should point out that these vignettes represent situations that have arisen in a number of different universities.

1. A was a senior, very experienced educational developer, highly regarded within her own university and beyond. She was very committed to

---

[1] Eliot, T S (1925) *Poems 1909–1925*, Faber and Faber, London

her role, and had a deep concern for students and their learning. Her institution was in a period of considerable change. Faculties were being restructured, and there was much uncertainty and low faculty morale. In the apparent absence of a focused strategic direction, and in the real absence of clear operational planning to manage the change, A increasingly found herself 'firefighting': being parachuted in to different faculties to help solve problems whose root cause was often poor change management and unclear communication. Increasingly, A found herself working with disgruntled, and sometimes aggressive, members of faculty. A attempted, in what she saw as a constructive way, to feed up, through her line manager to the university's senior management, information about the problems she was encountering. She hoped to be able to influence the development of a clearer and better-communicated change strategy. She felt that her messages were never heeded – even when she tried to use her annual appraisal to raise the issues. Reflecting back on the situation now, A feels that the cumulative pressures over time slowly wore her down. As she felt less and less able to make the impact she felt she ought, she worked ever longer hours. As she worked longer hours, she grew tired, and knew that the quality of her work was not as high as usual. A vicious downward spiral developed, with A working ever harder to achieve less and less. Eventually, A became ill, and was off work on extended sick leave for several months. She is still concerned that some senior managers see her illness as a sign that she is not up to her job.

2. B was a junior member of an educational development team. His work was project based. The projects he managed were discrete and self-contained. He was always the only member of the development team involved with these projects, and worked with academic faculty, who sometimes treated him with little collegial respect and dismissed or ignored his professional competence. B began to feel very isolated professionally, and marginalized within the education development team. Not unlike A, B was also worried that he was not making the impact he ought, and he too started working ever longer hours, with diminishing success. His home life suffered, and his relationship with his partner and children came under stress. His line manager noticed that B was working overly long hours, but did not discuss this with B to try to identify the underlying causes. B's line manager decided that the problem was that B was inefficient and had poor time management skills, and therefore ordered B to attend a time management course. B perceived this as a criticism of a personalized failing, and saw the course not as developmental and supportive, but rather as punitive. He attended the course, resentfully, and his behaviours did not change as a result of it. His line manager interpreted this as further personal failure and said so to B. B became intermittently ill for over a year, and one of his children started

displaying very challenging behaviours, which B believes were triggered by the stresses at home.

3. C has worked in educational development for about seven or eight years. She is a very capable and committed educational developer. It is clear from talking to C that, like A, she is passionately committed to teaching and learning, and to ensuring the high quality of students' learning experiences. She has worked in both pre- and post-1992 universities. Her current post is in a pre-1992, research-intensive university. She has found it increasingly difficult to reconcile her values and beliefs to the post she holds, because the institution in which she works so clearly values, promotes and rewards research over teaching and learning. Eventually, she decided that her future career lay outside higher education (HE). While she is excited about the new direction she is now pursuing, she also feels sad and guilty about having left behind educational development.

The first thing that strikes me about these stories is the terrible human cost they all involve. They also, however, share a number of other features: loss of control; guilt; becoming overwhelmed; lack of support; marginalization; losing sight of the big picture in the deluge of detail; losing sight of yourself; life becoming unbalanced; stress and illness.

There is, of course, an enormous body of literature – and a huge training industry – designed to help us face these problems. The 'self-help' section of any bookstore is stacked high with books on stress management (Race, 2001: ch 6); time management (Brown and Smith, 1999); meditation and relaxation (Richardson, 2000); coping with difficult people (O'Connor and Seymour, 1994); having a more high-powered career (Mulligan, 2000). Much of this advice is extremely valuable, of course, but there remains the problem of how we often use (or, rather, fail to use) these resources, or, like B, how we respond to training opportunities. Often, we receive good advice, or learn helpful techniques, with every intention of adopting these, but we then fail to carry our learning through into our behaviours. We remain under Eliot's Shadow, reverting to old, damaging habits and patterns.

Worse still, we sometimes use our knowledge of better, more productive ways of behaving and managing ourselves as a stick to beat ourselves with: *I know I should/shouldn't be doing this, I know better – but I just can't help it – I must be useless/stupid/lacking in willpower/no good at this job...* and if there's one thing guaranteed to make us repeat a behaviour or a pattern, it's self-oppressive guilt. Guilt drives us to repeat a thing again and again and again in the unacknowledged hope that one day we won't feel so bad about what we're doing; but that release never happens, so round and round the loop we go.

Rather, then, than spending the rest of this chapter repeating the excellent advice that is already readily available elsewhere, I am going to discuss an effective way to scaffold growth and development; a framework within which it becomes possible to act, simply because acting comes to feel more attractive than staying where we are. I will share with you that I am writing as much from personal experience as from a knowledge of the literature and experience as a trainer. Some years ago, I became ill through stress and over-work. The ideas and activities in this chapter are all ones I have used and found helpful. They have helped me to stay on track, stay in control and move forwards. I have also used some of these techniques with groups. Colleagues' evaluations of such sessions, together with the evidence of their actions over the following months, suggest that many other people have found these activities very valuable as well. These are activities you can use alone, or with groups of learners, or in self-support groups.

The important thing, of course, is that you do use them! If reading this chapter is to be of any lasting value to you then you need to interact with it. In the first section that follows, I present two interconnected models for planning personal development and then seeing it through. After this, I outline many of the most common stresses that we face as developers. I then offer a number of exercises and activities that can be used either alone or with groups, and I conclude with some thoughts about how to use these resources well. A very productive way to get the most from this chapter is to read it through and then select just two of its activities: the one that *most* attracts you and the one that *least* attracts you. Why is that? What might you learn immediately from those instinctive reactions? Now undertake the activity you identified as attractive – either with a friend or colleague or alone. Decide to do just one thing within a week as a result of the exercise. Monitor how that goes. Congratulations! You are taking control.

GROWING SMARTLY: TWO INTERCONNECTED MODELS TO HELP US COPE AND DEVELOP

> 'Cheshire Puss,' she began, rather timidly, as she did not at all know whether it would like the name... 'Would you tell me, please, which way I ought to go from here?'
> 'That depends a good deal on where you want to get to,' said the Cat.
> 'I don't much care where –', said Alice.
> 'Then it doesn't matter which way you go,' said the Cat.
> (Lewis Carroll, *Alice's Adventures in Wonderland*)

An increasing number of already successful professionals are learning the benefit of being coached. Coaching helps individuals to set and realize higher goals than they might have thought possible, and to align these with their own deepest-held values and beliefs. There is not, after all, a one-model-fits-all standard of what counts as success, or of what counts as a happy and fulfilled life. One way of gaining intensive benefit from coaching is to employ the services of a professional life coach, but we can also use some simple, and highly effective, techniques from coaching for ourselves (Whitworth, Kimsey-House and Sandahl, 1998; Zeus and Skiffington, 2000).

As developers, we are all familiar with a cyclical model of learning: one has an experience; reflects on that experience; considers whether it is possible to theorize or generalize from it; and actively experiments to test out that theorization (Cowan, 1998: ch 4; see also Chapter 12). Planning our own futures is a congruent process. Coaching is a way of enabling us to reflect, plan and take action, and in this way, through being action and outcome focused, it is rather different from a process such as counselling, say.

Two basic models used in coaching that help us to set, work towards and achieve our goals are the GROW model (Downey, 2002: ch 3) and the setting of SMART goals (Grant and Greene, 2001: 172–202). The latter is best embedded within the GROW process, and not seen as separate.

GROW stands for *G*oals; *R*eality; *O*ptions; *W*ill. In order to achieve progress, we need *goals*. If, unlike Alice in Wonderland, we want to be able to move forwards in a concerted way, then we need a clear and specific destination. This is why the most effective goals (effective in the sense that they are helpful to us rather than burdensome, and are most likely to be achieved) are SMART goals. SMART goals are *S*pecific; *M*easurable; *A*ttractive; *R*ealistic; and *T*ime bound.

Goals need to be *specific*, because it is impossible to work towards vague ones; it is hard to break down the pathway towards them into clear, logical steps, and it is also hard to know whether you really are making progress towards them. For example, your initial idea for a goal may be 'to get fitter'. This, however, is not a goal; it is a process you would undergo on the way to achieving a goal. How would you know when you are as fit as you wish to be? A specific goal would be something like: I will complete the London Marathon next year; or I will be able to swim 20 lengths without stopping.

Similarly, goals need to be *measurable*; if there is nothing clearly at stake, there is no real motivation to act, but if there is a specific bottom line that enables us to know absolutely clearly whether we have achieved our goals or not, then we are much more likely to persevere until we are successful. A recent project has followed the careers of one cohort of Harvard University graduates. The most significant factor in predicting their business success has been not the subject they studied, nor the quality of their degree, nor their IQ, but how well they have set and pursued clear goals. Tellingly, the most successful of all have kept track of their goals and progress *in writing* ever since they were undergraduates. The second most successful group claim to have set themselves specific goals but have never written them down or worked with someone else to evaluate how well they were doing in achieving their goals. The least successful group have not set themselves goals at all.

Third, goals need to be *attractive*. We need to want to achieve them; the goals need to be our own wish-list and aspirations, not someone else's. Of course, in our professional lives, we all have short- and medium-term goals, some of which we set, some of which we negotiate and some of which are imposed. Which of these do you find most compelling? Most enjoyable to work on? Most fulfilling? For longer-term personal and professional growth, we must own our own goals – even if someone else works alongside us in helping us to identify them.

Although the best goals are the highest ones – a goal too easily achieved leads to little progress, whereas a tough goal moves us on very much further – nevertheless they should also be *realistic*. If we set ourselves unrealistic, unattainable goals, we will become disheartened by their non-achievement, and often slip back into self-punitive behaviours and beliefs. The best goals nurture us! They stretch us, increase our capacity and confidence, take us to the limits of what we thought we could achieve, help us move into new territories – but remain in the realms of the possible.

Finally, good, usable goals for growth are always *time bound*. An attitude of 'this week, next week, sometime, never' is not a productive one when it comes to achieving our desires. This is one reason why working with a friend or colleague is really excellent – a regular checking in, the focus of which should be on actions taken and their effect plus a clear decision about the next steps, is a great way to keep on track.

So much, then, for setting SMART goals. Over and above this process, the GROW model alerts us to three other dimensions necessary for success: the need to check *R*eality, explore *O*ptions and have the genuine *W*ill to act.

The *R*eality aspect of the GROW model takes us beyond just thinking about how realistic our goals are. We need to take a clear look at the reality of our current situation and of past history. Some things are beyond our capacity to change and influence. If these are things that are weighing heavily on us then we need to reframe our goals and expectations into terms that are within our own control. It is no good at all to set a goal that depends on someone else changing their behaviour (no matter how desirable that may be to us!). For example, a colleague with whom I have worked felt very unsupported by his line manager. His initial wish was for his line manager to change her behaviours, and to look after him better. He had taken the initiative to express his needs to her in a constructive way, but this had not led to any lasting change. A reality check with him led us to the conclusion that in this case the leopard was indeed not going to change its spots. This hard reality enabled him to redefine his goal: what he needed was to create support for himself, but this support did not need to come only (or even at all) from his line manager. He built a community of colleagues and friends who agreed to support his professional development, worked with a coach, and set up a self-help group, modelled on a professional action learning set. This has given him the support and confidence he needed.

We all operate professionally within two spheres: the sphere of our influence and that of our concern (Covey, 1990). I visualize these as two concentric circles: our sphere of influence is a smaller circle set within our sphere of concern. The more we stay in the outer ring – outside our sphere of influence, but worrying about things that concern us – the more stressed and disempowered we will feel. By staying within our sphere of influence as much as possible, we remain able to act and feel more confidently in control. My observation time and again has been that colleagues who adopt this strategy (whether consciously or not) find, over time, that their sphere of influence grows, because they are seen as professionals who are in control of themselves and get things done. Conversely, colleagues who waste (generally negative) energy on things they are concerned about but cannot influence find that their sphere of influence diminishes over time.

The flip-side of *Reality* checking is that we often carry unacknowledged limiting beliefs about what we can and cannot do; about how others will react to us in given situations; about the limits of what is possible; about how flexible we can be; about history repeating itself. The aspect of being coached I have found most exciting, most daunting, most scary and most exhilarating is uncovering my own limiting beliefs and acting as if they did not exist – because once you act and achieve something you had told yourself was impossible (because... because... because...) then the limiting belief is exposed as a fraud, and no longer holds sway over you.

This aspect of reality checking links to the next element of the GROW model, which is to explore our *Options* for action. Here, the key to success is brainstorming, suspending disbelief, being outrageous. You can always come back to edit and select later (but you'll be surprised how often the option that initially seems the wildest is precisely the one that shows you the way forward). Several of the activities outlined below are designed to help open up our options. My rule of thumb for personal development is never to decide what you are going to do until you have come up with at least five options. Often our options and ideas become smarter as we go along, each idea sparking the next and building up a better and better picture of what we can do.

The final stage – the *Will* to act – requires that we are rigorously honest with ourselves. Having decided which option to pursue, ask yourself, 'On a scale of 1 to 10, how committed am I to doing this?' What you are asking yourself is whether the proposed action is something you really want to do – not something you feel you should or ought to do. If you cannot give yourself 10 out of 10, then you need to revisit your options and come up with another. If that sounds tough, it is – but it is far, far better to be rigorous at the outset and then commit yourself to a course of action that you will follow through than to begin half-heartedly and in doubts, and then, inevitably, fail to achieve what you had intended.

Once you are committed to an action, then the three watchwords are *outcome, acuity, flexibility*. To see something through, we need to be clear what we intend to achieve; to notice whether or not we are achieving it; and to be prepared to try something else if our initial approach is not working. Doing something else, note, is hardly the same as just giving up!

COMMON STRESSES FOR DEVELOPERS

I hope that we will have as many different, exciting personal aspirations as there are readers of this book – and I would celebrate that diversity. If you are planning to work specifically on your professional development, however, then the list below may trigger off some feelings of recognition that may be a starting point for deciding which kinds of issues to identify and resolve. I have worked with many different groups of both academics and developers, and talked to many other staff and educational developers, and from this work and these discussions a number of commonly recurring themes about particular professional stresses for us as a group emerge:

- lack of professional recognition within our institutions;

- lack of a clear career pathway and career progression;

- institutional, and individual, resistances to our work – finding ourselves undermined and marginalized;

- constantly finding ourselves at the leading edge of change;

- not being involved in planning change, but being expected to deliver and implement it;

- working in stressed, or under-resourced, teams;

- being buried in detail and minutiae;

- work not feeling fun any longer;

- a lack of clarity about roles and expectations/working with other academic and administrative colleagues across poorly defined boundaries;

- multi-tasking;

- working within rapidly changing contexts – where perhaps the speed of change means that things are not always seen through or where teams are constantly forming and re-forming;

- walking the tightrope between being seen as 'a tool of management' and being 'one of the people'.

In thinking about your reaction to this list, it is important to distinguish between the kinds of things we might feel after a particularly stressful or bad day or week, and chronic situations we would like to take control of – either by changing the situation; or by changing how it affects us; or by creating better support for ourselves to deal with it.

ACTIVITIES

I think it is incumbent upon us as developers to model and use good practices of personal development. My personal professional aspiration is to do a job well, a job that I regard as worthwhile, exciting and stimulating; that allows me to work with other people and have a positive impact in their lives; and within which I can continue to grow and learn. The vast majority of the time, that is exactly how I feel about my current role. If I stop feeling that, I will certainly move on. I am not, however, a naïve optimist, and I fully acknowledge that I do have some terrible, loathsome days! The activities below have helped, and continue to help, both myself and many colleagues to cope with the inevitable problems and sometime lows of personal and professional life; to celebrate the high points and achievements; to keep track of our own ongoing development and growth; and to motivate us to work towards an end goal of nurture, balance and fulfilment. In order to learn from the activities that follow, you will need first to undertake them, and then to reflect on their results. The combination of the results you achieve and your reflections on them will enable you to gain greater clarity about the direction you want to take, the goals you wish to set yourself, and the first steps required to achieve those goals.

The Wheel of Life

The Wheel of Life is a very good initial exercise, and is a useful one to which to return every so often, as it helps us to keep track of the overall balance in our lives.

Draw a circle and divide it up into eight segments, like slices of a cake. Label each segment with one of the eight most important aspects of your life. A fairly common combination would look something like this: health / your home / finances / fun and recreation / partner and relationship / friends and family / work and career / creativity and personal growth. This is an illustrative combination, so feel entirely free to adapt it to suit your current needs. Now you need to assess (honestly and fairly!) how satisfied – on a scale of 1 to 10 – you are with each of these aspects in your life. As well as deciding an overall score, jot down the key factors that made you decide on that score. Next, colour in each slice of pie in proportion to its score. An aspect of your life scoring 10 would be fully coloured in; one getting 5 would be half-filled; and one scoring 0 would not be coloured in at all. This gives you an immediate, and powerful, visual sense of how you are currently feeling about your life – both your general sense of contentment and the balance between different aspects of your life. This exercise is very helpful in identifying areas for development. Repeat it every so often, and observe how the pattern changes over time. (For other versions of this exercise see Gaskell, 2001: 18–30; Whitworth, Kimsey-House and Sandahl, 1998: 198–207.)

Draw a graph – plot the rhythm – identify the patterns

This is another useful 'survey' tool – and is one particularly well suited to those of us whose lives are influenced by the pattern of the academic year.

Take a large sheet of paper – a flipchart sheet is ideal. Position it in land-scape format and draw a vertical and a horizontal axis on it, near the bottom and left-hand edges. The horizontal axis will be used to plot time. You can survey any length of time using this method. I have found that surveying either the past term/semester or the past year leads to particu-larly helpful insights. The vertical axis can be used in a number of ways. Different ideas for what to record include how professionally satisfied you felt at a given time; how contented; how healthy; how successful you perceived yourself as being; or how high your energy levels were. There is no hard-and-fast rule here, other than to find a measure for the vertical scale that is meaningful to you and that reflects how you react to your own ups and downs. Plot this measurement over the time span you have selected; look at the overall shape of the graph you have produced and make yourself brief notes on the graph to account for its key features. Why was that period so good? Why was this time so difficult? What caused that sudden downturn, or this marked upswing? Were you more or less on a level, or does the line track major swings between positive and dreadful periods? From this exercise, what patterns can you identify? Do you have certain triggers or stresses that you are not currently managing success-fully? Are particular times in the term/ academic year particularly difficult, and how can you plan for those better? When does it make most sense for you to take leave and to rest? Can you figure out how to plan to do this *before* you get exhausted?

Poem exercise/creative visualization/writing in another form

Sometimes, particularly if you feel 'stuck' with a problem or situation, what you most need is to be able to find a different way of looking at it. From a new perspective, fresh insights and solutions often flow. One very good way to achieve this change of perspective, of course, is simply to talk to a trusted friend or colleague. There are, however, other ways in which we can achieve a similar end by ourselves. Draw a picture. Write the situation out in a different form: as a letter to a problem page in a really tacky magazine, perhaps, and then write the agony aunt's reply. Make this fun. Or outrageous. Or both. I was once instructed to write about a particular situation in rhyming iambic pentameters! It was the first time I had ever encountered this exercise, and I was profoundly sceptical. Nevertheless, I had a go, and to my amazement I found that the restrictive form took my attention (and panic) far enough away from the problem itself that I actually became very clear about what the real, underlying issue was and what I intended to do about it.

Thirty questions

'Thirty questions' is an excellent group brainstorming exercise that I first encountered during an Institute for Learning and Teaching in Higher Education workshop led by Sally Brown. It works best in groups of between four and six people, all of whom need to have identified a particular problem or situation with which they are feeling stuck and would like some help. Each person needs to have formulated their problem clearly, in writing, in only two or three sentences. In turn, each person presents his or her issue to the group, and, if needed, group members should ask any questions they need for clarification and to ensure that they all understand the issue clearly. Group members then brainstorm and shout out (non-judgemental) questions they think the individual could usefully be asking him- or herself with regard to that person's chosen issue. The individual writes all these down *without responding to them in any way at all.* This process continues until 30 questions have been written down.

What works very well about this process is that it is not threatening. We tend to accept or reject advice in a very immediate way, or hear it very partially, but questions stay with us longer and resonate more. It is important to keep on going until all 30 questions have been put, even if there are longish pauses during the process, as it is very often the case that the last few questions are the most valuable to the individual – and, having undertaken this exercise many times, I can honestly say that it is always possible to find 30 questions.

The individual then needs to look over the list. Some questions they will already know the answer to; some will genuinely not be relevant to the situation; and some, the most important ones, generally half a dozen or so, will really give the individual pause for thought. These are the questions that immediately resonate – that make us wince! Paying attention to those questions is powerful, and I have known several individuals who were feeling very blocked make extraordinary progress as a result of this exercise.

Letters to and from the future

There follow two letter-writing exercises – which are both, in different ways, spurs to action. One focuses us on where we want to go, and the other holds us to our own promises.

In the 'letter *from* the future' exercise, you are invited to imagine that you are 90, and are writing a letter from your future self to your present self, looking back on your life. This exercise is useful for helping us to focus on what is really important to us. What is it about our own experience and our journey through life that we will come to see as really valuable – and what's just incidental? For any process of change to work well, what we need is to be able to tell ourselves a story. Change is a human process, and often needs to find an expression in the human terms of a story or a narrative. The difference with this particular genre of story is that we need to write the ending first. If we have an exciting, attractive and thoroughly imagined ending (What will I be doing? How will I feel? What will it look like? And so forth) then figuring out the steps to get there is a much simpler, secondary process. The point is that no effective process of change ever starts from a bullet point list of actions – it needs the vision of the destination first.

The 'letter *to* the future' is a way of helping us to keep to the actions we have planned – and is an exercise I often use with groups. Write down for yourself the action you intend to take, and by when. Put this in a stamped, addressed envelope. Give it to a reliable friend and tell the friend when you would like him or her to post it to you. Align this with your deadlines for action. When the letter arrives – have you done what you promised yourself? If not, what are you going to do about that? When? (Different versions of this exercise are to be found in Grant and Greene (2001: 51–61).)

SOME WAYS OF USING THESE RESOURCES

There is a strong movement in HE to achieve quality assurance through quality enhancement. The idea is that if you are engaged in an ongoing cycle of evaluating your strengths and weaknesses, planning action accordingly, monitoring and evaluating the impact of that action, re-evaluating your strengths and weaknesses, and thus starting the cycle over again, this process of constant quality enhancement should itself ensure that quality can be assured. It aligns quality with a process of growth and development, and not with one of static bureaucracy. The title of this chapter refers both to coping and to growth. I see the relationship between these as parallel to that of quality enhancement and assurance: if we are engaged in an ongoing process of growth, we will also be excellent at coping. This is not, of course, to say that personal growth is an easy ride, or that the exercises and processes described in this chapter are some kind of magic panacea, but even when the journey gets rough, this chapter offers you some tools to give you the tenacity to stay on course.

Try some of these exercises alone. Consider finding a friend or colleague with whom to work in an ongoing relationship. I have a wonderfully supportive ongoing co-mentoring relationship with a colleague from another institution, and we swap time by phone every fortnight. The regular rhythm of this contact I find tremendously supportive. Use some of these exercises when you are leading team activities; there is always something new to be learnt no matter how often you do them. Think how your immediate work team could use these kinds of ideas. My unit meets every week, and we always spend some of that time engaged in personal development exercises. I think we are a well-functioning, close team, and that this is in very large part due to the effort we put into our own, and each other's, growth and development.

As I wrote at the beginning of the chapter, as developers we are often surprisingly poor at practising the developmental processes we preach. My hope is that something in this chapter will trigger a moment of realization of something you would like to change in either your personal or your professional life. For readers who learn well through theory, considering the GROW and SMART models may well be the best place to begin. Readers who learn through reflections on experience – their own and that of others – might like to begin by focusing on their reactions to the case histories or the list of common stresses. Activists might do best to plunge straight in with an activity. Whichever approach works best for you is fine. Notice what is triggered in your mind, and use that to identify a significant area for your own development. And then act, for it is only in action that progress is made and solutions are found. If your personal approach to constant goal setting and growth becomes habitual, not only will you find yourself engaged in a constant, exciting process of personal development, you will also find that you manage the inevitable stresses of your professional role much more successfully. And through this, we finally become personally congruent with our professional role: developers who are themselves developing.

REFERENCES

Brown, S and Smith, B (1999) *Academic Survival Strategies*, Staff and Educational Development Association (SEDA) Special Number 8, SEDA, Birmingham
Covey, S (1990) *The Seven Habits of Highly Effective People*, Fireside, New York
Cowan, J (1998) *On Becoming an Innovative University Teacher*, Society for Research into Higher Education and Open University Press, Buckingham
Downey, M (2002) *Effective Coaching*, Texere, London
Gaskell, C (2001) *Your Pocket Life Coach*, Thorsons, London
Grant, A and Greene, J (2001) *Coach Yourself: Make real change in your life*, Pearson Education, Harlow
Mulligan, E (2000) *Life Coaching for Work*, Piatkus, London
O'Connor, J and Seymour, J (1994) *Training with NLP*, Thorsons, London
Race, P (2001) *The Lecturer's Toolkit*, 2nd edn, Kogan Page, London
Richardson, C (2000) *Take Time for Your Life*, Bantam Books, London
Whitworth, L, Kimsey-House, H and Sandahl, P (1998) *Co-active Coaching: New skills for coaching people towards success in work and life*, Davies-Black Publishing, Palo Alto, CA
Zeus, P and Skiffington, S (2000) *The Complete Guide to Coaching at Work*, McGraw-Hill Australia, Roseville, NSW

FURTHER RESOURCES

Two particularly useful Web sites are:

http://www.lifecoachingacademy.com/
The Coaching Academy is Europe's largest training organization for coaches. It also gives prospective clients information on the standards to expect from a coach.

http://www.trevorcousins.com
A clear introduction to coaching by a coach who has experience of working with academics.

Appendix: further sources of information for staff and educational developers

Bland Tomkinson

This appendix describes some of the resources available to staff and educational developers to assist in their task. These resources are grouped under a number of headings: Books; Journals; Web sites; Networks.

No account, particularly one as brief as this, could hope to be comprehensive, but the description aims to cover a variety of sources that I have found particularly useful. The glossary that follows this appendix also serves to outline some of the main organizations, funding bodies and networks active within UK higher education (HE) that are referred to in various chapters.

BOOKS

Academic practice/teaching and learning

Biggs, J (1999) *Teaching for Quality Learning at University*, Buckingham, Society for Research into Higher Education (SRHE) and Open University Press (OUP). John Biggs takes a clear and scholarly approach to his topic. His book, encouraging in tone and well illustrated, is used on a growing number of courses on teaching in HE.

Fry, H, Ketteridge, S and Marshall, S (eds) (2003) *A Handbook for Teaching and Learning in Higher Education*, Kogan Page, London. This book is a staple volume for designing and running programmes for the training of staff new to teaching. It covers most of the headings that educational developers would wish to use and is useful as a course text for participants.

Grasha, A F (1996) *Teaching with Style*, Alliance Publishers, Pittsburgh. Tony Grasha takes a novel approach to pedagogy, looking at both learning styles and teaching styles. This is quite a refreshing book but British readers may find that the US style jars a bit. This text is also useful for relatively experienced lecturers.

Harb, J N, Hurt, P K, Terry, R E and Williamson, K J (1995) *Teaching through the Cycle*, Brigham Young University Press, Provo, UT. Less well known but shorter than Grasha and more practical. It is particularly useful for ideas when one is working with engineers.

Knight, P E, Aitken, N and Rogerson, R J (2000) *Forever Better: Continuous quality improvement in higher education*, New Forums Press, Stillwater, OK. Has a focus on the continuous improvement of teaching quality and is, therefore, a book that can be used with more experienced teachers as well as new lecturers. A little trite in parts, it nonetheless offers perspectives from around the English-speaking world.

Knight, P T (2002) *Being a Teacher in Higher Education*, Open University Press, Buckingham. Peter Knight's book combines scholarship with encouragement and practical guidance, in line with its aim to help the new teacher 'develop a sense of oneself as a good teacher'.

McKeachie, W (ed) (1999) *Teaching Tips: Strategies, research, and theory for college teachers*, 10th edn, Houghton Mifflin, Boston. Bill McKeachie's work has stood the test of time and is widely recognized around the world as a good starter text for new academics. The title suggests that it might be purely anecdotal but it does contain some solid theory. The 10th edition has contributions from a couple of British authors, but even without these manages to stand above the different international teaching cultures.

Ramsden, P (1992) *Learning to Teach in Higher Education*, Routledge, London. Ramsden is sometimes regarded as a bit 'old hat' but this book clearly provides the springboard for many others. In a clear and thoughtful way, it combines practical advice, scholarship, and a clear understanding of the realities of being a new teacher in HE.

Assessment

Andresen, L, Nightingale, P, Boud, D and Magin, D (1993) *Strategies for Assessing Students*, Standing Conference on Educational Development (SCED) Paper 78, Staff and Educational Development Association, Birmingham. Out of print, but provides a useful and practical grounding in assessment and may still be available in libraries.

Angelo, T and Cross, P (1993) *Classroom Assessment Techniques*, 2nd edn, Jossey-Bass, San Francisco. To some extent about formative assessment but also about self-evaluation. This text can be useful in staff development contexts as well in university teaching and represents a novel and useful approach.

Brown, S and Glasner, A (1999) *Assessment Matters*, SRHE and Open University Press, Buckingham. At once scholarly and pragmatic and challenges the orthodoxy of much university-level assessment.

e-Learning

Broadbent, B (2002) *ABCs of e-Learning: Reaping the benefits and avoiding the pitfalls*, American Society for Training and Development (ASTD) and Jossey-Bass, San Francisco. A basic introduction aimed at work-based learning but has lessons that apply equally to staff and educational development.

Fallows, S and Bhanot, R (eds) (2002) *Educational Development through Information and Communications Technology*, Kogan Page, London. Considers the ways in which ICT can be used to enhance learning and teaching, both on- and off-campus, and how educators and institutions have tackled the issues associated with the adoption of new approaches and technologies.

Group work

Jaques, D (2000) *Learning in Groups*, 3rd edn, Kogan Page, London. A comprehensive introduction to the theory and practice of teaching and learning in groups. The theoretical introduction goes much wider than just learning in groups and provides a sound basis for the more practical suggestions that follow.

Tiberius, R G (1999) *Small Group Teaching: A trouble-shooting guide*, Kogan Page, London. A more pragmatic approach. Starts from problems in groups, moving on to possible causes and thence to suggestions for improvement. This is a handy book to dip into when problems arise.

Management development

Middlehurst, R (1993) *Leading Academics*, SRHE and Open University Press, Buckingham. Looks at issues of university management and is important for those about to embark on programmes for senior academic management.

Pedagogy

Laurillard, D (2002) *Rethinking University Thinking*, 2nd edn, Routledge, London. Diana Laurillard's authoritative work is a useful trigger for any work in educational development, though it is perhaps more widely used by those with a technological bent.

Leach, J and Moon, B (eds) (1999) *Learners and Pedagogy*, Paul Chapman Publishing, London. Also from the Open University stable and represents an intriguing mix of articles about pedagogy, at a variety of levels of education, with many from different subject perspectives.

Problem-based learning

Boud, D and Feletti, G (eds) (1998) *The Challenge of Problem-based Learning*, 2nd edn, Kogan Page, London. A very informative work for those considering any form of inquiry-led learning, but especially for those contemplating Problem-based Learning (PBL).

Savin-Baden, M (2000) *Problem-based Learning in Higher Education: Untold stories*, SRHE and Open University Press, Buckingham. Also a useful read for those embarking on PBL, and gives some interesting and useful case studies.

Scholarship of teaching and learning

Hutchings, P (ed) (2000) *Opening Lines: Approaches to the scholarship of teaching and learning*, Carnegie Foundation, Menlo Park, CA. Presents a series of essays reflecting on case studies in the scholarship of teaching.

Smith, B and Tomkinson, B (eds) (2003) *Critical Encounters*, LTSN Generic Centre, York. Echoes the Hutchings volume with UK case studies.

Staff and professional development

Brew, A (ed) (1995) *Directions in Staff Development*, SRHE and Open University Press, Buckingham. An overview of staff development in HE. Although slightly dated in parts, it nevertheless provides useful material, especially to those new to staff development in the higher education context.

Gillespie, K H, Hilsen, L and Wadsworth, E (eds) (2002) *A Guide to Faculty Development*, POD and Anker, Bolton, MA. Provides a variety of pithy advice for the educational developer, founded on both scholarship and practical experience.

Mabey, C and Iles, P (eds) (1994) *Managing Learning*, Kogan Page, London. The title of this book might mislead the casual observer into expecting a text on educational development, although it is much more oriented to staff development. It provides a useful collection of journal articles from writers eminent in their fields.

Wilson, J P (ed) (1999) *Human Resource Development*, Kogan Page, London. A useful primer for staff developers; attempts to link theory and practice. Some of the chapters also have value for those who consider themselves educational developers.

Zuber-Skerritt, O (1992) *Professional Development in Higher Education: A theoretical framework for action research*, Kogan Page, London. This is the pre-eminent text on action research and builds on the work of others to develop an underpinning theoretical approach for both staff and educational development. A companion volume gives examples and reflections.

SEDA Series (*all* Kogan Page, London)

This series (http://www.kogan-page.co.uk/asp/booklist.asp) provides a useful starter to any library collection; in addition to Fallows and Bhanot (see above), recent volumes include:

Jenkins, A, Breen, R, Lindsay, R and Brew, A (eds) (2002) *Reshaping Teaching in Higher Education*. This volume is concerned with examples of how academic research activity can be linked with academic teaching to mutual benefit.

Macdonald, R and Wisdom, J (eds) (2002) *Academic and Educational Development: Research, evaluation and changing practice in higher education*. This volume recognizes the need for research and scholarship to underpin changing practices in higher education.

Yorke, M, Baume, C and Martin, P (eds) (2002) *Managing Educational Development Projects*. This volume illustrates good practice in successfully managing projects in academic and educational environments.

SRHE Series (*all* Open University Press, Buckingham)

This series covers a wide range of interests in higher education and includes Biggs, Brew, Brown and Glasner, Middlehurst, and Savin-Baden (see above). Recent titles include:

Duke, C (2002) *Managing the Learning University*. This volume tries to set out a management style for higher education, based on a knowledge of management theory but without jumping on business management bandwagons.

Eggins, H and MacDonald, R (eds) (2003) *The Scholarship of Academic Development*. This volume provides a well-researched underpinning to academic development as a profession.

JOURNALS AND MAGAZINES

I have avoided selecting specific articles from journals – the list would be far too long – but the following journals are of particular interest:

- *Active Learning in Higher Education* – the journal of the Institute for Learning and Teaching in Higher Education. Has practitioner-based articles, often with a subject focus.

- *ALT-J* – the journal of the Association for Learning Technology, with a focus very much on learning technologies, though some articles take a wider view of educational or staff development.

- *Education, Technology and Society* – online journal of the International Forum of Education, Technology and Society. Has articles from developers and practitioners but mostly with a technology bent.

- *Educational Developments* – published by the Staff and Educational Development Association; provides a useful variety of articles on changes in higher education and their implications for staff and educational development.

- *Higher Education Research and Development* – the journal of the Higher Education Research and Development Society of Australasia. Mostly with an Australian focus, with some subject-based articles and possibly more articles on international/multicultural education than comparable journals elsewhere.

- *Innovation in Education and Teaching International* (formerly *Innovation in Education and Training International*) (IETI) – the journal of the Staff and Educational Development Association. The bulk of its refereed articles are about research and development in teaching and learning, though it contains some about educational, rather than staff, development. Some articles are subject based but most have wide applicability.

- *International Journal for Academic Development* (IJAD). IJAD is the journal of the International Consortium for Educational Development, and wholly concentrates on research and development in academic – meaning staff and educational – development. It carries contributions from academic developers in a wide range of countries.

- *Studies in Higher Education* – the journal of the Society for Research into Higher Education. Research-based articles on many aspects of higher education.

Other journals in the field of higher education, or more generally in education, often have articles of relevance to educational developers but these are not listed here. Also, there are numerous journals concerned with subject-specific education and these are felt to be too specific for inclusion.

WEB SITES

For UK users, the Learning and Teaching Support Network Web site http://www.ltsn.ac.uk (accessed February 2003) provides a link through to Subject Centre sites that cover teaching and learning in 24 disciplinary areas, as well as to the Generic Centre. This is particularly handy in researching subject-specific materials: many of the Subject Centre sites have links through to reports on projects that the LTSN has funded.

In the field of learning technologies, the RESULTS portal http:// www.results.ac.uk (accessed February 2003) is a useful though underused link to other resources.

In the United Kingdom, the Deliberations Web site has an iconoclastic collection of material relevant to educational developers: http://www. lgu.ac.uk/deliberations/ (accessed February 2003)

In the United States, the National Teaching and Learning Forum Web site http://www.ntlf.com/ (accessed February 2003) has an informative newsletter and provides an accessible route to discussion of ideas. The University of Kansas Center for Teaching Excellence Web site http://www.ku.edu/~cte/resources/websites.html (accessed February 2003) has links to a range of other sites both in the United States and in other countries. Richard Lyons also provides a list of useful Web sites at http://www.developfaculty.com/online/index.html (accessed February 2003)

Also, the Educational Resources Information Center (ERIC) database http://ericir.syr.edu/Eric/ (accessed February 2003) is a mine of information.

The TLT Group is perhaps best known for the Flashlight Program http://www.tltgroup.org/ (accessed February 2003).

A useful online selected bibliography can be found at

http://www.carnegiefoundation.org/CASTL/highered/bibliography.htm (accessed February 2003).

For new teachers, First Words provide brief, lively and practical guidance: http://www.brookes.ac.uk/services/ocsd/firstwords/fwconts.html (accessed February 2003).

NETWORKS

There are essentially two, inter-related types of network: the human and the electronic. Professional bodies, societies and agencies active in this field include:

- ALT – Association for Learning Technology (UK) [Online] http://www.alt.ac.uk/ (accessed February 2003);

- ASTD – American Society for Training and Development (USA) [Online] http://www.astd.org (accessed February 2003);

- EDUCAUSE (US) [Online] http://www.educause.edu/ (accessed February 2003);

- HEDG – Heads of Educational Development Group (UK);

- HERDSA Higher Education Research and Development Society of Australasia (Australia) [Online] http://www.herdsa.org.au/index.html (accessed February 2003);

- HESDA – Higher Education Staff Development Agency (UK) [Online] http://www.hesda.org.uk/index.html (accessed February 2003);

- IFETS – International Forum on Education, Technology and Society (US/NZ) [Online] http://ifets.ieee.org/ (accessed February 2003);

- ILTHE – Institute for Learning and Teaching in Higher Education (UK) [Online] http://www.ilt.ac.uk/index.html (accessed February 2003);

- POD – Professional and Organizational Development Network in Higher Education (US) [Online] http://www.podnetwork.org/index.htm (accessed February 2003);

- SEDA – Staff and Educational Development Association (UK) [Online] http://www.seda.ac.uk/ (accessed February 2003);

- SRHE – Society for Research into Higher Education (UK) [Online] http://www.srhe.ac.uk/ (accessed February 2003);

- STLHE /SAPES – Society for Teaching and Learning in Higher Education (Canada) [Online] http://www.tss.uoguelph.ca/STLHE/ (accessed February 2003).

Most of these have associated discussion lists – some busier than others! In the United Kingdom, a number of discussion lists are based around the JISCMail service http://www.jiscmail.ac.uk/ (accessed February 2003). Some of these are the discussion lists managed on behalf of organizations listed above; others active at February 2003 include:

- staff-development@jiscmail.ac.uk

- web-based-staff-dev@jiscmail.ac.uk

- lang-asst-trg@jiscmail.ac.uk (related to the development of Language Assistants/Lectors)

- escalate@jiscmail.ac.uk (related to the Learning and Teaching Support Network for Education)

- isl@jiscmail.ac.uk (related to the annual Improving Student Learning conferences).

Other JISCMail lists cover specific educational development projects, specific regions of the United Kingdom and particular subjects or specialities.

The prolific Ted Panitz lists a number of United States-based list servers concerned with teaching in HE – too many to reproduce here, but the list can be viewed at http://home.capecod.net/~tpanitz/lists.htm (accessed February 2003).

Glossary

This glossary is based on one compiled by the UMIST Teaching and Learning Support Centre and is reproduced with permission.
See also:

[Online] http://www.nwlink.com/~donclark/hrd/glossary.html (accessed February 2003)
[Online] http://www.jisc.ac.uk/glossary/index.html (accessed February 2003)

AAHE American Association for Higher Education (USA).

action research A process of planning a novel action in the work (teaching) situation, putting that action into practice and then monitoring and evaluating the effects of the action.

affective Relating to feelings and emotions; used to describe one of Bloom's learning domains.

ALT Association for Learning Technology (UK).

assessment The evaluation of student performance and attainment. *See also* formative assessment.

ASTD American Society for Training and Development (USA).

AVCC Australian Vice-Chancellors' Committee (Australia)'

benchmark A standard point of reference that enables comparisons to be made; *subject benchmark statements* are intended to act as a point of reference for academic programmes in a subject, usually at undergraduate level.

Bloom's Taxonomy A system of classifying learning named after Benjamin Bloom, who chaired the steering group.

cognitive Concerned with the act of knowing. *See also* learning; learning style.

cognitive strategy A plan of action adopted in the process of knowing, conceiving or perceiving.

cognitive style A distinctive and habitual manner of knowing, conceiving or perceiving.

Curriculum 2000 A UK government initiative to change the curriculum and examination schemes for 16- to 19-year-olds.

CVCP Committee of Vice-Chancellors and Principals. Now Universities UK (*qv*).

deductive Obtained by a process of deduction; that is, a process of inference in which the conclusion about the particular follows necessarily from general premises.

DfES Department for Education and Skills (UK) (formerly DfEE, Department for Education and Employment).

didactics The study of teaching of, and the contents of, a subject or discipline.

discourse A formal and methodical expression of thought on a subject; ways of constituting knowledge, not just ways of thinking and producing meaning, which, together with social practices, forms of subjectivity and power relations, form a natural and integral part of such knowledge.

distance learning A form of study where the learner is remote in distance from the provider of tuition and relates to the tutor by communication that is other than face to face.

EDUCAUSE A non-profit association that aims to advance higher education by promoting the intelligent use of information technology (USA).

epistemology The study of how the mind knows what it knows; of the nature of knowledge or ways of knowing, particularly in the context of the limits or validity of the various ways of knowing.

ESRC Economic and Social Research Council (UK).

evaluation The consideration or examination of something in order to judge its value, quality, worth, completeness or importance.

evaluative The expression of a judgement about something, or assigning a value to it, as opposed to describing a fact.

FDTL Fund for the Development of Teaching and Learning (UK) – part of the Teaching Quality Enhancement Fund. Now in its fourth round; each round applies only to a specific range of subjects.

FE Further education.

feedback The giving of evaluative or corrective information to the originator about an action or piece of work; *also*, the information so transmitted.

FIPSE Fund for the Improvement of Post-Secondary Education (USA).

flexible learning A description applied to forms of study that are not under the continuous, immediate supervision of tutors but that nevertheless benefit from the planning, guidance and tuition of a teaching institution.

formative assessment   Assessment that is undertaken largely with the intent of providing feedback to the student to aid his or her development.

HE   Higher education.

HEDG   Heads of Educational Development Group (UK).

HEFCE   Higher Education Funding Council for England.

HEFCW   Higher Education Funding Council for Wales.

HERDSA   Higher Education Research and Development Society of Australasia.

hermeneutics   The study of the principles of interpreting meaning. It includes the whole question of how a particular text is 'received', especially understanding the social and philosophical context.

HESDA   Higher Education Staff Development Agency (UK).

ICED   International Consortium for Educational Development – a grouping of national organizations promoting good practice in academic development.

IFETS   International Forum of Education, Technology and Society – a subgroup of the IEEE Learning Technology Task Force.

ILTHE   Institute for Learning and Teaching in Higher Education (UK).

inductive   Obtained by a process of logical induction; that is, inference of a general conclusion from particular instances.

inquiry-based learning   A student-centred approach to learning with a focus on inquiry, information creation and self-directed learning.

JISC   Joint Information Systems Committee, with a remit covering higher education and further education throughout the United Kingdom.

learning   The acquisition of knowledge, skill or understanding by example, experience or receipt of instruction. *See also* distance learning; flexible learning; inquiry-based learning; open learning; problem-based learning.

learning outcome   The knowledge, skill or understanding that is the desired result of a learning process.

learning preference   The favouring by a learner of one particular mode of teaching over another.

learning strategy   A plan of action adopted in the acquisition or imparting of knowledge or skill through study, experience or teaching.

learning style   A distinctive and habitual manner of acquiring or imparting knowledge through study, experience or teaching. Learning styles and cognitive styles are differing but complementary concepts (*see* E Sadler-Smith (1996) Learning styles and instructional design, *Innovations in Education and Training International*, **4**, pp 185–93). *See also* cognitive strategy; cognitive style; learning preference; learning strategy.

lecture   A discourse given before an audience or class in order to convey knowledge; *also*, the act of giving such a discourse.

LSC   Learning and Skills Council – both the central council (which took over the Further Education Funding Council and some of the central Training and Enterprise Council (TEC) functions) and regional councils (which replaced local TECs) (England)

LTSN   Learning and Teaching Support Network (UK) – funded by the Teaching Quality Enhancement Fund (*qv*). It comprises:

- an Executive, based within the Institute for Learning and Teaching in Higher Education (*qv*), which manages and co-ordinates the network;

- a Generic Centre offering expertise and information on learning and teaching issues that cross subject boundaries;

- 24 Subject centres, based in higher education institutions throughout the United Kingdom, offering subject-specific expertise and information on learning and teaching;

- a Technologies Centre, funded by the Joint Information Systems Committee, which looks at and develops new learning technologies in higher and further education.

meta-portfolio   A comprehensive, organized collection of documents or ephemera, or both, arranged such that other portfolios (*qv*) may be drawn from it for specific purposes.

module   A short course of study that forms part of a degree programme.

NCT   National Co-ordination Team (UK). A service operated by the Open University on behalf of the Higher Education Funding Council for England to co-ordinate initiatives under the Teaching Quality Enhancement Fund (*qv*).

NDT   National Disability Team (UK). A service, based at Anglia Polytechnic University, that co-ordinates initiatives by the Higher Education Funding Council for England to improve access for the disabled.

NTFS   National Teaching Fellowships Scheme – a scheme of annual competitive awards for teaching that is administered by the Institute for Learning and Teaching in Higher Education.

ontology   The study of the nature of existence, of things as they actually are. Cf epistemology (*qv*).

open learning   Learning where students have a choice as to where they learn, when they learn, how they learn and the pace at which they learn.

pedagogy   The study of the science or profession of teaching, encompassing aims, curriculum content and methodology.

phenomenography   The study of the qualitatively different ways in which people understand the world around them. In education, the most important elements of this are that data are collected directly from learners and that the content and setting are those actually involved in learning.

POD Professional and Organizational Development Network in Higher Education (USA).

portfolio A comprehensive collection of documents or ephemera, or both, collated so as to convey information about the skills, experience or development needs of its author, normally with a covering narrative. *See also* meta-portfolio; proto-portfolio. (Definitions after B Tomkinson (1997) Towards a taxonomy of teaching portfolios, Staff Development Occasional Paper 2/97, UMIST, Manchester.)

problem-based learning A student-centred instructional strategy where tutor-constructed problems form the organizing focus and stimulus so that knowledge is acquired through self-directed learning.

programme A collection of study modules leading to a degree or other qualification.

proto-portfolio A collection of documents or ephemera, or both, brought together for the purpose of conveying information about the skills or experience of its author, but without organization or narrative.

QAA Quality Assurance Agency for Higher Education (UK). An autonomous body set up by the Committee of Vice-Chancellors and Principals and the funding councils to promote public confidence that quality of provision and standards of awards in higher education are being safeguarded and enhanced.

qualitative Based on or relating to qualities or the general aspect without involving measurement.

quality Degree of excellence.

quality assurance The systematic monitoring and evaluation of the various aspects of a programme, service or facility to ensure that standards of quality are being met.

quality enhancement Refers to a programme for the continuous improvement of the various aspects of a programme, service or facility.

quantitative Based on or arrived at by measurement.

RDN Resource Discovery Network (UK). A set of subject gateways sponsored by the Joint Information Systems Committee providing access to electronic resources.

reflective practice A professional approach characterized by deep, careful thought backed up by action and review.

SEDA Staff and Educational Development Association (UK).

seminar A meeting for giving and discussing information, often in an informal setting.

SRHE Society for Research into Higher Education (UK).

STLHE Society for Teaching and Learning in Higher Education (Canada).

summative assessment   assessment that is undertaken largely with the aim of producing a mark or score that is used to decide relative success or failure in a formal procedure.

teaching   Imparting knowledge, skill or understanding to someone by instruction, example or through an experience.

TLRP   Teaching and Learning Research Programme (UK) – a programme of educational research funded by the funding councils and administered by the Economic and Social Research Council. It was intended that the focus of the programme should be on higher education and that it should involve practitioners.

TLTP   Teaching and Learning Technology Programme (UK) – a series of three programmes funded by the Higher Education Funding Council for England specifically aimed at introducing more learning technology into the curriculum.

TQEF   Teaching Quality Enhancement Fund (UK) – an umbrella programme of the Higher Education Funding Council for England that funds the Fund for the Development of Teaching and Learning, the Learning and Teaching Support Network, the National Teaching Fellowships Scheme and institutional programmes.

tutorial   A class conducted by a tutor for one individual or a small number of students.

Universities UK   A national body representing UK universities that seeks to provide mutual support for vice-chancellors and other chief academic officers and to speak with a common voice on issues of moment for higher education. Formerly CVCP (*qv*).

Index